LAW FOR ARCHITECTS

WHAT YOU NEED TO KNOW

ROBERT F. HERRMANN

and the Attorneys at Menaker & Herrmann LLP

W. W. Norton
New York • London

TO OUR CLIENTS, who have expanded our understanding of their world and honored us with their trust.

The matter contained in this book is provided for information purposes only, and is not intended to be, nor should it be, construed as legal advice. It should not replace the advice of your own legal counsel.

AIA documents reproduced with permission of The American Institute of Architects, 1735 New York Avenue, NW, Washington, DC, 20006.

This publication incorporates licensed copyrighted or other proprietary material of ACORD Corporation. All rights reserved. Used with permission of ACORD Corporation. The name ACORD and the ACORD logo are registered marks of ACORD Corporation. This document and any opinions it may contain are solely the product of its author(s) and are neither endorsed, nor warranted, by ACORD.

Blumberg form reprinted with permission. It may be purchased from BlumbergExcelsior, Inc. (www.blumberg.com). Reproduction prohibited.

For information about permission to reproduce selections from this book, write to:
Permissions, W. W. Norton & Company, Inc., 500 Fifth Avenue, New York, NY 10110

For information about special discounts for bulk purchases, please contact:
W. W. Norton, Special Sales at specialsales@wwnorton.com or 800-233-4830

Manufacturing by Quad/Graphics, Versailles
Book design by Jonathan D. Lippincott
Page makeup by Ken Gross
Production manager: Leeann Graham

Library of Congress Cataloging-in-Publication Data

Herrmann, Robert F.
    Law for architects : what you need to know / Robert F. Herrmann and the attorneys at Menaker & Herrmann LLP.
        p.   cm.
    Includes bibliographical references and index.
    ISBN 978-0-393-73345-7 (hardcover)
    1. Architects—Legal status, laws, etc.—United States. 2. Architectural practice—United States. 3. Construction contracts—United States. I. Menaker & Herrmann LLP. II. Title.
    KF2925.H47 2012
    343.7307'7872—dc23   2012001530

ISBN: 978-0-393-73345-7

W. W. Norton & Company, Inc., 500 Fifth Avenue, New York, N.Y. 10110
www.wwnorton.com
W. W. Norton & Company Ltd., 15 Carlisle Street, London W1D 3BS

10 9 8 7 6 5 4 3 2

CONTENTS

Foreword 7
Preface and Acknowledgments 11

1: Why Do I Need an Agreement? 13
Getting Started: What Should an Initial Proposal Contain? 14
What Are the Benefits of Using American Institute of Architects
    Forms of Agreement? 15
How Is the Typical Architect/Owner Agreement Structured? 16
Consultants: Who Should Engage Them, the Architect or the
    Owner? 45
What Do I Need to Know if I Am Working on a Project in a Foreign
    Country? 47
How Is My Role Different If I Am Just the Design Architect? 50
The Owner's Agreement with the Contractor: What Should I Know? 51

**2: What Is My Intellectual Property and How Do I
Protect It?** 55
What Is Copyright? 56
What Are Derivative Works? 58
Who Owns A Copyright? 59
As the Copyright Owner, How Do I Protect My Work? 62
How Long Does Copyright Last? 63
What Is Copyright Infringement? 63

How Does a Court Decide Whether a Copyright Has Been
Infringed? 66

What Are the Remedies for Copyright Infringement? 70

As the Copyright Holder, Can I Put Pictures of the Building on My
Website? 71

What Are My Intellectual Property Rights When Working Abroad? 73

What About My Rights in Electronic Documents? 73

Does Using Building Information Modeling Software Change My
Rights? 76

What Is a Trademark? 77

Can Any Word or Symbol Be Trademarked? 78

What Are the Penalties for Trademark Infringement? 79

What Is a Patent? 80

What Are the Penalties for Patent Infringement? 81

3: Why Do I Need Insurance? 83

What Exactly Is Insurance? 84

What Role Do Insurance Brokers Play? 85

What Does Professional Liability Insurance Cover? 88

What Does Commercial General Liability Insurance Cover? 91

What Does Workers' Compensation Insurance Cover? 92

What Does Commercial (Business) Automobile Insurance Cover? 92

What Does Business Office Insurance Cover? 92

What Does Employment Practices Liability Insurance Cover? 93

What Does It Mean to Be an Additional Insured? 93

What Insurance Should My Consultants Carry? 94

What Is Project Insurance? 95

What Is a Waiver of Subrogation? 95

How Are My Professional Liability Insurance Premiums
Calculated? 95

4: What Do I Need to Know About Getting Paid? 97

What are the Different Means of Determining the Framework for
Compensation? 97

What Happens If My Client Fails to Pay? 100

What Is a Lien? 101

What Is my Last Resort? 104

5: What Do I Need to Know About Forming and Organizing An Architectural Firm? 105

What Form of Entity Should I Have? 105

Why Do I Need a Written Agreement with My Other Owners? 111

Can I Practice Architecture with Other Professions? 120

What Do I Need to Know About Practicing in Other States? 120

What Do I Need to Know About Expanding Ownership of My Firm or Merging My Practice? 123

6: What Employment Issues Do I Face as an Architect? 127

What Do I Need to Know About Hiring? 127

What Workplace Issues Should I Be Aware Of? 136

What Can I Do to Avoid Litigation if I Have to Terminate Employees? 146

7: How Do Construction Disputes Get Resolved? 151

What Does a Construction Claim Look Like? 152

What Is Meant by the Term "Claim"? 153

When Do I Need to Get a Lawyer Involved? 154

What Are the First Steps in Addressing a Claim? 155

What Should I Do When the Claim Is Against Me? 156

Why Is It Critical to Save My Records? 156

What Are the Main Dispute Resolution Vehicles? 157

How Are Disputes Resolved Informally? 158

How Can Monetary Claims Be Resolved Informally? 159

How Can Non-Monetary Claims Be Resolved Informally? 159

Should Dispute Resolutions Be Documented? 161

What Are the Main Types of Formal Claims Resolution? 161

How Does Mediation Work? 162

How Does Arbitration Work?　166

How Do I Enforce a Favorable Arbitration Award?　170

How Does Litigation Work?　171

What Are Appeals?　176

8: I May Have Committed Malpractice: What Is My Legal Exposure?　179

Under What Sorts of Laws Can Someone Sue Me for
　Damages?　180

What Sorts of Things Can I Be Sued For?　184

What Are "Economic Losses"?　189

Who Can Sue Me for Economic Losses?　192

For How Long After a Project Can I Be Sued?　196

9: How Do I Become Qualified to Practice Architecture?　199

What Kind of Activities Require a License?　199

Why Are Architects Required to Be Licensed?　201

Who Decides Who Gets Licensed?　202

What Are the Requirements to Become Licensed?　203

Do I Have to Be Licensed in Every State Where I Provide Architectural
　Services?　204

Does My Firm Need to Be Licensed?　206

What Do I Need to Do to Keep My Architecture License?　206

What Happens If I Am Not Licensed?　206

So If I Have a License and Keep It, Is That All I Need to Do?　207

10: How Do I Choose an Attorney to Help Me?　211

Notes　214
Index　216
About the Authors　223

FOREWORD

As I read *Law for Architects: What You Need to Know* by Robert Herrmann and his colleagues at Menaker & Herrmann LLP, twenty-six years of experience with Robert A. M. Stern Architects, twenty-three of them as managing partner, flashed through my mind. If I had only had this guidance at the beginning rather than at the end of my tenure! I found myself grading my own performance chapter by chapter. Full disclosure compels me to point out that the authors were my legal and business advisers and confidantes for twenty-five of these years.

Architects are trained to have design skills. Architects who advance in the profession develop technical design, marketing, and project management skills as well. But those who aspire to establish a practice or become a principal in an architectural practice need an understanding of the array of legal and business issues firms face. Few of us start out thinking about liability or employment issues, or tax and accounting issues, or the many legal issues that swirl around the construction industry. Eventually most of those who continue in the profession need to know enough about all such basic matters to be able to make intelligent decisions, and to understand the language spoken by the advisers we select to help us make such decisions. Every new architecture graduate will find in this volume wide-ranging help in understanding the complexity and seriousness of the professional practice of architecture.

Many of us took the often obligatory class in professional practice while in school. Often the most interesting aspects were the bizarre course a mistake in practice could take on its way to resolution. There are plenty of examples here, but the response we might have had in school ("how could they make such an obvious mistake?") is replaced by awed respect for the way that small misunderstandings, mistakes, or omissions can spin out of control. We know what the consequences might be for omitting the flashing, but who thinks closely about the consequences of omitting a copyright notice or failing to obtain a waiver of consequential damages. *Law for Architects* reminds us of all of them, and the prospect can be intimidating. To the new architect it offers a leg up in growth and advancement, and a place to turn when you are sent on your first site visit or even to review your first set of shop drawings. It shows what each of these assignments entails in terms of risk to the firm employing you, or what your client or the contractor may or may not understand about what you are doing. For the seasoned architect it provides an articulate check list and point of reference for those things to which you know you should be attentive on every project but sometimes just do not quite find time to examine. And it provides you with a great teaching tool for rising employees.

The beauty of the content here is that the basics are presented in language design professionals can understand, and the format is such that you can seek and find the information you need, even when it simply helps you to decide you need more expert assistance from the resources suggested in many of these chapters. I learned a great deal more about some of the issues with which I have been dealing during most of my professional life.

As I read, it came home to me once again how complex is the process of designing and building a structure to be occupied by real people; how many parties there are to the process, and what overlapping but also divergent interests they often have. Behind each paragraph here there is a body of knowledge and professional expertise, often in more than one discipline. A lot of valuable information is compressed into a concise package—many topics are presented that could warrant a full-blown essay or even a book. With what awe must we as architects face our tasks of drafting plans, negotiating with owners, contractors, building officials, and consultants! When we finish our site report, what consequences may depend on correctly and completely recording that the reinforcing has been properly placed. The clues are all here as to the importance and consequences of our actions.

Fortunately we are also reminded of the many sources available to us for support from our professional organizations, consultants, insurance, tax and accounting professionals, human resources and information technology professionals, and, most of all, from experienced legal counsel. As you will become aware as you read through the topics, appropriate legal counsel is key to becoming fully informed and resolving most of the issues that may arise. This volume will help you to understand the basics of many of the business and legal issues that can arise, and the language to communicate with the advisers who can help you make the right decision.

To be sure, legal affairs are not what drew you to the architectural world in the first place. This volume is all about making sure that potential problems do not become big problems that will take your time and resources away from doing what you do best: being an architect.

— Robert S. Buford, *managing partner, retired,*
Robert A. M. Stern Architects

PREFACE AND ACKNOWLEDGMENTS

Law for architects? Why would practicing architects or students studying architecture want to read a book about the law? After all, architects are creative people who chose their profession to express their creative energies. Surely, reading a book about the *legal* aspects of the design profession is the last thing an architect would want to do. As it turns out, however, while architecture may be a creative profession, it is also a business. In our increasingly complex world, a successful practice needs not only good design skills but also an understanding of the legal framework that is key to survival in a competitive and complex business environment. Gaining this understanding not only helps keep you out of trouble but also goes a long way toward making your practice a thriving business.

In the early 1990s, with the encouragement of the then dean of the Columbia University School of Architecture, Bernard Tschumi, I developed a course on architecture and the law. Not surprisingly, not enough students signed up for the course for it to be offered. However, whenever I have told architects about this failed course, they have uniformly said that they wished they had taken such a class. So it is fair to say that the seeds for this book were planted almost twenty years ago.

This is not a book that you necessarily want to read in one sitting. Rather, it may serve as a useful resource when questions come up and you want a quick understanding of the issues. The legal aspects governing the practice of architecture are constantly changing, so I strongly encourage you to recognize that although this book will help you understand many of the issues you face in your practice, it is not a substitute for consultation with an attorney.

This book would not be possible without the help of my partners Yao Fu Bailey, Michiel A. Bloemsma, Cheryl L. Davis, Paul M. Hellegers, Richard

G. Menaker, and Rebecca Northey, who wrote various chapters reflecting their areas of expertise. I also want to thank Greg Kumm of Prosurance Redeker Group for taking the time to read and comment on the insurance chapter.

Special thanks go to our firm's design clients. We work with some of the most talented design professionals in the world, and through that work we have gained better insights into issues that our clients face on a daily basis.

I wish to thank Rob Buford, former managing partner of Robert A. M. Stern Architects, for writing a foreword to this book and for giving me the opportunity to work with him and his firm for more than twenty-five years.

Finally, I would like to thank Carol Rose, copy editor and Nancy Green, senior editor at W. W. Norton for all their help in making this a better book. In particular, Nancy had a key role in developing the concept of this book as a guide really for architects and not for architects' attorneys.

— Robert F. Herrmann

ONE

WHY DO I NEED AN AGREEMENT?

"Get it in writing!" Nothing could be simpler or more important in establishing a sound relationship between you and your client. Written, signed agreements are a necessary evil so both parties can limit the surprises down the road and know what to expect of each other.

For more than a hundred years the American Institute of Architects (AIA) has published forms of agreement for use by architects. Over time these agreements have become longer and more complicated, a response to increasingly more sophisticated projects and, perhaps, also a reflection of our more litigious society. The number of contract forms the AIA offers continues to increase. At the same time, some owners and even some architects choose to develop their own forms of contract. In an ideal world, a handshake would be all you needed to start designing the project. This is not an ideal world.

Whether it is a full-blown AIA form contract or a short letter agreement, the importance of having a written agreement cannot be overemphasized. Proceeding on the basis of an oral agreement is full of pitfalls. Recollections may vary, and the parties may disagree on the terms. It may turn out that an oral agreement is not enforceable. Oral agreements can never contain all the terms that would be in a written agreement. A written agreement serves as a road map for the project and a guide to facilitating the relationships and communications between you and your client. Two of its very valuable functions are: (1) to define everyone's expectations so that the parties understand what is expected of them and (2) to establish the rights and responsibilities of the parties in the event that something goes wrong during the project. In theory, once a written contract is signed and the project has begun, you can file the contract away to gather dust in your file cabinet and not look at it again. But if issues arise, as so often happens, you can pull out the agreement and, hopefully, derive from it guidance for resolving the issue. Only one thing is more comforting than secure guidance from your contract—a happy client at the completion of the job.

Any written agreement for services between you and an owner should contain some basic provisions. You must include a comprehensive description of your scope of work, specifying who is responsible for various consulting services. You also need to clearly state the fee and payment method for such services. Any agreement should also give you some basic legal protections as the design professional. These provisions include, among others, defining who owns your work product and how it can be used, a clear definition of your responsibilities during the design and construction phases, and dispute resolution and termination rights for both you and your client.

GETTING STARTED: WHAT SHOULD AN INITIAL PROPOSAL CONTAIN?

Agreements between an owner and an architect often start with a letter proposal from the architect setting out the proposed scope of the project and the fees. These letter proposals can, but often do not, contain legal provisions. The proposals can either be legally binding on the parties or, as is more customary, nonbinding, with the understanding (spelled out in the proposal) that you and your client will enter into a formal, binding agreement at some later date. Although the expectation is that the parties will enter into a subsequent written agreement, sometimes parties, for whatever reason, never get around to it. Work starts, relationships are good, and it is just not a high priority for anyone to formalize the relationship. That result can be disastrous. The project may well evolve and, as is often the case, expand, and yet the parties are still working from a short, bare-bones letter proposal at best. A proposal to renovate the bathroom and a closet may turn into renovation of an entire house, and yet you and the owner might simply be proceeding on the basis of a letter proposal for the bathroom and closet renovation.

Unless it is crystal clear that a binding agreement will be entered into promptly and you know that you will be diligent in getting it, even your initial proposal should contain at least some standard terms and conditions addressing basic legal issues for your protection, including intellectual property rights, payment terms, termination rights, and limitations on your liability. These provisions, and others, will re-emerge in the more extensive agreement that should follow the accepted initial proposal. We discuss them in detail below.

WHAT ARE THE BENEFITS OF USING
AMERICAN INSTITUTE OF ARCHITECTS FORMS OF AGREEMENT?

Since the late nineteenth century, the AIA has provided forms of agreement for use by architects, owners, and contractors. Using the AIA forms of agreement offers many benefits. First, some owners, particularly the more experienced, are familiar with the agreements. Moreover, the terminology used in the AIA agreements is generally understood by the owners' representatives, architects, contractors, and even some owners. Finally, if disputes arise, you have a body of case law and commentary by attorneys and construction professionals interpreting various provisions found in the standard AIA agreements to turn to for guidance. Each of these factors militates in favor of using the AIA forms as a starting point in documenting the owner/architect agreement.

The AIA periodically revises its forms to address the changing world of construction. For example, the AIA agreements now address "green" design issues and electronic transfer of documents.

Many commercial and institutional owners are skeptical of the AIA agreements, noting that, since the AIA forms are developed and presented by an organization of architects, the forms may be biased toward the architect. Perhaps so. A review of any AIA owner/architect form agreement reveals that it is replete with limitations on your responsibilities and qualifications for any services you render. Indeed, some owners extract selected sections of AIA form agreements, tweak them in their favor, and incorporate them into their own standard forms of agreement. Some owners have also begun to use a set of documents known as ConsensusDOCS. These forms, created by a consortium of construction industry organizations, seek to reflect input from a variety of parties to the construction process.

If you are using an AIA form of agreement, do not simply fill in the blanks and send it to your client without carefully reviewing the standard terms and conditions. The AIA, in crafting documents to be used in a variety of contexts throughout the United States and overseas, has made assumptions regarding what services an architect typically provides. The assumptions are not always applicable. Since every project is unique, you must review the AIA forms to be sure that your services include what the AIA deems basic services. For example, in some AIA form agreements the architect's basic services include mechanical, electrical, and structural engineering services. This imposes on the architect the duty to engage consultants (and assume the liability for their performance) in each of those specialized fields. In reality, some projects do not require all of them, or, in some cases, the owner engages some or all of these consultants directly. You must modify the standard provision in the AIA form agreement accordingly. Another example is the requirement that the architect review contractors' applications for payment. On larger projects the owner's representative or construction manager may perform that function so this standard provision should be modified. Additionally, the AIA details the architect's role in bidding out the work, but that may not in fact be part of your deal with your client. To avoid confusion and strife, carefully review and adjust as necessary any such provisions in the form. If the agreement is not modified and a problem arises, your client can always argue you failed to provide a service that was set forth in the agreement, even though neither party had really intended that you provide that service.

HOW IS THE TYPICAL ARCHITECT/OWNER AGREEMENT STRUCTURED?

Here, as elsewhere in this chapter, we refer to the AIA B101 2007 Standard Form of Agreement Between Owner and Architect (2007 B101 Agreement), the AIA form used by architects on many projects. However, the AIA offers other owner/architect forms that you should consider, depending on your project. Currently, the AIA has forms of owner/architect agreement for complex projects, projects of limited scope, and residential or small commercial projects.

Initial Information

The standard owner/architect agreements issued by the AIA, including the 2007 B101 Agreement, all generally have a similar structure. The first part identifies the parties, describes the project, and may detail other initial information such as the owner's budget, names of consultants on the project, the schedule for completion, and the like.

Standard of Care

Many owners expect to receive the pinnacle of service, a perfect work product, and a guarantee from you that every step will be flawless. But you probably are not superhuman. You certainly do not practice in Valhalla, nor do those who work with you and for you and whose contribution you take responsibility for. Errors can and do occur. Omissions are inevitable. That being the reality of the matter, you should include an appropriate definition of your standard of care in every contract.

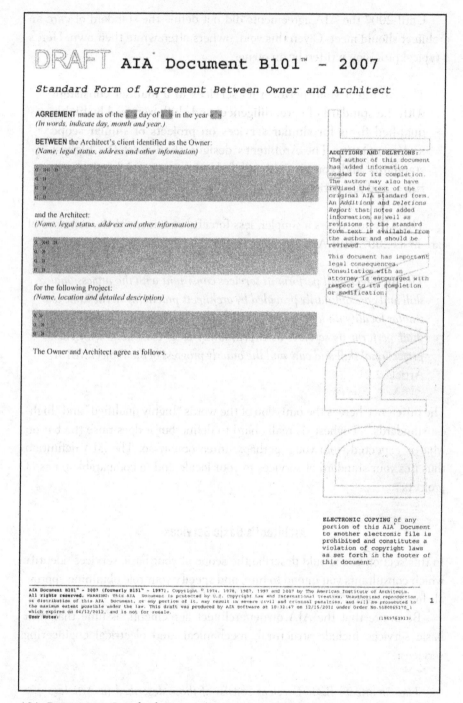

AIA B101 2007 Standard Form of Agreement Between Owner and Architect, page 1

Until 2007 the AIA agreements did not define the standard of care an architect should meet. Given this void, owners often wrote their own. Here's a typical provision written by an owner:

> The Architect shall perform its services in a manner consistent with the standard of care, diligence, and skill exercised by highly qualified firms for similar services on projects of similar scope and complexity. The Architect's designs shall meet the highest standards and comply with all federal, state, and local codes, rules, and regulations.

The AIA now offers a simpler, less forceful statement of the standard of care in its 2007 B101 Agreement:

> *The Architect shall perform its services consistent with the professional skill and care ordinarily provided by architects practicing in the same or similar locality under the same or similar circumstances. The Architect shall perform its services as expeditiously as is consistent with such professional skill and care and the orderly progress of the Project. (B101, Article 2.2)*

The difference here is the omission of the words "highly qualified" and "highest standards." "Highest" is really hard to define but it does raise the bar on what is expected from you—perhaps unreasonably so. The AIA definition thus ties your standard of services to your locale and to comparable types of projects.

Architect's Basic Services

In this section you should describe the scope of your basic services, identify which consultants you intend to hire, and specify your role obtaining approvals for the project.

Be aware that the AIA owner/architect agreements assume that your basic services include structural, mechanical, and electrical engineering services:

> *The Architect's Basic Services consist of those described in Article 3 and include usual and customary structural, mechanical, and electrical engineering services. (B101, Article 3.1)*

If you do not intend to provide these engineering services, modify this provision. If, for example, you are not hiring the structural engineer, your agreement should state that you can rely on what the engineer designs. The 2007 B101 Agreement provides in Article 3.1.2 as follows:

> *The architect shall be entitled to rely on the accuracy and completeness of services and information furnished by the Owner and the Owner's consultants.*

Countless other consultants may be needed on a particular project, so be sure to specify which ones you are responsible for.

Most agreements have a section defining your design responsibilities. On a typical large project, the architect's services are often broken into five phases: (a) schematic design, (b) design development, (c) construction documents, (d) bidding or negotiation, and (e) construction administration. On smaller projects, the agreements may compress one or more of these phases so that there may only be a design and construction administration phase. The construction phase provisions address all aspects of an architect's role for this phase of the project: site visits, review of shop drawings and submittals, review of applications for payment, changes in the work, and inspections upon project completion.

Scope descriptions in the AIA documents are typically quite general. If you are using an AIA form, review the descriptions to be sure they reflect what you are going to do and consider whether to expand the descriptions so that your clients have a better sense of what you do during the design phase.

For example, Article 3.2.5 of the 2007 B101 Agreement provides in the Schematic Design Phase Services section the following:

> *Based on the Owner's approval of the preliminary design, the Architect shall prepare Schematic Design Documents for the Owner's approval. The Schematic Design Documents shall consist of drawings and other documents including a site plan, if appropriate, and preliminary building plans, sections and elevations; and may include some combination of study models, perspective sketches, or digital modeling. Preliminary selections of major building systems and construction materials shall be noted on the drawings or described in writing.*

This article seems from a quick read to be general and innocuous. However, it merits careful reading. Are you providing a site plan? Are you agreeing to provide digital modeling? Are you going to provide preliminary selections of building systems or is that the purview of the engineers hired by your client? These questions apply to all the articles in any AIA contract that describe your scope. You must review the descriptions and carefully revise them to reflect what your actual scope of services is.

You also need to consider what limitations, if any, you place on revising your plans as the project progresses. You may have an owner who really does not know what he or she wants and asks you for countless initial sketches and drawings or numerous revisions along the way as the design takes shape. Are you willing to do this for the fee you originally proposed, or are you going to limit the number of drawings or revisions you make for that fee?

If you are not using an AIA form of agreement, you must write your own scope description of your services. Again, be as clear as you can be when describing your services so that there are no misunderstandings down the road. If you are using your own form of agreement, consider developing a set of your own standard terms and conditions to attach as an exhibit to your proposal, specifying your scope of work and fee. If you are designing a residential project, describe your services in detail so that your client can see what rooms/features are included in your proposed scope of work. You do not want to find out halfway through the project that your client expected you to design a library off the living room and you did not know that when you started work. If you can get your client to give you a written program (or if you write one with the client) you can avoid some future misunderstandings.

Increasingly, clients are requiring (and architects are recommending) that designs incorporate environmentally responsible design alternatives. The 2007 B101 Agreement has added provisions addressing this issue:

> The Architect shall consider environmentally responsible design alternatives, such as material choices and building orientation, together with other considerations based on program and aesthetics, in developing a design that is consistent with the Owner's program, schedule and budget for the Cost of the Work. The Owner may obtain other environmentally responsible design services under Article 4. (B101, Article 3.2.5.1)

If you are not going to consider these kinds of design alternatives, strike this provision. If your client is seeking more than this—for instance, certification of compliance with the standards of the U.S. Green Building Council (USGBC)—address that work in your agreement. The USGBC has established an internationally recognized certification system known as the Leadership in Energy and Environmental Design (LEED) Green Building Rating Systems. Different levels of LEED certification are achieved through a point system. Levels are, in ascending order, Certified, Silver, Gold, and Platinum.

A client who desires to have a LEED-certified project may propose a provision such as the following:

> It is understood that the Project will be designed as necessary and desirable to achieve LEED Gold certification by the United States Green Building Council.

Many variables can impact whether a project meets a LEED standard. Some of those are outside of your control. Therefore, if you are designing to a LEED standard, consider qualifying language as more fully documented in the section on indemnification, warranties, and guarantees in this chapter.

Designing to meet environmental goals is a changing area; you should welcome the opportunity to meet evolving environmental standards but be aware of the pitfalls when designing to specific goals.

Architect's Additional Services

In addition to the basic services provisions, the standard AIA owner/architect agreements identify potential additional services. A non-AIA agreement should do the same. Additional services typically fall into two categories. The first involves those services that the parties identify at the beginning as not part of basic services—typically those services offered by other disciplines such as landscape architecture, interior design, civil engineering, security, and telecommunications design. Other services that the AIA considers outside the typical scope for an architect are detailed cost estimating, on-site project representation, tenant-related services, furniture, fixtures and equipment design, and LEED certification. Many of these additional services have their own AIA form of supplemental agreement that you can attach and incorporate into the basic agreement if you are going to provide the service. At the time you are negotiating your contract, list and identify these additional services and the party responsible for providing them.

The second category of additional services encompasses changes to your basic services due to unforeseen developments during design or construction. The following services are typically defined as additional services due to changes in the project:

- Providing new and different services necessitated by a change in your client's initial information, instructions or approvals, or a material change in the project such as a change in size, quality, complexity, the owner's schedule or budget or method of project delivery.
- Changing or editing previously prepared drawings required by the enactment or revision of codes, laws, or regulations or by official interpretations.
- Preparing for and attendance at a public meeting or hearing.
- Preparing for and attendance at a dispute resolution proceeding, except where you are also a party.
- Reviewing a contractor's submittal out of sequence from the submittal schedule originally agreed to by you.
- Responding to a contractor's requests for information that are not prepared in accordance with the contract documents or where such information is available to the contractor from a careful study and comparison of the contract documents, field conditions, other owner-provided information, contractor-prepared coordination drawings, or prior project correspondence or documentation.
- Preparing change orders and construction change directives that require evaluation of the contractor's proposals and supporting data or the preparation or revision of drawings or specifications.

These additional services are often subject to negotiation with your client. The client may insist long after you have signed the basic agreement that a certain number of public presentations or attendance at public hearings be included in basic services for your basic service fee. He or she may claim to expect you to cooperate without charging a fee if there is a dispute between the client and a contractor. Clients may expect their architects to make multiple versions of designs and to be willing to change them to accommodate their wishes later in the project without incurring additional fees. In negotiating these issues, keep in mind the time and cost for the new work in relation to your overall fee proposal. Preparing for and attending a public hearing before a planning board can add hours of work, none of which will be compensable if you agree to include the work as a basic service. The fee section of your agreement can include contingent arrangements for additional services and provide for additional fees if those services become necessary.

Unless your fee arrangement is hourly, you should also consider providing to be compensated for additional services should the project continue for longer than initially anticipated or be delayed. The 2007 B101 Agreement in Article 4.3.4 has a provision addressing this issue:

> If the services covered by this Agreement have not been completed within _____ ( ) months of the date of this Agreement, through no fault of the Architect, extension of the Architect's services beyond that time shall be compensated as Additional Services.

Notwithstanding having this provision in your agreement, your clients may try to blame you for any delays or simply argue your fee is sufficient without further payments based on time.

Owner's Responsibilities

The AIA agreements also spell out certain responsibilities for your owner/clients. These responsibilities may include providing you with a written program, providing a budget and updating it as the project progresses, identifying a representative to act on the clients' behalf, providing legal documentation regarding the site, and furnishing, if necessary, services of geotechnical or other engineers. The nature of both the project and the client determines what information your client is responsible for providing to you. If you know at the beginning of a project what information you need from your client, be sure to ask for it and refer to that material in the agreement you are negotiating.

You need to be particularly aware of who has the final say when your client is not one individual. For example, in a single-family residential project where the husband and wife are both signatories to the agreement, whose direction takes precedence? You don't want to find yourself in the position where one spouse makes many expensive changes along the way and then the other spouse later questions those charges, as well as the attendant additional fees for your extra services, and resists paying. On commercial projects, determine who represents the owner, who may be in another state or country. Who can make decisions on a timely basis so the project does not get bogged down while you wait for a decision?

Cost of the Work

If your fee is tied to cost, the agreement should also provide for a definition. The "cost of the work" is typically defined as the cost of work for the portion of the project that has been specified or designed by you as the architect. This concept can be unclear in actual practice. For example, what if the owner engages some of the consultants, such as structural or mechanical engineers, whose specifications and designs are incorporated into your plans? You may still be expected to oversee and coordinate the work of those consultants, but will the structural or electrical work designed by them be considered "cost of the work" that is taken into account in computing your compensation? It's a question that needs to be addressed when negotiating an agreement.

The AIA agreements provide that you and your client can agree upon the budget for the project. The agreement also addresses what happens if the projected cost of the work exceeds the agreed-upon budget. Several possible scenarios can dramatically affect your workload and compensation. If you have agreed to design within the limits of a prearranged budget, then a contractor's estimated cost of the work that exceeds the budget may result in your having to redesign without further compensation to you to bring the project within budget. However, if there is no prearranged budget for the project, then you have a right to be paid for additional services if your client eventually determines that the contractor's estimated cost of the work is too high and requires redesign of the project. There really *must* be a clear understanding at the beginning of a project what the client's expectations are regarding a budget for the work.

Clients commonly change their minds as a project progresses. How many times has a client fallen in love with your initial designs and agreed to increase the budget or, better yet, said cost is no concern? At the same time, that client may suffer financial reverses or simply change his or her mind during the design or construction phase and require budget cutbacks. This can lead to misunderstandings about what you are entitled to be paid when your client asks for major redesign to save money part way into the final construction document design phase. Arguing over your additional compensation at this point can poison the relationship and put you in an awkward position going forward. And when there is a conflict over the budget, the owner sometimes unfairly seeks a fee reduction from you. All too often, at the end of the project, an owner complains about the cost, the time it took, and various other factors outside your control, and then blames you for all of them. By simply providing in the agreement for how you get paid if changes are made midstream, you can strengthen your position if your client later attempts to renegotiate your fees.

Ownership and Use of Instruments of Service

One of the most contentious issues in your contract negotiations with a client today concerns ownership and use of your work product. We deal with this subject in more detail in Chapter 2, but we touch briefly on the issue here since it frequently comes up in contract negotiations. Architects rightfully take pride in their creative talents and the designs they create. The work product you develop by applying your training, experience, and natural talent is precisely what your client hired you for in the first place. Architects have a right to protect their work and not see a house they have designed being built down the block by the same or a different developer. (This is not just a question of pride but of liability as well.) At the same time, an owner who has paid for a design might expect to be able to use it in any way he or she chooses. Conflict is inevitable unless you and your client can reach agreement at the beginning of a project on who owns what rights and who can use and in what circumstances the designs you have created.

The AIA agreements start with the proposition that the architect owns the intellectual property rights in his or her work product and controls the copyright. Although owners sometimes wish to own the copyright in the plans created for their project (known as a work made for hire), owners are generally more interested in the right to use the work product to (a) complete the project should the architect be terminated, (b) use the work product to make modifications or additions to the project following completion of the architect's services or termination of the architect during the design or construction phases, and (c) make use of the work product on other projects. Owners often make the simple but appealing argument that they should get to use what they have paid for without limitation.

Over the years, the AIA has struggled with how to address the perplexing issue of ownership and use of architects' work product. In an attempt to meet clients' concerns regarding use, the AIA provides in the 2007 versions of the AIA owner/architect agreements that a client may use your work product to complete, modify, or expand a project without your involvement, provided that the client (1) performs its obligations under the agreement, and (2) agrees to indemnify and hold you harmless from claims arising out of use of your plans without your involvement. This right, combined with the client's right to terminate an agreement for convenience, is a concession to the clients' side of the debate. This compromise seems a reasonable solution to a tricky issue and avoids what were often contentious negotiations. What the AIA agreements still do not address is the issue of use of your name if you are terminated before your services are complete. Therefore, in working through these termination and use issues, you need to consider adding that your client will retain a new architect of record and will not use your name on the project unless you consent. Here is a provision to address this concern:

> In the event of termination prior to completion of the Architect's services, Owner agrees to retain a new architect of record and not to use the Architect's name in connection with the Project without the Architect's prior written consent.

Cost Estimating

The standard AIA contracts state that the architect as part of basic services shall provide cost estimating services. However, the language is qualified as follows:

> *Evaluations of the Owner's budget for the Cost of the Work, the preliminary estimate of the Cost of the Work and updated estimates of the Cost of the Work prepared by the Architect, represent the Architect's judgment as a design professional. It is recognized, however, that neither the Architect nor the Owner has control over the cost of labor, materials or equipment; the Contractor's methods of determining bid prices; or competitive bidding, market or negotiating conditions. Accordingly, the Architect cannot and does not warrant or represent that bids or negotiated prices will not vary from the Owner's budget for the Cost of the Work or from any estimate of the Cost of the Work or evaluation prepared or agreed to by the Architect.* (B101, Article 6.2)

The qualifications in this paragraph simply reflect the reality that an architect cannot guarantee or warrant that a contractor's bid will meet what was projected.

The standard AIA contracts also provide that *detailed* cost estimating is an additional service. Cost estimating is a minefield for architects. Architects often estimate in terms of a cost per square foot based upon experience with a particular type of project. More detailed estimating may be beyond your professional experience, requiring you to engage a person with that specialty. Therefore, whenever possible, encourage the client to engage the cost estimator directly.

Many AIA contracts require, as part of basic services, the architect to redesign the project should the design come in over the projected budget. Where the owner provides a budget and engages a cost estimator, the contract can provide that the architect shall receive additional services compensation in the event redesign is needed because the cost estimator understated a material item of cost.

Schedule for Services

AIA contracts also require architects to provide a schedule for services. The 2007 B101 Agreement requires the architect to provide "as soon as practicable after the date of this Agreement" a schedule with anticipated dates for commencement of construction and for substantial completion of the work (Article 3.1.3). Schedules are always difficult to determine at the beginning of a project, so if you provide one, include appropriate caveats as outlined in this section and update the schedule periodically.

Owners, particularly commercial owners and residential developers, are obsessed with timely completion of a project, as prompt completion has obviously significant impact on the profitability of the project. The store that cannot open for the holidays due to delays by the architect may have multimillion-dollar losses in sales. The homeowner who cannot move in when anticipated and who must therefore continue to pay rent elsewhere has potentially significant additional costs. The concert hall that cannot open due to an architect's errors in design may have to scramble to find alternative and expensive venues for the scheduled performances. The university dormitory not completed by the beginning of the semester may require the college to house students in temporary and expensive housing. The pressures on you to complete your work quickly are immense and, therefore, create not only stress but also the potential for errors as speed takes precedence over careful drafting.

Because of concerns over speedy completion, clients often insist on a provision commonly known as a "time is of the essence" clause. A typical version of this clause may read like the following:

> Time is of the essence for performance of the Architect's services and if the Architect fails to meet the design schedule the Architect shall be liable to reimburse Owner for all damages incurred as a result of failing to meet the schedule.

Not only does the "time is of the essence" clause put pressure on you, it also often compels you to notify your client of every potential delay to your performance caused by the client or others over whom you have no control and thereby "make a record" of any potential delay to avoid a claim of default on your part (more on this in Chapter 7). You should always try to avoid "time is of the essence" clauses in your agreements. Propose instead the language that the AIA has incorporated into its standard forms of agreement:

> *The Architect shall perform its services as expeditiously as is consistent with such professional skill and care and the orderly progress of the Project.* (B101, Article 2.2)

If, however, you are unsuccessful in removing a "time is of the essence" clause, be sure your project schedule incorporates plenty of leeway for deadlines and includes explicit time frames for responses by your client or your client's consultants and reviews of your plans and specifications. If you encounter any delays, notify your client *in writing* in a timely manner (e-mail usually suffices).

You should also insist on a provision commonly known as a "force majeure" clause. A "force majeure" clause extends time for performance of all parties due to changes in the work, labor disputes, fire, or other causes beyond your reasonable control. A "force majeure" clause might read as follows:

> **The Architect shall be excused from performance hereunder arising from a cause beyond its reasonable control that it could not by the exercise of due diligence have avoided, including an act of any governmental authority, an act of God, extraordinary weather conditions, flood, and accidents such as fire or explosion not due to the negligence of the Architect.**

Construction Administration

In any agreement, you must carefully define the services that you provide during the construction phase. Owners often expect the architect to be their "eyes and ears" on the project and to keep them informed of every project detail. But unless you are on site every day, you may not be able to meet your client's expectations. Therefore, your agreement with the owner should properly define and qualify your responsibilities for such matters as site visits, shop drawing and submittal reviews, certification of applications for payment, and determination of substantial and final completion. The AIA does so in its form agreements, and you should sit down with your client at the beginning of the project to explain your administrative role during construction.

Site Visits

Most architects visit a project site only once or twice a week (or month) during the construction phase. As a result, unbeknownst to you, construction sometimes deviates from your plans and specifications. Walls might be closed before you get to the site, making it impossible to determine if the proper insulation was installed. Or doors, windows, or stairways may be installed improperly or in wrong locations without your being present to make corrections and necessitating time-consuming reconstruction. The AIA contract forms recognize your limited role during site visits such as, for instance, in the 2007 B101 Agreement, Article 3.6.2.1, where the architect's responsibilities for site visits are defined as follows:

> The Architect shall visit the site at intervals appropriate to the stage of construction, or as otherwise required in Section 4.3.3, to become generally familiar with the progress and quality of the portion of the Work completed, and to determine, in general, if the Work observed is being performed in a manner indicating that the Work, when fully completed, will be in accordance with the Contract Documents. However, the Architect shall not be required to make exhaustive or continuous on-site inspections to check the quality or quantity of the Work. On the basis of the site visits, the Architect shall keep the Owner reasonably informed about the progress and quality of the portion of the Work completed, and report to the Owner (1) known deviations from the Contract Documents and from the most recent construction schedule submitted by the Contractor, and (2) defects and deficiencies observed in the Work.

The 2007 B101 Agreement actually provides for you to specify the number of site visits you intend to make during construction (B101, Article 4.3.3.2).

If you are responsible for preparing minutes of project site meetings, be sure to take careful and accurate notes. You should send minutes promptly to those in attendance at the meeting and others who should be kept advised of what transpired. Your minutes should always have, at the end, a statement such as the following:

> Please provide any comments on these minutes within seventy-
> two hours.

If someone, such as the contractor or construction manager, is responsible for preparing minutes, be certain to review them and comment as needed. Years later, when a dispute arises, minutes are often the best record of what was happening at a particular point in time at the project.

Rejecting/Stopping Work

Imagine arriving at the job site during installation of stucco and discovering that the contractor is not installing it the way you think it should be. Your client is in Europe and not reachable. What to do? In some circumstances it may be necessary for you to tell the contractor to stop work. But if you do and it turns out that the contractor was doing the work correctly, there is a distinct possibility you will be caught up in a delay claim by the contractor.

You do not want to get involved in telling the contractor how to do his or her job. The means and methods of construction are the contractor's responsibilities, not yours. Further, you risk the possibility of being caught up in a delay claim.

The AIA agreements provide that an architect has authority to reject (but not stop) work that does not conform to the contract documents. The 2007 B101 Agreement in Article 3.6.2.2 provides as follows:

> *The Architect has the authority to reject Work that does not conform to the Contract Documents. Whenever the Architect considers it necessary or advisable, the Architect shall have the authority to require inspection or testing of the Work in accordance with the provisions of the Contract Documents, whether or not such Work is fabricated, installed or completed. However, neither this authority of the Architect nor a decision made in good faith either to exercise or not to exercise such authority shall give rise to a duty or responsibility of the Architect to the Contractor, Subcontractors, material and equipment suppliers, their agents or employees or other persons or entities performing portions of the Work.*

Deciding how to proceed when confronted with defective work is fraught with pitfalls. Ideally you notify your client, who then instructs the contractor to stop work per their owner/contractor agreement. Sometimes, though, you may not have that luxury and have to deal directly with the contractor.

Shop Drawing and Submittal Reviews

Another area where architects and their clients may disagree is in their respective expectations about shop drawing and submittal reviews. Shop drawings are drawings, diagrams, schedules, and other data created by a contractor, subcontractor, manufacturer, supplier, or distributor to illustrate some portion of the work they are performing or supplying. The AIA agreements limit your responsibility for shop drawing review to checking for conformance with information given and design concepts expressed in the contract documents.

Owners often expect you to provide more detailed reviews and for you to confirm dimensions and compliance of the shop drawings with applicable codes. You may also do a more detailed review on your own initiative to be sure dimensions are correct. If you do undertake this more detailed role, you then may be at risk if problems arise with the item you reviewed. The 2007 B101 Agreement attempts to limit your responsibilities for shop drawings and submittal review and provides as follows:

> In accordance with the Architect-approved submittal schedule, the Architect shall review and approve or take other appropriate action upon the Contractor's submittals such as Shop Drawings, Product Data and Samples, but only for the limited purpose of checking for conformance with information given and the design concept expressed in the Contract Documents. Review of such submittals is not for the purpose of determining the accuracy and completeness of other information such as dimensions, quantities, and installation or performance of equipment or systems, which are the Contractor's responsibility. The Architect's review shall not constitute approval of safety precautions or, unless otherwise specifically stated by the Architect, of any construction means, methods, techniques, sequences or procedures. The Architect's approval of a specific item shall not indicate approval of an assembly of which the item is a component. (B101, Article 3.6.4.2)

You should also be sure that shop drawing stamps, used when reviewing submittals and shop drawings, are consistent with the stated limitations in your contract. A typical shop drawing stamp for the architect of record on a project may look something like this:

FILE NO._____ SUBMISSION NO._____

☐ NO EXCEPTION TAKEN
☐ REJECTED
☐ REVISE AND RESUBMIT
☐ SUBMIT SPECIFIED ITEM

Review is for general conformance with the design concept of the Project and general compliance with the information given in the Contract Documents. Corrections or notations made on Shop Drawings do not relieve the Contractor from complying with requirements of the Contract Documents. Approval of a specific item shall not include approval of an assembly of which the item is a component. The Contractor is responsible for confirming and correlating all quantities and dimensions, selecting fabrication processes and techniques of construction, coordinating its work with the work of others, and performing its work in a safe and satisfactory manner.

By: _____ Date:_____

Architect Proj No._____ Proj Name_____

ARCHITECT'S NAME
Address

If you are asked to review a shop drawing by a contractor where the submittal is subject to review of other consultants, you may want to use a stamp like the one on the next page.

Try to avoid the temptation and, at times, pressure from the owner to go beyond your contractual obligations when reviewing shop drawings. If you do, you do so at your own peril. The last thing you want is to suddenly take on liability for some fabrication detail because of the way you analyzed and commented on it.

FILE NO._____ SUBMISSION NO._____

☐ NO EXCEPTION TAKEN
☐ REJECTED
☐ REVISE AND RESUBMIT
☐ SUBMIT SPECIFIED ITEM

This submittal has been reviewed for design compliance only as it applies to Architect's design intent. This submittal is primarily subject to the review and approval of other Consultants whose disciplines are responsible for the construction trade work in this submittal.

By: _____ Date:_____

Architect Proj No._____ Proj Name_____

ARCHITECT'S NAME
Address

Certificates of Payment to Contractor

Architects are often expected to review and approve contractor applications for payment. The nature of the review may depend upon the terms of the contract between your client and the contractor. If that contract provides that the contractor build the project for a lump sum, including the cost of the work and contractor's overhead, insurance, and fee, then the applications for payment traditionally request payment based on a percentage of completion of the entire project or a particular phase. If, on the other hand, the contractor has a "cost-plus agreement," meaning that the contractor gets reimbursed for the actual cost of each item of work plus a fee, then the applications for payment must contain backup documentation showing the costs actually incurred by the contractor, and you may be expected to review that documentation. This is an immense headache. Few architects have the back-office support or accounting expertise to review every invoice a contractor has paid on a cost-plus project. You need to make clear to your client at the time you enter into your agreement the limitations you have reviewing the contractor's invoices and back-up documentation. Review with your client the payment forms that your contractor will submit and explain how you will analyze them. The task can be out-sourced to a construction management firm or a qualified accountant at a fee to the client.

There is real potential for trouble when the contractor does not have the capability to provide proper cost documentation. This happens at times on single-family residential projects where the contractor may be a master builder but just cannot manage the paperwork. It then becomes tempting for the architect to take on the responsibility of trying to make sense of the contractor's billings by generating summaries and documentation for the owner. Be careful of stepping into this potential minefield—your client relies on you and, if you are given incorrect information, the contractor's poor bookkeeping suddenly becomes your problem.

The standard AIA agreement undertakes to define and qualify your responsibilities when reviewing a contractor's certificate for payment. The 2007 B101 Agreement, Article 3.6.3, reads as follows:

> The Architect shall review and certify the amounts due the Contractor and shall issue certificates in such amounts. The Architect's certification for payment shall constitute a representation to the Owner, based on the Architect's evaluation of the Work as provided in Section 3.6.2 and on the data comprising the Contractor's Application for Payment, that, to the best of the Architect's knowledge, information and belief, the Work has progressed to the point indicated and that the quality of the Work is in accordance with the Contract Documents. The foregoing representations are subject (1) to an evaluation of the Work for conformance with the Contract Documents upon Substantial Completion, (2) to results of subsequent tests and inspections, (3) to correction of minor deviations from the Contract Documents prior to completion, and (4) to specific qualifications expressed by the Architect. (B101, Article 3.6.3.1)
>
> The issuance of a Certificate for Payment shall not be a representation that the Architect has (1) made exhaustive or continuous on-site inspections to check the quality or quantity of the Work, (2) reviewed construction means, methods, techniques, sequences or procedures, (3) reviewed copies of requisitions received from Subcontractors and mate-

rial suppliers and other data requested by the Owner to substantiate the Contractor's right to payment, or (4) ascertained how or for what purpose the Contractor has used money previously paid on account of the Contract Sum. (B101, Article 3.6.3.2)

Substantial Completion/Punch Lists/Final Completion

The standard AIA contracts provide for the architect to sign off on contractors' substantial completion and final completion of a project. Substantial completion is typically defined to be that point in the project where your client can use the project (or a portion of the project) for its intended purposes. This usually means, in connection with new construction or a major renovation, that your client can live in the house or that a temporary or permanent certificate of occupancy has been obtained and the owner can move in, although some work remains to be completed.

Substantial completion has major significance for all participants on the construction project. For the contractor, this often means that a portion of the contractor's billing, which may have been withheld during the course of the project (retainage), is released. If the owner can take occupancy and use the premises, even though the contractor still must do work, the owner's insurance may kick in at that point and take over for the contractor's insurance.

You as the architect, when it appears that the project is substantially complete, are called upon to make a close inspection of the work to determine whether it satisfies the standard for substantial completion. The level of review is higher than what is expected during normal site visits during the construction phase. Substantial completion may also be a point in time when written warranties from vendors and suppliers are turned over to your client. Normally, you are expected to obtain from the contractor and forward to your client the written warranties and related documents required by the contract documents and assembled by the contractor. Determining Substantial Completion also has significance for you as the architect. Under Article 4.3.2 of the 2007 B101 Agreement your final payment is due the earlier of the date of Substantial Completion or the anticipated date of Substantial Completion (if set forth in your agreement). Services provided thereafter are considered additional services.

Once you have determined that the project is substantially complete, you and your client should generate a punch list for the contractor. This punch list, which identifies minor work still to be done, is an important document since its completion sets the terms for final completion and final payment to the

			Punch List			1/16/2012
4th Floor						
Room #	Room Name	Sub	Issue/ Scope	Date submitted	Date Resolved	
401	Guest bedroom	Electrician	Install the 4 sconce. Installed however the junction box is still visible.	28-Dec		
		AV Contractor	Install the 2nd TV as requested by the owner	28-Dec		
		Decorator	The 4 sconce that had the bell covers modified to cover the junction boxes still do not cover. Please advise if they should be removed and sent back to empire metal?	16-Jan		
		GC	(1)Install the radius grilles. Delivery date schedule for the 1st week in January.(2)Install the sash stays on both windows.(Recently ordered)	28-Dec		
402	Vestibule	Electrician	Install ceiling light fixture. Onsite and ready for installation.	28-Dec		
403	Bathroom	Millworker	"Install edge pulls on the vanity doors, please mortise for the edge pulls. Edge pulls onsite and ready for installation!"	28-Dec		
404	Closet	GC	Install the closet pole.	28-Dec		
405	Bedroom	Painter	Touch up the window sill paint	28-Dec		
		GC	(1)Complete the GWB to glass transition cleanup.(2) Change out the shutter knob set screws to brass.	28-Dec		
		Millworker	Adjust the access panel to sit flush with the wall.	28-Dec		
406	Bath	Painter	Touch up the ceiling paint	28-Dec		
		Plumber	(1)Install the permanent faucet once returned from modification and the drain componets once received back from Metal man.	28-Dec		
407	Closet	GC	(1)Label access panel.(2) Install the closet pole	28-Dec		
408	Hall	Decorator	The wall covering will stay & all the door color to remain the same.	4-Jan		
409	Powder Room	Plumber	Replace the existing wall mounted faucet as requested by client. Options are currently being reviewed.	28-Dec		
		Decorator	PA to advise on the final wall covering finish decision. The faucet handles from 403 have been installed temporarily in this room for client review.	4-Jan		
410	Utility Room	Millworker	Remove the installed shelf. RA to advise if enough material is left over to create a wall to wall shelf to live above the safe cabinet	28-Dec		
		GC	Label access panel	28-Dec		
		Client	GC is awaiting the final decision for the floor & ceiling finish?	16-Jan		
411	Elevator Vest.	Carpenter	Install permanent hinges on the elevator door. Pending delivery from Vendor.	4-Jan		
		Decorator	Wall covering to remain	25-Jul		
		GC	Label the access panel.(2) Replace the elevator door stay.	28-Dec		
412	Family Room	Painter	(1)Paint the wall sensor.(1) Paint the white curtain track to match the wall paper.	28-Dec		
		Electrician	"Drop the chandelier 3 1/2"" as requested by PA."			
		AV Contractor	Client/ Client rep to confirm permanent location of the I POD dock. GC can review the scope.	28-Dec		
		Plumber	Provide colored sprinkler caps & install.	28-Dec		
		Metal Worker	"Please adjust the S-wall railing stand offs to have the same dimension from the teak cap to the coup link as the railing to the coup link. Currently all dimensions are different and one post is not secure.(2) The teak railing is not secure at the intersection where it meets the teak panel., please complete this."	16-Jan		
		Decorator	"Please confirm whether of not the curtain tracks will be powder coated or painted,"	16-Jan		
		Millworker	(1)Mortise & install edge pulls upon delivery.(2) Removed the bar cabinet doors to apply a refinishing coat. Continue the same process to the façade boards around the bar.	28-Dec		
		GC	Label the access panels throughout the room. Install the dishwasher kick plate. Cut out for & install access panel under the bulkhead stair case.	28-Dec		
414	Terrace	GC	Complete brick & mortar repairs at perimeter walls.	28-Dec		
		Landscaper	Complete the irrigation & landscape lighting testing.	28-Dec		
		Mason	Complete the stucco above the terrace doors. The final color must mirror the bluestone threshold.	16-Jan		

Sample Punch List

contractor (and possibly to you if your client has tied your last payment to the contractor's final completion of the project). Be certain that there is an agreement by and among the contractor, you, and your client as to what items are on the punch list.

As the contractor completes the punch list, items are removed and the list updated. After fully addressing the punch list, the contractor seeks your sign-off that the project is complete and final payment can be made. Many projects as they near completion seem to grind on and on, and the contractor never finishes the punch list. You can do little in this situation. If possible, avoid having your final fee installment dependent upon the contractor's finishing the punch list. The AIA forms of contract address this concern in part by providing that your services end when you issue the Final Certificate for Payment. Notice that the agreement says "issue," and that it is not keyed to actual "payment." Owners may not pay, but that does not mean you are still responsible for providing services until the owner finally gets around to paying.

Indemnification, Warranties and Guarantees

Because of your client's often heightened expectations, issues associated with indemnification, warranties for, and guarantees of your work frequently arise in contract negotiations. You should make sure that you have the benefit of professional liability insurance to protect you in the event of a claim for indemnification, or breach of warranty or guarantee. We discuss insurance in more detail in Chapter 3.

Clients often seek to be indemnified or, in another formulation, "held harmless" from claims by third parties arising out of your work. Therefore, your clients may seek to add indemnity clauses in their owner/architect agreements protecting them and their related entities or family members from claims by third parties. The claims in question would generally be personal injury or property damage claims arising at the project site. Someone visiting the project site might suffer an injury when floorboards give out. A neighbor's car might be damaged by a wall that collapses. In these situations the owner also often looks to the architect to defend any claim. The only problem is that many insurance companies providing professional liability coverage do not step up to defend a "claim" that has not matured into a finding of liability on your part. Rather, insurance companies provide coverage for costs incurred by an owner, including legal fees, after the architect's liability is established (see Chapter 8). You should do what you can to avoid having to commit to any obligation to "defend" your client in the event a claim is made against the client.

Here is a typical indemnity clause that your client may want to insert in the agreement:

> To the fullest extent permitted by law, the Architect shall defend, indemnify, and hold harmless Owner, its officers, directors, members, managers, agents, and employees from and against any and all claims, actions, suits, damages, losses, and expenses resulting from the acts or omissions by the Architect and the Architect's consultants in the performance of their respective professional services pursuant to this Agreement. The provisions of this paragraph shall survive expiration or termination of this Agreement.

Here is the same clause with modifications that, if accepted by an owner, should allow you to avail yourself of your professional liability insurance coverage:

> To the fullest extent permitted by law, the Architect shall indemnify and hold harmless Owner, its officers, directors, members, managers, and employees from and against damages, losses, and expenses resulting from the negligent acts or omissions by the Architect and the Architect's consultants in the performance of their respective professional services pursuant to this Agreement. The provisions of this paragraph shall survive expiration or termination of this Agreement.

This provision omits the duty to "defend" and further provides that the indemnity triggering event be limited to your negligent acts or omissions. The provision also removes "agents" from the indemnity obligation since the term is not defined and therefore encompasses a whole range of parties you may not know about. Your professional liability insurance should cover you for such acts or omissions under this provision.

Architects should avoid making any "guarantee" of their work product. Guaranteeing that a design complies with applicable codes, rules, and regulations raises the standard by which you are measured in the event of a claim. Most clients believe an architect should be willing to agree to design a project in compliance with all applicable laws, codes, rules, and regulations. Against this, however, many architects would argue that they are not perfect, many factors and considerations can affect the practical application and effect of a design, and mistakes inevitably happen.

A prime example of problems you may encounter when you are asked to "guarantee" your work is compliance with the Americans with Disabilities Act (the ADA). The ADA is a statute that requires buildings to be designed in certain ways to meet the needs of disabled persons. Precisely what should be done to meet those needs can be subject to differing interpretations. Guaranteeing compliance may get you in trouble. You therefore may want to consider a provision in your agreement that reads something like the following:

> The Owner acknowledges that the requirements of the ADA may be subject to various and possibly contradictory interpretations. The Architect will use its reasonable professional efforts to interpret applicable ADA requirements as they apply to the Project. The Architect, however, cannot and does not warrant or guarantee that the Project will comply with all interpretations of the ADA.

Another example where there could be potential problems with any guarantee of your plans is in the area of LEED certification. You and your client may have agreed that the building you are designing meet a silver LEED-certification level. However, attaining the certification depends on a number of factors beyond your control, including how the building is operated. Therefore, any agreement providing that you design to meet a certain LEED certification should contain a provision along these lines:

> In its design of the Project, the Architect shall exercise all reasonable efforts consistent with its standards of care as provided in the Agreement to assist the Owner in attaining LEED Silver Certification and energy efficiency; however, the Architect cannot guarantee that the Project will achieve such certification or will be energy self-sufficient because the Architect shall not have control over how the Owner or other users of the Project will carry out the design intent and meet the requirements to achieve certification or maintain the Project as energy self-sufficient.

A strict standard of care does not recognize the reality that architects cannot completely insulate against human error. Still, it is hard to argue with a client who asks you to commit in writing that your work product comply with applicable laws and regulations. That is about as far as you should go in promising error-free results, but do so with appropriate caveats such as the ones mentioned in this section.

Dispute Resolution

For many years, the standard AIA contracts provided for arbitration as the sole means to resolve any dispute. Arbitration is a private proceeding, usually held either in a lawyer's office or the offices of the organization administering the arbitration, such as the American Arbitration Association. The rules of evidence are not formally enforced in most arbitration proceedings and the proceedings are totally confidential. In 1997, the AIA added nonbinding mediation as a prerequisite to arbitration. Mediation is also a private process where a neutral party who has no authority to make decisions or render a binding ruling on the merits endeavors to resolve disputes by meeting together and separately with the parties. In 2007, recognizing that many owners found arbitration to be biased toward architects either because some arbitrators are architects or because arbitrators have a reputation, albeit not necessarily correct, that they tend to resolve claims by providing compromise "split decisions," the AIA modified the provisions. But many owners, particularly institutional and commercial owners, insist upon litigation as the means to resolve disputes. Accordingly, the AIA now has in its contracts a check-the-box approach to dispute resolution. There is a box for arbitration, a box for litigation, and a box marked "Other." For a detailed discussion of claim resolution, see Chapter 7.

Limiting Damages

Closely tied to the provisions of your contract on dispute resolution are those relating to what damages can be recovered. For example, an error in the architect's design may require that a wall be replaced. The cost to replace that wall (and to redesign it) is a direct damage resulting from the architect's negligent error and omission. If replacement of the wall delays completion of the project and the project is a new store expected to open in time for the Christmas holiday season, then a claim by the owner for the lost profits due to the store's not opening would be a "consequential damage" of the negligent design. These losses, which include lost profits, loss of income from not being able to use a new facility, or additional rent paid pending moving in to the new facility, are all losses that would be considered consequential damages. The 2007 B101 Agreement has a specific provision addressing consequential damages:

The Architect and Owner waive consequential damages for claims, disputes or other matters in question arising out of or relating to this Agreement. This mutual waiver is applicable, without limitation, to all consequential damages due to either party's termination of this Agreement, except as specifically provided in Section 9.7. (B101, Article 8.1.3)

Keeping this provision in the agreement is well worth fighting for in many instances. No matter how much insurance you may have, a catastrophic loss due to your negligence could result in damages exceeding your policy limits. Obviously, the nature of the project may have a bearing on how important the consequential damages waiver is for you. A small apartment renovation may have little or no potential damages, so fighting for the provision in negotiation may not be that important and you can focus on other issues as appropriate.

As a further way to prevent catastrophic damages, you may try to limit your maximum exposure to the fees you are paid. This argument is most appealing when you have a relatively small fee compared to the cost of construction and therefore to the potential damages if something goes wrong. A provision limiting your liability to your fees or a set amount would read something like this:

Neither the Architect, nor the Architect's consultants, shall be jointly, severally, or individually liable to the Owner in excess of the compensation to be paid pursuant to the Agreement or _____ Dollars ($_____), whichever is greater by reason of act or omission, including breach of contract or negligence not amounting to a willful misconduct.

If you cannot get agreement on limiting your liability to your fee or a certain sum, then you may be successful in getting your liability for damages to your client limited to the amount of professional liability insurance coverage you carry. A provision with this limitation would read as follows:

In recognition of the relative risks, rewards, and obligations of the Owner, the Architect, the Architect's consultants, and building contractors, the Owner agrees that the Architect's liability under this Agreement shall be limited to the amount of Architect's professional liability insurance.

Third-Party Beneficiaries

If you are the architect for a new condominium, purchasers of new units will review your floor plans and other written material your office prepares for the developer marketing the units. The last thing you want to see is some disgruntled purchaser who finds the apartment not to his or her liking suing you. If a client of yours has a lender who periodically asks for updates on the program of construction, you certainly do not want the lender to be able to sue you over the reports you have provided.

You have a contract with your client. You do not have a contract with a purchaser of a new condominium apartment or with your client's lender. Yet, both the purchaser and lender may have cause to sue you based on the legal theory that they are a beneficiary of your agreement with your client and can stand in the shoes of your client and sue for breach of contract.

To help deter and, ideally, prevent these lawsuits the 2007 B101 Agreement has a standard provision reading as follows:

> *Nothing contained in this Agreement shall create a contractual relationship with or a cause of action in favor of a third party against either the Owner or Architect.* (B101, Article 10.5)

Many lenders want the right to take over a contract should their borrower (your client) default on a construction loan. The issue here often becomes whether the lender should be responsible for the owner's obligations to you that predate the owner's default. If your client is in default on the loan, chances are that the client is also behind in payments to you. When the lender takes over, you ideally want the lender to be required to pay any past-due amounts owed to your firm. The 2007 B101 Agreement requires the lender to assume all of the owner's obligations.

> *The Owner and Architect, respectively, bind themselves, their agents, successors, assigns and legal representatives to this Agreement. Neither the Owner nor the Architect shall assign this Agreement without the written consent of the other, except that the Owner may assign this Agreement to a lender providing financing for the Project if the lender agrees to assume the Owner's rights and obligations under this Agreement.* (B101, Article 10.3)

Lenders often ask you to sign their own forms of consent during the course of the project. Be sure to read the proposed consent carefully, because lenders often seek to disclaim any responsibility for their borrower's obligations that predate a default on the loan.

Insurance Provisions

Architects need to understand not only what insurance they should have but also what insurance the contractors and owners should carry. Some of the AIA agreements published in 2007 require you to list the insurance limits you have for (1) professional liability insurance to cover negligent errors and omissions in the design work, (2) general liability insurance to cover what is commonly referred to as "slip and fall" situations, (3) automobile insurance if the architect has or rents a car or cars, and (4) workers' compensation insurance to cover injury claims by your employees.

Clients often insist that you carry insurance for a number of years following completion of the project. It is not unreasonable for an owner to require that the architect maintain professional liability coverage for several years after completion, but any such requirement should, if possible, be couched in terms of the coverage being "reasonably commercially available."

The client and the architect often have to negotiate appropriate limits of coverage. There is no right or wrong number for the amount of professional liability or general liability insurance you should carry, especially in today's litigious environment. But if the owner seeks to impose what you consider to be excessive limits, then the additional cost should be factored into your fee negotiations. The client who insists on extraordinary insurance protection should be prepared to pay for it.

Insurance is addressed in more detail in Chapter 3.

Electronic Transfer of Documents

More and more architects who use software to create their drawings transfer those drawings electronically to the client or to a third party such as a contractor. The AIA now recognizes this possibility and provides in its agreements that a standard form of electronic transfer agreement be part of the agreement. Documents sent electronically may get corrupted in the process, resulting in a critical issue: who is liable for the resulting errors that, if undetected, can create big problems for the project? We discuss the

AIA's approach to the issue in its form documents in more detail in Chapter 2. Here, though, we stress the need for you to be clear with your client as to which set of documents serves as the permanent record—the files transferred electronically or the hard copy that your office generates.

Termination

Any owner/architect agreement should provide both you and your client the right to terminate for a breach of contract, also referred to as termination "for cause." Cause would certainly include your client's failure to pay you in accordance with the terms in your agreement. The AIA agreements give you the option of terminating or suspending services if you are not being paid. If you plan to terminate, provide written notice to the other party to allow an opportunity for the other party to cure the alleged default.

The termination for cause provision in the 2007 B101 Agreement reads as follows:

> *Either party may terminate this Agreement upon not less than seven days' written notice should the other party fail substantially to perform in accordance with the terms of this Agreement through no fault of the party initiating the termination.* (B101, Article 9.4)

To afford a party an opportunity to cure, the provision could be rewritten as follows:

> **Either party may terminate this Agreement upon not less than seven days' written notice should the other party fail substantially to perform in accordance with the terms of the Agreement, provided, however, that prior to exercising the right to terminate, the party seeking to terminate shall provide the other party with a detailed written statement of the reasons and at least seven (7) days to cure any alleged default.**

The AIA agreements provide that if the architect terminates an agreement for cause the architect is entitled to anticipated profit on the value of services not performed (see Article 9.7 of the 2007 B101 Agreement). This is one of the first provisions owners seek to delete.

The AIA agreements also give the owner the right to terminate for convenience:

The Owner may terminate this Agreement upon not less than seven days' written notice to the Architect for the Owner's convenience and without cause. (B101, Article 9.5)

The AIA forms do not, however, give you the same right to terminate for convenience. It is very unusual for a professional such as an architect to have the luxury of just being able to walk away from an engagement without good reason. This can put you in an awkward spot sometimes. You may find yourself with a difficult owner who may be making your life miserable through constant phone calls or e-mails or simply an inability to make design decisions. Yet you cannot just stop working. In these circumstances the best you can do is to try to have a straightforward conversation with your client, tell him or her it would be better to get a new architect, and then offer to cooperate with the new architect.

If your client has the right to terminate for convenience, you should also provide for some additional compensation if your client intends to use your work product to complete the project. In Article 11.9, the 2007 B101 Agreement provides for a further payment (a licensing fee) but leaves it to you and the owner to fill in the amount. It is not easy to determine the amount when negotiating an agreement. Nor is it an easy subject to discuss. It is awkward to be talking about termination and licensing fees before you have even started work.

CONSULTANTS:
WHO SHOULD ENGAGE THEM, THE ARCHITECT OR THE OWNER?

At the very beginning of your negotiations with your client, you should come to agreement on who will engage consultants. If you are going to engage consultants, you should have a written agreement with each of them that is consistent with your agreement with your client. Often architects obtain proposals from their consultants before submitting a proposal or contract to an owner. The consultants may submit not only a proposed scope of work but also a list of terms and conditions applicable to those services. Those terms and conditions may turn out to be inconsistent with the terms and conditions you later agree upon with your client, which could subject you to conflicting obligations on such contractual elements as scheduling, approvals, and payment. The best way to avoid inconsistency is to use an AIA form C401-2007 or other similar form of consulting agreement template that incorporates the terms of the prime agreement between you and your client and then define the scope and fee for your consultant. To the extent possible, you want all your consultants to be subject to the same terms and conditions.

There are pros and cons in deciding whether you or your client should retain the consultants. On the negative side, if you retain the consultants, then you may be responsible for any claims by your client arising from the consultants' services. That makes it imperative that the consultants have proper insurance and submit to the same dispute resolution procedures that have already been agreed to between you and your client. Including consultants as part of your scope of services increases your billings. This increase could impact the amount of your professional liability insurance premiums which is based, in part, on your firm's billings. On the positive side, if you retain the consultants, you have direct control over their services. In all likelihood, whether or not you engage the consultants you will be brought into any owner/consultant disputes because the architect is normally charged with monitoring and coordinating the services of the consultants, regardless of who formally engages them.

Who retains the consultants can have significant implications for compensation, however. If you retain the consultants and later have problems getting paid by the client, you may still be on the hook for payment of the consultants' services. Suddenly you find that you are the guarantor of payment for a deadbeat client. Having the consultants contract directly with the client eliminates that possibility. In the end, the client may insist that he or she wants a single point of responsibility for the design team and therefore demands that you engage at least the major consultants (for example, the structural, mechanical, and electrical engineering, and plumbing design work for the project). In that event, be sure your contracts with the consultants provide that you pay them after you are paid by the client.

If you are engaging the major consultants, your client may still hire some specialty consultants, such as technology, lighting, or kitchen consultants. Are you going to be responsible for coordinating their services? If so, be sure to consider how this impacts your fee or schedule for services and provide appropriately for it in your contract. So if you expect that coordinating your client's consultants merits an additional fee, consider adding the following provision to your agreement:

> **Time incurred coordinating the services of Owner's consultants, including attendance at all meetings and correspondence, shall be billed hourly as Additional Services.**

WHAT DO I NEED TO KNOW
IF I AM WORKING ON A PROJECT IN A FOREIGN COUNTRY?

Many of the issues we reviewed so far apply to negotiations for projects without distinguishing between whether they are in the United States or in a foreign country. But if you are engaged for a project outside of the United States, special factors warrant your consideration. Unless you are going to be the architect of record responsible for filing requirements and code compliance (which would be highly unusual), you need to have clear provisions in the contract with the client delineating your role and that of the architect of record. It should be clear who will engage the architect of record—you or the owner. It should also be clear that you will rely on the architect of record for compliance with local codes and regulations. A provision such as the following addresses this issue:

> The architect retained by the Owner (hereafter, the "Architect of Record") shall be responsible for compliance of the plans, drawings, and specifications with local laws, rules, regulations, ordinances, zoning, and building codes; coordination of local engineering and other consulting services; coordination and preparation of materials for governmental approvals where necessary; document translations if appropriate; review of the Design Architect's documents for appropriateness of material selection and consistency with local building trade practices; preparation of final construction documents; and construction contract administration and construction phase observation, including approval of contractors' applications for payment and certifications required by the Owner and local authorities.

Even if you are not the architect of record, you may need to consider whether your firm needs to be licensed in the foreign jurisdiction. Whether such is required depends, in part, on where your work will be performed and how often you or your employees will be at the project site.

A client from a foreign country may insist that foreign law, either the law of the project location or the client's location (if different), govern any dispute. This may make it difficult to anticipate or understand how the law could affect you. To reduce that uncertainty, the choice of the means for dispute resolution is critical. You should consider requiring a dispute-resolution forum in a neutral country and under a forum sponsor whose rules and regulations are clearly stated. A dispute resolution provision for an agreement for work in a foreign country might read as follows:

> Dispute Resolution: In the event of a dispute arising out of or relating to this Agreement or the services to be rendered hereunder, the Owner and the Design Architect agree to attempt to resolve such disputes as follows:
>
> a. In the first instance, the parties agree to attempt to resolve such disputes through direct negotiations between the appropriate representatives of each party so empowered;
>
> b. If such direct negotiations are not fully successful, the parties agree to attempt to resolve any remaining disputes by formal nonbinding third-party mediation conducted in accordance with rules and procedures to be agreed upon by the parties in writing; and
>
> c. If the dispute or any issues remain unresolved, the parties agree to submit the dispute to binding arbitration under the rules and procedures of the [name of arbitration organization]. Such arbitration proceedings shall take place in [name of city/country]. A decision of the arbitrator(s) shall be final and shall be enforceable in courts of appropriate jurisdiction.
>
> d. Fees and reasonable costs of dispute resolution procedures shall be shared equally by the parties pending final settlement.

A number of organizations sponsor arbitrations and mediations in various countries that provide a neutral setting for dispute resolution. You should consult a knowledgeable attorney about this to discuss the options.

Agreements for foreign projects also need to specify what language governs if the agreement is drafted in one language and then translated into another. To the extent possible, you presumably want the English version to govern. If the foreign language version is to govern, have someone you trust translate the version into English or review the translation made by your client.

Getting paid when you are working overseas can also be an issue. Before entering into an agreement, get answers to these questions: Can you easily move funds out of the country if you are being paid in the country? Can U.S. dollars be wired out of the country easily? Will you be subject to local taxation? Your preferred choice is to be paid in U.S. dollars by wire transfer into your U.S. bank account. To be paid inside a foreign country can trigger requirements to obtain a business license or to pay local taxes. Remember to get a sufficient retainer deposit up front to be held to the end of the project if possible. In certain countries it takes time for your client to transfer payment to the United States; your client may first need to obtain government approval to wire U.S. dollars overseas.

Finally, if there are taxes on fees paid for design services, you want your client to cover them or gross up what is paid to you so that you can pay them and still get your full fee. Consider adding a provision such as the following to any agreement for a project outside the United States:

> Fees and other compensations are exclusive of Value Added Tax (VAT) or other forms of foreign taxation or fees. The Design Architect is solely responsible for payment of U.S. taxes. Where VAT or other foreign taxes or fees may be payable under this Agreement, the Owner agrees to either pay such taxes on behalf of the Design Architect or increase the Design Architect's compensation by an amount necessary to pay such taxes. The Owner agrees to indemnify, defend (at the Design Architect's option), and hold the Design Architect, and its agents, partners, employees, and consultants harmless from and against any and all claims, liabilities, damages, judgments, suits, losses, and expenses (including reasonable attorney's fees and disbursements) arising from or associated with the payment of such foreign taxes or fees. The provisions of this paragraph shall survive expiration or earlier termination of this Agreement.

Special insurance issues may also arise when you work on an overseas project. Consider, for example, whether your insurance policies in force in this country cover non-U.S. work. Some countries require that you have insurance with a firm licensed or qualified in that country. You may discover that the company issuing your U.S. policies may not be licensed or qualified in that country. When negotiating an agreement for an overseas project, explore the jurisdiction's insurance requirements and the costs of new or additional coverage. You do not want to sign an agreement with your client and later find that you have to get another insurance policy at a cost that you had not factored into your compensation.

The AIA has a form of architect/owner agreement for overseas projects (the B163) but many foreign clients insist on their own forms, which are often much less detailed than the typical agreement for a project in this country.

HOW IS MY ROLE DIFFERENT IF I AM JUST THE DESIGN ARCHITECT?

Often you may be asked or may only want to be the design architect on a project with someone else taking responsibility for preparation of the construction documents, for compliance of those documents with the applicable codes, and for construction administration services. If you take on a role of a design architect, you cannot use the standard AIA agreements because they provide a much broader scope of services and responsibilities. Instead you need to define your role clearly and limit your liability as much as possible.

Your agreement should provide that you can rely on the architect of record for review of your work product for compliance with the applicable codes. The agreement might have a provision as follows:

> The Owner shall engage an architect of record (AOR) for the Project who shall be responsible for compliance of plans and specifications with all applicable laws, codes, rules, and regulations. The Design Architect shall be entitled to rely upon the AOR for compliance of the Design Architect's work product with all applicable laws, codes, rules, and regulations.

In addition, as the design architect, you probably want to have some role during the construction documents and construction administration phases to determine that the plans and then construction conform to your design intent. If your client does not agree to your involvement, you should have a provision in your agreement that your name not be associated with the project without your consent. If you are involved during the construction phase you should carefully limit your responsibility during site visits to review for compliance of the work with your design intent. Do not agree to review the work for compliance with the construction documents you did not prepare.

When you are a design architect and someone else is the architect of record responsible for construction documents and code compliance, your shop drawing stamp should be different from the stamp you use as an architect-of-record and might look something like the box on the next page.

The critical difference between this stamp and the architect-of-record stamp (shown earlier in this chapter) is the statement here that your review is only for "general conformance with the design concept of the project" and *not* for "general compliance with the information given in the Contract Documents."

FILE NO._____ SUBMISSION NO._____

☐ NO EXCEPTION TAKEN
☐ REJECTED
☐ REVISE AND RESUBMIT
☐ SUBMIT SPECIFIED ITEM

Corrections or notations made on Shop Drawings do not relieve the Contractor from complying with requirements of the Contract Documents. Review is for general conformance with the design concept of the Project. Contractor is responsible for confirming and correlating all quantities and dimensions, selecting fabrication processes and techniques of construction, coordinating its work with the work of others, and performing its work in a safe and satisfactory manner.

By: _____ Date:_____

Architect Proj No._____ Proj Name_____

ARCHITECT'S NAME
Address

THE OWNER'S AGREEMENT WITH THE CONTRACTOR: WHAT SHOULD I KNOW?

Your client has a contract not just with you but also with the contractor. Sometimes, particularly on a residential project, you are asked to recommend a contractor and a form of agreement. You can provide some informed assistance, as long as you make it clear you are not a contract expert and do not claim to be providing legal advice. It is challenging enough to perform one professional function without assuming responsibility for the duties of another profession.

The AIA offers a large number of forms of agreement for use by an owner with a contractor/construction manager. Which form is appropriate depends on the nature of project, what role the owner envisions for the contractor or construction manager, and how the contractor or construction manager bills for its services. A project may be lump sum, with the contractor's fee as part of the lump sum quote, or the project may be cost-plus, with the owner responsible for paying all costs of the work, as defined in the agreement, plus a fixed or percentage amount for the contractor's fee, overhead, and insurance. Some construction projects have what is known as a guaranteed maximum price, where the contractor agrees that the cost of work (based on the plans presented at the time of contract signing) will not exceed a certain sum. Some owners have an owner's representative or construction manager as an adviser, with the owner contracting with the general contractor. Be careful here. You are not an attorney, so your role should be limited to discussing different means of project delivery: cost-plus or fixed-sum or guaranteed-maximum price agreements and any discrepancies with your own agreement. Avoid preparing the owner/contractor agreement!

All AIA owner/contractor agreements incorporate in some fashion what are known as the General Conditions of the Contract for Construction (General Conditions). These General Conditions may be set forth in the body of an owner/contractor agreement or as a separate document that is incorporated by reference into the agreement. The General Conditions help define the respective responsibilities of the contractor, owner, and architect during the construction phase of a project. They address issues such as how changes in the work should be handled, dispute resolution, insurance, termination rights, contractor warranties and guarantees, correction of work, and substantial and final completion.

The General Conditions impose certain responsibilities on the architect that are not found in the typical owner/architect agreement. Paramount among these is the appointment of the architect as the initial decision maker (IDM) in addressing disputes between the client and contractor. As the IDM, the architect is assigned the task of making an initial decision on claims between the owner and contractor before either the owner or contractor may go to a dispute resolution process. If you do not want to have this responsibility, ask the owner to choose a different IDM or have the provision removed entirely.

It is most important that you understand the agreement your client intends to use with a contractor or construction manager. This means you should receive a copy of that agreement at an early date so you can review the contractor's expectations and be sure that your client and the contractor do not attempt to impose responsibilities on you that may be unreasonable. Such an attempt should not actually be binding on you since the owner/contractor agreement in question is not something you have agreed to in the contract between you and the owner. Nevertheless, the potential for conflict between the two contracts can create issues. For example, the owner and contractor might agree (behind your back) that you should respond to requests for information or change orders within three days of receipt, although there is no such requirement in your contract with the owner and the short time-frame is unworkable. Say, then, that you do not respond within three days to a change order request, and the contractor objects that he or she is now being delayed as a result. You have done nothing wrong under your agreement with your client, yet the contractor may now have a valid delay claim against the owner under their contract. The owner and contractor will have a dispute, the owner will have no recourse against you, but you will still look bad to the owner— your client—for not responding to the change orders sooner. It all could have been avoided by your being aware of the unreasonable notice period in the owner/contractor agreement right at the start of the project and getting it changed.

You should also make certain that the owner/contractor agreement requires the contractor to provide evidence of insurance for the project and, if possible, makes you an additional insured (see Chapter 3). Then, if there is a claim against you arising out of acts by the contractor, you can turn to the contractor's insurance company and request a defense and indemnification in any lawsuit.

* * *

Since every project you might design is, in some way, different from the last one you designed, there is no one type of agreement that works for all your projects. The AIA forms of agreement offer a good starting point, but any AIA agreement you use must be carefully reviewed and edited for the specific project. Many of our clients use the AIA forms for some projects and letter agreements when working on projects of limited scope or where they are design architects with a limited role. Projects overseas offer different challenges, since the custom in each country as to what kind of contract is appropriate will vary.

Much depends on who the clients are and their level of sophistication and experience with construction. Whatever you ultimately agree upon with your client, however, should by all means be in writing and signed by both parties and dated.

TWO

WHAT IS MY INTELLECTUAL PROPERTY AND HOW DO I PROTECT IT?

Let's start with the basics—just what is "intellectual property"? If you own a home or an apartment you own what lawyers call "real property." (This is not to say that other forms of property aren't equally "real"; it's just a matter of legal terminology.) That BlackBerry®, iPhone®, or other personal digital assistant (PDA) you rely upon? That's "personal property." To put it in layman's terms (or, if you prefer, in architect's terms), your intellectual property can be described as the product of your mind. According to Victoria Espinel, who was appointed in December 2009 as the nation's first Intellectual Property Enforcement Coordinator (in belated recognition of the importance of intellectual property to the United States' economy), intellectual property is "the ideas behind inventions, the artistry that goes into books and music, and the logos of companies whose brands we have come to trust."[1] Ms. Espinel went on to say, "my job is to help protect the ideas and creativity of the American public." The idea behind this chapter is to help you learn a bit about protecting your own ideas and creativity.

While intellectual property may not be as tangible as some other forms of property, it is just as respected—and protected—by the law. Intellectual property law has its basis in the United States Constitution, which expressly authorizes Congress "[t]o promote the Progress of Science and useful Arts, by securing for limited Times to Authors and Inventors the exclusive Right to their respective Writings and Discoveries."[2] The key words here are "exclusive" and "limited." "Authors" and "Inventors" have a federally approved, constitutionally "exclusive Right" to exploit their "respective Writings and Discoveries" (meaning no one else can copy and sell them) —but only for a "limited" period of time. The underlying purpose of the law is to encourage authors and inventors to keep creating new works of art and science by granting them a monopoly in their work. However, since many works of art and inventions are inspired by or are an expansion upon the work of others, the monopoly is limited, so the creativity of subsequent authors and inventors is not hampered.

Our federal statutes protect intellectual property via copyright, patent, or trademark. As a general matter, copyrights primarily protect works of art, music, or literature (such as *Death of a Salesman* or prints by Andy Warhol), while patents protect works of scientific innovation. While your architectural designs can be protected by the copyright law, if you were to develop a new type of building facing, or a new construction material, those developments might be protected by patent law. Trademark differs from copyright or patent in this respect: the law in the latter areas protects the work product itself (the design or the invention), while trademark protects the goodwill generated by the person or company that provides the work product, as that goodwill is reflected in a trade name or logo (such as Coca-Cola® or Microsoft Windows®). Thus, for example, an architect who also designs furniture or lighting fixtures and wants consumers to identify a particular design quality or style as hers may choose to trademark her own name and market her designs (for example, Jane Architect Furniture Collection®).

WHAT IS COPYRIGHT?

Since most of your work product as an architect comes under the protection of the copyright law, let's tackle this area first. What exactly is copyright and just what does it protect?

In its most basic sense, copyright is exactly what the name says it is—the "right" to "copy" the work in question. The United States copyright statute expands on the (very) brief protection set out in the Constitution, and states that a copyright owner has the exclusive right to (1) reproduce the copyrighted work; (2) create derivative works based upon the copyrighted work (more on this later); and (3) distribute copies of the copyrighted work to the public by sale or other transfer of ownership, or by rental, lease, or lending. While the copyright holder has certain additional rights with respect to music and other works with a performance element, those rights are not relevant to most architects, so we do not address them here.

Does the copyright law protect every "work" out there, or even everything an architect can create? No, it does not. As the federal statute provides, copyright protects rights in "original works of authorship." That doesn't mean that every aspect of your work must be unique or completely uninspired by preexisting work, but simply that you independently created your work (in other words, that you did not simply copy someone else's work) and it must have some minimal degree of creativity.

As for "works of authorship," the law defines them as: (1) literary works; (2) musical works; (3) dramatic works; (4) choreographic works; (5) pictorial, graphic, and sculptural works; (6) motion pictures and other audiovisual works; (7) sound recordings; and, as of 1990, (8) architectural works. An "architectural work" is defined as "the design of a building as embodied in any tangible medium of expression, including a building, architectural plans, or drawings. The work includes the overall form as well as the arrangement and composition of spaces and elements in the design, but does not include individual standard features."[3]

While architectural drawings and designs have received protection under copyright law as "pictorial and graphic works" since the Copyright Act of 1909, not until the Architectural Works Copyright Protection Act of 1990 (AWCPA) did architectural works themselves become expressly protected under copyright law. This act was prompted by the United States' becoming a signatory to the international Berne Convention for the Protection of Literacy and Artistic Works in 1988. Since the language of the Berne Convention protected copyright in architectural works, the United States had to clarify and strengthen its protection of architectural works.

Buildings themselves were not originally protected under the copyright law largely because of the distinction copyright law makes between the type of works that are deemed copyrightable work and uncopyrightable "useful articles." The copyright statute defines a "useful article" as "an article having an intrinsic utilitarian function that is not merely to portray the appearance of the article or to convey information."[4] Examples of useful articles include clothing, furniture, and lighting fixtures. Since the purpose of the copyright law is to provide a limited monopoly in a work, deeming a chair a protectable work under the copyright law might unreasonably result in someone having a monopoly on a seat, four legs, and a back (with or without two arms). This is why the copyright law only protects those aspects of useful articles that are clearly separable from the utilitarian aspects of the work. A carving on the back of a chair or a fabric pattern on a shirt may be protectable under the copyright law, while the design of the chair or shirt itself (unless the design is unique in some way) would not be.

Prior to the passage of the AWCPA, unless the aesthetic elements of a building were distinguishable from its design (such as a sculptural element), a building was not protected under the copyright law. As Paul Goldstein, a commentator, stated: "Structures built from architectural plans will often fail to qualify as pictorial, graphic, or sculptural works because their 'intrinsic utilitarian function' makes them 'useful articles.'"[5] The AWCPA now expressly makes buildings protectable.

The author's right to control reproduction of his or her work, or actual copying, is fairly clear. As for the right to control the distribution of the work, at least one court has addressed whether leasing out apartments constructed from infringing plans can violate an architect's exclusive right to "distribute" a work. In *Looney Ricks Kiss Architects, Inc. v. Bryan,*[6] the court said: "[A]s a matter of law, this Court finds that holders of architectural copyrights have the exclusive distribution rights of their architectural works. In this instance, this Court finds as a matter of law that under these circumstances in this case the [owners of the apartment building] . . . could be susceptible for claims of direct infringement for each rental of the apartments that they own."[7]

WHAT ARE DERIVATIVE WORKS?

As stated earlier, under the copyright law, the author has the exclusive right to create derivative works. Derivative work is defined by the statute as "work based upon one or more preexisting works."[8] This doesn't mean that a new work cannot be *inspired* by preexisting works, by the architect's "standing on the shoulders of giants," but rather that a new work cannot be perceived as being based on a prior work. For example, in the literary arena, sequels (or prequels) to a work are usually found by the courts to be derivative works. In the visual area, a photograph of a work of art or sculpture can also be a derivative work of the original artwork.

So, if a building is now protected by the copyright law, and if a photograph can be a derivative work, does this mean that an architect has the right to prohibit anyone from taking a photograph of a building he or she has designed? If the building is visible from a public area, the answer is no. This makes sense as a practical matter, since there is clearly a social and cultural value in the ability to portray structures, urban landscapes, and city skylines that must be balanced against the intellectual property rights of the architect, leaving aside the impracticality of requiring innocent holiday photographers to airbrush buildings from their photos before posting them on Facebook®. To make this point clear, the copyright law states: "The copyright in an architectural work that has been constructed does not include the right to prevent the making, distributing, or public display of pictures, paintings, photographs, or other pictorial representations of the work, if the building in which the work is embodied is located in or ordinarily visible from a public place."[9]

Since an architect owns the copyright in the design of a building, would an alteration to that building that was unauthorized by the architect constitute a "derivative work" that would infringe upon the architect's copyright? As any architect can imagine, if the copyright law were to be interpreted that way, owners would be in an uproar. The AWCPA amended the copyright law to clarify this point: "Notwithstanding the provisions of [the section stating that only the copyright owner may create or authorize the creation of derivative works], the owners of a building embodying an architectural work may, without the consent of the author or copyright owner of the architectural work, make or authorize the making of alterations to such building, and destroy or authorize the destruction of such building."[10]

WHO OWNS A COPYRIGHT?

The copyright law refers both to the "author" and the "owner" of a work. As a general matter, the "author" usually means the creator of the work—the writer, painter, sculptor, the person who puts pen to paper or hand to clay. The author usually owns the copyright of his work.

If, however, your employee creates the work as part of the ordinary course of employment, then something called the "work for hire" principle comes into play. Where the work is created in the course of employment, the employer, not the employee, is considered the author of the work. This is because the law presumes that the employer controls, or has the power to control, the creation of the work, and is therefore the true "author" of the work. Under this principle, the copyright in the work of an architect who is acting as an employee of an architecture firm is owned by her employer. Even if the work is not created by an employee but by an independent contractor, the "work for hire" principle can still apply. In that case, however, the contractor would have to agree in writing to transfer his or her copyright.

As you can see, just like any other kind of property, ownership of a copyright need not remain with its original owner (namely the author of the work), but can be transferred, either as a matter of law or by agreement between the transferor and the transferee. Many owners assume (incorrectly) that by paying for the architect's services, the designs, or intellectual property, are automatically transferred to them as well. Fortunately, the AIA's form contracts clearly state that the architect owns the instruments of service and the intellectual property therein. In 1997, the AIA agreements between owners and architects stated:

> *Drawings, specifications and other documents, including those in electronic form, prepared by the Architect and the Architect's consultants are Instruments of Service for use solely with respect to this Project. The Architect and the Architect's consultants shall be deemed the authors and owners of the respective Instruments of Service and shall retain all common law, statutory and other reserved rights, including copyrights.* (B141, Article 1.3.2.1)

Your ownership of the copyright in building designs has more than theoretical legal value. Without the permission of the copyright owner (i.e., the architect), the building owner cannot make copies of the designs or authorize such copies to be made (thus depriving contractors of plans to work from). Since a building is effectively a derivative work of the plans, the copyright owner can bar the building owner from completing the construction process on the grounds of copyright infringement.

Please bear in mind that, since copyright actually consists of several distinct rights—the right to copy, the right to authorize copying, and the right to create derivative work—any one of these rights can be transferred without the others. For example, an architect may authorize the building's owner to copy the plans to construct the building in question, but may draw the line at permitting the building's owner to use those same plans to create an identical building.

Even if various rights are not actually transferred, they can be—and usually are—licensed. The 1997 B141 Agreement provided:

> *Upon execution of this Agreement, the Architect grants to the Owner a nonexclusive license to reproduce the Architect's Instruments of Service solely for purposes of constructing, using and maintaining the Project, provided that the Owner shall comply with all obligations, including prompt payment of all sums when due, under this Agreement.* (B141, Article 1.3.2.2)

The 1997 B141 Agreement went on to say that if the contract itself were to be terminated, the owner's license would be terminated as well:

> *Upon such termination, the Owner shall refrain from making further reproductions of Instruments of Service and shall return to the Architect within seven days of termination all originals and reproductions in the Owner's possession or control.* (B141, Article 1.3.2.2)

This meant that if the owner decided to terminate the contract purely because of a desire to find another, less costly architect, by doing so the owner would lose any right to retain any copies of the design, let alone provide them to a successor architect so he or she could use and benefit from the prior architect's work product.

The language of the 1997 B141 Agreement, however, stated that if the owner terminated the agreement "for cause" (for example, if the architect failed to meet his or her own obligations under the agreement) and the architect was judged to be in default, then the owner could use the instruments of service to complete the project:

> *If and upon the date the Architect is adjudged in default of this Agreement, the foregoing license shall be deemed terminated and replaced by a second, nonexclusive license permitting the Owner to authorize other similarly credentialed design professionals to reproduce and, where permitted by law, to make changes, corrections or additions to the Instruments of Service solely for purposes of completing, using and maintaining the Project.* (B141, Article 1.3.2.2)

The use of the phrase "adjudged to be in default" is vital here. The 1997 B141 Agreement does not say that the architect must be "thought" or "believed" to be in default, it says she must be "adjudged" to be in default. Thus the 1997 B141 Agreement permitted the owner to proceed with construction using the architect's plans, but only *after* the architect had been found by a judge or arbitrator to have failed to comply with his or her own obligations under the agreement. To get such a ruling, the owner would have to incur additional expense and lose even more time from the construction process, which would probably be stalled pending resolution of the claim. Note that under this agreement, even where the architect was adjudged to be at fault, the copyright was not transferred outright to the owner; instead, the owner received a revised license, again limited to permit the construction and maintenance of the building at issue.

When the AIA was in the process of revising its form agreements, it took into consideration the realities of the marketplace and the complaints of the owners. The 2007 version of the B101 now permits the owner to continue using the instruments of service when he or she terminates the agreement for cause, but removes the requirement that the architect first be adjudged to be in default before the owner can use the work product.

If the owner terminates the agreement for convenience, or if the architect terminates the agreement because the client suspended the project for more than ninety days, the 2007 B101 Agreement provides that the owner must pay a licensing fee for continued use of the instruments of service (Article 11.9). However, since no licensing fee is specified in the agreement, you and your client should negotiate in advance and agree upon such fee in the event the agreement is ultimately terminated. The 2007 AIA language does not address whether the owner can continue to use the original architect's name in connection with the project if the agreement is terminated, nor does it state whether the project must be refiled with the stamp of the new architect of record; you should discuss (and ideally resolve) these issues as part of the overall negotiation of the agreement.

AS THE COPYRIGHT OWNER, HOW DO I PROTECT MY WORK?

The right to copyright protection arises upon creation of a work—as soon as an author puts pen to paper, applies hand to clay, or uses a mouse to configure a drawing. Let me repeat that: a copyright exists once a work is set in tangible form; nothing more is needed. However, to be able to bring suit in federal court and demand statutory damages (which can be larger than the "lost profit" type of damages), as well as attorneys' fees, you as the author must *register* your work.

Like many other things in the twenty-first century, the copyright registration process has become digitized and is primarily done via the Internet.[10] While paper application forms can still be submitted, they must now be ordered from the Copyright Office and entail an additional fee. Otherwise, applicants must go to the website www.copyright.gov, and follow the instructions to register a work. Each application must include a copy of the work that is to be registered.

How do people know you have every intention of protecting your copyright? Because you tell them by placing a copyright notice on your work. Once a work has been made tangible, or "fixed" (even before registration or application), the author should promptly place a copyright notice on the work. Prior versions of the copyright law made this a legal requirement, and failing to provide such notice could result in the loss of copyright protection. While this is no longer required, it is still wise to put a copyright notice on every design, drawing, or other expression of a design concept that you want to protect.

Copyright notice is very basic. It usually appears in one of two forms: © Architect, 2012, or, in the more spelled-out form, Copyright 2012, Architect. If you do business as an entity such as a professional limited liability corporation, your copyright notice should use your name—for example, Architect, PLLC 2012.

HOW LONG DOES COPYRIGHT LAST?

Under prior versions of the copyright law, copyright protection lasted for one term of 28 years, which could then be renewed for another 28-year term. The 1976 amendment of the law extended the copyright term to last for the life of the author of the work plus 50 years. As of this writing, copyright protection (for works created after January 1, 1978) has been extended to last for the life of the author plus 70 years. But, as you can see, the length of copyright protection can change along with the copyright law.

What if the author is a corporation, as in the case of a work made for hire? Since a corporation can "live" for untold years, does that mean that a corporation's copyright can also last forever? No, that would go against the concept of "limited monopoly," which is at the heart of intellectual property law. Therefore, the law limits copyright in a work made for hire to 95 years from the date of its first publication or 120 years from the year of its creation.

WHAT IS COPYRIGHT INFRINGEMENT?

Infringement is the copying of protected matter or the creation of a derivative work without permission of the copyright owner. We've discussed the concepts of who the "copyright owner" is and what a "derivative work" is. Here we have another legal concept—that of "protected matter."

Even after a work is created, set down in tangible form, and registered, that does not mean that every aspect of it is entitled to protection under the copyright law. For example, the concept behind a work is not subject to copyright protection; artistic and scientific progress could be stifled if one author could monopolize an idea. This is the same principle that prevents useful articles from receiving the protection of copyright's limited monopoly. The copyright law distinguishes between an idea and the expression of that idea. Only the *expression* of an idea is entitled to copyright protection.

For example: a boy and girl from two warring families meet and fall in love. This is an idea and not protectable; anyone and everyone can use this idea (and so many artists have). Once this idea is given expression, however, you can have a work that is protected under the copyright law. The boy and girl are given names, personalities, set in a specific environment, given a defined conflict, and you end up with works as different as *Romeo and Juliet, West Side Story,* and *Avatar.* This idea/expression dichotomy applies in the architectural arena as well. In several well-known cases of alleged copyright infringement, the courts based their decisions on whether the purportedly copied work was an idea or the expression of an idea.

The case of *Eli Attia v. Society of New York Hospital* [11] involved an architect, Eli Attia, who was retained by New York Hospital to develop a plan for the renovation of the hospital. An outline of his proposal, including some architectural sketches, was presented to the New York Hospital board. Attia then prepared two booklets showing his proposals, including some more elaborate designs, and even registered the copyright in those booklets.

New York Hospital retained Attia to work with Taylor Clark Associates (TCA) as consultants for the project. When the relationship apparently "turned acrimonious," the consulting agreement was terminated, and New York Hospital paid Attia approximately $500,000 for his consulting services. The hospital later awarded the renovation project to a joint venture between TCA and Hellmuth Obata & Kassabaum (HOK), working together as architects. After seeing an article in *The New York Times* that included an illustration of HOK/TCA's plan, Attia brought suit for copyright infringement and for violation of the Lanham Act, which relates to trademarks and unfair competition, because HOK/TCA had falsely designated themselves as the source of the design (more about this subject later).

The Second Circuit Court of Appeals looked at what had allegedly been copied from Attia's work and found that what was purportedly copied was not protected under the copyright law:

The problem underlying Plaintiff's claim of copyright infringement, however, is that not all copying from copyrighted material is necessarily an infringement of copyright. There are elements of a copyrighted work that are not protected even against intentional copying. It is a fundamental principle of our copyright doctrine that ideas, concepts, and processes are not protected from copying.[12]

The court found that what had been copied were only "ideas":

> As a generalization, to the extent that such plans include generalized notions of where to place functional elements, how to route the flow of traffic, and what methods of construction and principles of engineering to rely on, these are ideas that may be taken and utilized by a successor without violating the copyright of the original author or designer.[13]

The court looked to the way the work was described in Attia's own booklet:

> Plaintiff's [Attia's] first Option 1A booklet, for instance, states that the following planning approach will suggest an *idea* that was recognized in the past, but not pursued until this point, and that this report is for the purpose of demonstrating a *concept*. It is not meant to suggest a specific configuration or functional plan, but rather to explore a significant opportunity to improve the facilities and health care which comprise New York Hospital.[14]

According to the booklet, "This report is meant as a first attempt to stimulate thinking and discussion amongst the participants of the planning Team and the Hospital."[15] This language makes Attia's work sound more like an idea—which by its nature is not protected under the copyright law—than the expression of an idea.

In comparing Attia's proposed designs to those of HOK/TCA, the court found that the placement of a new structure on FDR Drive, the use of truss technology to transfer weight, and the placement of the emergency department were "ideas and concepts," and therefore had not been infringed. In *Sparaco v. Lawler, Matusky, Skelly Engineers LLP,*[16] the Second Circuit Court of Appeals applied the *Attia* standard to another set of drawings. The court found these drawings entitled to copyright protection, stating:

In our view, the site plan was significantly different from Attia's proposal of ideas for the expansion of the hospital. Sparaco's site plan specifies more than vague, general indications of shape and placement of the elements. It provides detailed specifications for preparation of the site. . . . It was a plan only for the preparation of the site. As such, it appears to be a fully realized plan capable of being used to guide actual construction work on numerous site preparation tasks.[17]

HOW DOES A COURT DECIDE WHETHER A COPYRIGHT HAS BEEN INFRINGED?

Once the court establishes that the material in question is subject to the protection of copyright law, the next step is to determine whether copying actually took place. In the absence of an actual witness or other direct evidence of copying, the courts look to indirect evidence, such as access by the alleged infringer to the earlier work, and similarities between the works that would tend to prove copying.

Access, if it exists, is usually easy to prove. A design may be published on a website or in an article or otherwise made publicly available, or the owner may simply provide a new architect with a copy of the prior architect's plans. In the case of *Shine v. Childs*,[18] Thomas Shine himself had shown his designs to the architect he later accused of copying them.

In 1999, Thomas Shine was a student in the Masters of Architecture Program at the Yale School of Architecture. In December of that year, he presented his designs for what he called "Olympic Tower" to a jury of experts that had been invited to the school to review the students' work. As part of this presentation, Shine not only explained his tower's structural design, he displayed different structural and design models, renderings, floor plans, elevations, sections, a site plan, and a photomontage giving a visual impression of the tower's exterior. David Childs was one of the invited experts who witnessed this presentation. Childs not only noticed Thomas Shine's tower design, he praised it (as did other experts). The school's annual alumni magazine even published a photographic rendering of Shine's Olympic Tower, along with smaller inset photos of two of Shine's models; a compliment from David Childs was included in the publication.

Four years later, in the summer of 2003, David Childs was asked to be the design architect for what was expected to be the tallest building at the new World Trade Center site. Along with Studio Daniel Libeskind, Childs completed a design that was presented to the public at a press conference in December 2003. A number of computer-generated images of what was called "Freedom Tower" were presented, along with two scale models and a computer slide show elaborating on Freedom Tower's design principles.

Shine brought a lawsuit against David Childs and his firm (the "defendants") in 2004, claiming that his designs had been copied without his permission (i.e., copyright infringement). He demanded an injunction to prevent any further infringement of his work, as well as recovery of any financial damages he had suffered plus any profits the defendants had obtained as a result of the infringement. Since the Freedom Tower's design was changed for other reasons, his request for an injunction became moot.

The defendants moved to dismiss the case. The court found that Shine's Olympic Tower design was entitled to receive protection under the copyright law. Since there was no evidence of direct copying, the court looked to the issues of access and whether "similarities that suggest copying exist between the protected works and the alleged infringing work."[19] There was no question about access, and the defendants conceded that there was access to Shine's designs for the purposes of argument.

The court then looked to the issue of whether "reasonable jurors could find that substantial similarity exists between Olympic Tower and the Freedom Tower," stating that "'total concept and feel' is the dominant standard used to evaluate substantial similarity between artistic works in our Circuit."[20] The defendants argued that expert testimony should be used for this analysis, but the court said:

> Because the lay public's approbation usually is the foundation of returns that derive from a copyrighted work, an allegedly infringing work is considered substantially similar to a copyrighted work if "the ordinary observer, unless he set out to detect the disparities, would be disposed to overlook them, and regard their aesthetic appeal as the same."[21]

The court ultimately decided that "reasonable ordinary observers could disagree on whether substantial similarity exists between the Freedom Tower and Olympic Tower"[22]; the defendants' motion to dismiss the complaint was denied.

Courts have looked at a number of factors to determine whether there is "substantial similarity" to warrant a finding of copyright infringement. These include:

Bathrooms and closets—one court found that a "different juxtaposi-
tion of master bedroom and walk-in closets," [23] among other factors, argued against a finding of substantial similarity.

Building materials—a court found that the use of mitered glass in
the entrance way was one of "a remarkable number of similarities" [24] which led the court to find substantial similarity between
the designs. Different materials may not prevent a finding of substantial similarity, however. Another court found that although
"certain differences between the designs slightly affect the feel,
such as . . . the use of brick instead of siding in certain areas . . . .
Despite these differences, however, the two designs still have the
same overall feel based on the same combination of the unique
features."[25]

Doors and entrances—a court found that "[a] close scrutiny of the
objective similarities in the details of the home offices reveals distinguishable characteristics. The home office of the Purtell Home
has two entrances, allowing entry from the sun room and laundry
room. The Hoeffel Home's office has one entry. Thus, the specific
details of the home office floor plans create different traffic pat-
terns in the two homes. They are not substantially similar."[26]

Elevators—a court found that "[t]he expression of the elevator
towers also differs significantly. [Plaintiff's] elevator towers are
free-standing and are located within the space created by the alter-
nating convex and concave sections of the building. The Trump
Buildings' elevator towers are located within the solid structure
of the building. . . . The towers also differ in shape and orientation. [Plaintiff's] elevator towers are cylindrical, while those in the
Trump Buildings are ovals. In [Plaintiff's] designs, the towers are
clustered in the center of the building, and the middle tower is
thicker than the two outer two. The towers in the Trump Buildings are spread out evenly, and all three are equal in diameter.
Further, the two outer towers in the Trump Buildings 'are angled
inward so that the leading edge of all three towers orient toward a
focal point outside the building.'"[27] Because of this, among other
factors, the court did not find substantial similarity.

Garages—a court found that "the Purtell Home features a side-load
angled garage while the Hoeffel Home has a front-load garage set
at a ninety-degree angle. The contrasting garage locations give
the two homes immediately discernible appearances from a curb-

side point of view."[28] The court found there was no substantial similarity.

Rooms—the court found that although the two sets of plans "have the same layout in that the rooms are located in the same places. However, as the Eleventh Circuit has noted, there are only so many ways to place three bedrooms, bathrooms, a laundry room, a living room, family room and kitchen".[29]

Size—a court found that "[Plaintiff's] residence is larger than the Modified Grand Floridian by over 1000 square feet. . . . The Court finds that the differences in the elevations and sizes of the homes are significant, and constitute more than just superficial changes made in an attempt to disguise similarities."[30] The court found that there was no substantial similarity.

Supports—a court found that "[w]ith respect to the structure of the supporting platform over the FDR Drive, there are significant differences between plaintiff's and defendants' plans in both the configuration of the trusses and in the placement and number of supporting columns."[31]

Unique elements—a court found that "because the wind towers are essentially the same height and width and rise on either side of the domes, they create extremely similar building contours."[32] That, along with other factors, led the court to hold that a jury might find the designs to be substantially similar, and it reversed the lower court's decision to grant summary judgment dismissing the copyright infringement claim.

The question of whether there is "substantial similarity" between two designs involves not only an analysis of the specific designs at issue but also a determination of whether the "ordinary observer" would be deceived. It is difficult to determine in advance whether a court would be likely to find that an infringement took place. This can be an advantage for the architect whose designs have arguably been copied, since it means that a court would be less likely to dismiss a case, but it is a notable disadvantage for architects on the other side of the equation—namely, the accused infringers. If you take over a project from another architect, you can be sued for using the prior architect's designs. It is a wise precaution for new architects to get a representation from the owner that such use is permitted under the owner's agreement with the prior architect, as well as indemnification or other protection from the owner should the representation prove to be false or if it fails to prevent a lawsuit.

You might consider a provision such as the following:

> The Owner represents and warrants that it has the right to use the plans and specifications prepared by the prior architect and agrees to indemnify, defend (at the Architect's option), and hold harmless the Architect from and against any and all claims, damages liabilities, losses, and costs and expenses, including reasonable attorneys' fees and expenses, by the prior architect arising out of use by the Architect of the prior architect's plans and specifications.

Access to and "substantial similarity" between the alleged copy and the original do not necessarily indicate copyright infringement; a finding of infringement depends on how the architectural plans were used. For instance, courts have held that copying a building purely by observation (without copying any of the plans or specifications) does not violate the architect's copyright in the design. However, the court implied in *Guillot-Vogt Associates, Inc. v. Holly & Smith*[33] that if a person were to "go to a building, take measurements, make sketches, or otherwise record the building, and replicate the building without obtaining permission from the original designer," such conduct might violate the copyright law.

WHAT ARE THE REMEDIES FOR COPYRIGHT INFRINGEMENT?

Under Section 502 of the copyright law, a court can issue an injunction "to prevent or restrain infringement of a copyright." This means that a court can issue an order bringing construction of an infringing building to a halt or preventing such construction from starting (injunction was one of the remedies requested in the *Shine v. Childs* case discussed above).

A monetary recovery, known as damages, may also be available in cases of infringement. Under Section 504 of the copyright law, an infringer of copyright is liable for either (1) the copyright owner's actual damages and any additional profits of the infringer or (2) statutory damages. Actual damages would include lost fees, which could either be spelled out in the contract between the owner and the architect, or could be calculated based on the architect's hourly rate. A copyright owner is not permitted to recover *all* the profits the infringer might have earned in connection with the project, but only those profits attributable to the infringement itself. For example, construction phase fees earned by the successor architect might not be attributable to the infringement of the original architect's design.

As an alternative, the federal statute provides that instead of demanding the infringer's actual damages and profits, a copyright owner can ask for an award of statutory damages—meaning damages under Section 504 of the copyright law. Where the copyright owner elects to receive statutory damages, it is within the discretion of the court to order "not less than $750 or more than $30,000 as the court considers just."[34] Where the infringement is found to be willful (such as where the infringer knew that he or she was violating the law), the court can order damages of up to $150,000 per infringement. Since each copy of a separate plan or specification is arguably a separate infringement, statutory damages can mount very high, very fast.

The court also has the power under Section 505 of the copyright law to order payment of costs and "a reasonable attorney's fee to the prevailing party." This "prevailing party" language is of vital importance. It means that the winner of the litigation—which could well be the defendant—may recover his or her attorneys' fees from the losing party. In the *Attia* case, the suing architect had to pay the defendants' legal fees. Because this provision of the law cuts both ways, it can discourage a copyright owner with a weak or otherwise questionable claim from bringing a lawsuit.

A suit for copyright infringement can act both as a sword and as a shield. In *Robert R. Jones Architects, Inc.*,[35] the architect sued for—and won—an award of damages for infringement of his copyrighted designs. This is an example of copyright being used in an aggressive manner, as a sword. In contrast, copyright can be used as a shield, as a defense by the architect. In one situation, an owner terminated a contract with Architect A, hired Architect B, and then argued that Architect A should return his fees since he failed to do the necessary work. Architect A was able to show that Architect B used Architect A's designs; such infringement not only acted as a defense to the claim that Architect A had not done the requisite work, but provided Architect A with a separate claim for damages against the Architect B.

AS THE COPYRIGHT HOLDER, CAN I PUT PICTURES OF THE BUILDING ON MY WEBSITE?

As stated earlier, the copyright law doesn't prevent the making, distributing, or public display of pictures, paintings, photographs, or other pictorial representations of an architectural work, if the building in which the work is embodied is ordinarily visible from a public place. However, the architect's agreement with the owner may contain a limitation on such use or display. In the 2007 B101 Agreement, Article 10.7 states:

> The Architect shall have the right to include photographic or artistic representations of the design of the Project among the Architect's promotional and professional materials. The Architect shall be given reasonable access to the completed Project to make such representations. However, the Architect's materials shall not include the Owner's confidential or proprietary information if the Owner has previously advised the Architect in writing of the specific information considered by the Owner to be confidential or proprietary. The Owner shall provide professional credit for the Architect in the Owner's promotional materials for the Project.

Just like any other contract provision, this language is subject to negotiation and agreement of the parties. Here are some of the issues that might be subject to negotiation:

- *The architect's right to photograph the project.* Where a celebrity owner is involved, this may be a major issue.
- *The architect's right to use the owner's name.* Again, an issue may arise where a celebrity owner (or one reclusive for other reasons) is involved.
- *The owner's right to use the architect's name.* This may arise either where the owner and architect came to an "unfriendly" parting of the ways or where the architect is a celebrity whose name could give the owner a certain cachet. In this situation, the architect may want to include certain safeguards to ensure that his or her name is not damaged by being connected with a project that ultimately does not accurately reflect the architect's vision.
- *The owner's right to publish drawings or photographs of the project.* This may be a problem where the owner wishes to use the drawings for its own marketing purposes, which may or may not be compatible with the architect's wishes.

If you choose not to use an AIA contract, consider adding a provision to your contract that reads something like the following:

The Architect may, before and after the completion of the Project, photograph the Project and seek publication of drawings and photographs of the Project, provided, however, that the Architect shall not use the name of the Owner or address of the Project unless the Owner has given his prior written consent. If the Owner seeks to promote the Project in promotional materials, Owner shall not use the Architect's name unless the Architect has given his prior written consent. If the Owner seeks to publish drawings or photographs of the Project or is requested by another party to furnish drawings or photographs of the Project for publication, the Owner shall not permit the publication of the Project unless the Owner has obtained the Architect's prior written consent.

WHAT ARE MY INTELLECTUAL PROPERTY RIGHTS WHEN WORKING ABROAD?

The answer to this question depends on the country where you are providing architectural services. For example, if the country is a signatory to the Berne Convention or the Universal Copyright Convention, your rights may be similar to those when you design a project in the United States. If not, you need to determine not only what intellectual property rights the law of that country provides, but also what constitutes infringement under those laws. In any event, you should check the laws of a country before providing architectural services there.

WHAT ABOUT MY RIGHTS IN ELECTRONIC DOCUMENTS?

Many documents (if not all) are now transferred electronically, rather than in hard copy. This is to facilitate their prompt use by owners, contractors, and subcontractors and to allow other parties (such as engineers and consultants) to use them to create their own specifications or derivative works. While the electronic transfer of designs does not affect your intellectual property rights any more than other forms of transfer, once you have knowingly sent your work to another person in a manner that permits it to be altered, you should have a written agreement with the recipient of the electronic transfer that clarifies exactly what is and is not being transferred. This agreement should explicitly provide that the electronic transfer of a document doesn't transfer any rights in that document and detail acceptable methods and format for transfers.

In early 2007, the AIA issued the 2007 C106 Digital Data Licensing Agreement. This agreement states:

> *The Transmitting Party grants the Receiving Party a nonexclusive limited license to use the Digital Data solely and exclusively to perform services or construction for the Project in accordance with the conditions set forth in Article 3.* (C106, Article 2.1)

The language here is explicit: the recipient of the electronic document may use the document to perform the services or construction for that specific project only. While it is unlikely that a court would find that a transfer of rights had taken place if this language were absent from the agreement, the agreement repeats this limitation as clearly (and as often) as possible:

> *The transmission of Digital Data constitutes a warranty by the Transmitting Party to the Receiving Party that the Transmitting Party (1) is the copyright owner of the Digital Data, (2) has permission from the copyright owner to transmit the Digital Data and grant a license for its use on the Project, or (3) is authorized to transmit Confidential Information.* (C106, Article 2.2)

This language actually protects the recipient of the electronic document more than the architect. Nonetheless, the repetition of the fact that the architect is the copyright owner never hurts. Here is some additional protective language:

> *The Transmitting Party retains its rights in the Digital Data. By transmitting the Digital Data, the Transmitting Party does not grant to the Receiving Party an assignment of those rights; nor does the Transmitting Party convey to the Receiving Party any right in the software used to generate the Digital Data.* (C106, Article 2.3)

Again this repeats the point that the architect does not intend to transfer any rights in the document, except the limited license set forth above in Article

2.1. The 2007 C106 Agreement further reinforces the point with the following indemnification language:

> *To the fullest extent permitted by law, the Receiving Party shall indemnify and defend the Transmitting Party from and against all claims arising from or related to the Receiving Party's modification to, or unlicensed use of, the Digital Data.* (C106, Article 2.4)

This is a safeguard to protect the architect from potential liability if alterations made by the recipient of the document cause harm (or if the recipient misuses the document in a way that causes harm) or otherwise result in the possibility that the architect may be sued by a third party.

The agreement also has a section permitting the parties to specify additional conditions to the license granted in Article 2.1. This section usually includes rights or restrictions applicable to the recipient's use of the document, any requirements with respect to the format or method of the electronic transmission, and any other similar conditions.

The purpose of the AIA 2007 E201 Digital Data Protocol Exhibit is to set out agreed-upon procedures for exchanging digital data. This agreement repeats the language that (1) the electronic transmission "does not convey any right in the [document]," (2) the ability of the recipient to use the document "is specifically limited to the design and construction of the Project," and (3) if any claims are made "arising from or related to the receiving party's modification, or unlicensed use," the recipient will indemnify and defend the architect.

When electronically transferring data, make sure you are using validly licensed software. Doing so ensures that the software is adequately supported, any patches or fixes have been made, and you are not infringing upon the copyright in the software. This is not only a matter of ethics, but of economics as well. The same way an architect can bring suit for infringement of copyright, so too can software companies. And from time to time they do.

Installation and use of unauthorized software is far simpler than you might think. A student intern might, in all innocence and goodwill, install a copy of free educational software on a firm's computer. Since you are not permitted to use free educational software (unless you yourself are an architecture student), the firm's use of this program could constitute an act of copyright infringement. An otherwise valid copy of software could be (again innocently) installed on more than one computer; this is another potential act of copyright infringement. As you've seen earlier, the monetary damages for a copyright infringement action can mount very high, very fast.

DOES USING BUILDING INFORMATION MODELING SOFTWARE CHANGE MY RIGHTS?

In addition to using technology to transfer documents electronically, more and more contractors and designers use Building Information Modeling (commonly referred to as "BIM") as part of the design and construction process. The Associated General Contractors of America (AGC) defines BIM as follows:

> Building Information Modeling is the development and use of a computer software model to simulate the construction and operation of a facility. The resulting model, a Building Information Model, is a data-rich, object-oriented, intelligent and parametric digital representation of the facility, from which views and data appropriate to various users' needs can be extracted and analyzed to generate information that can be used to make decisions and improve the process of delivering the facility.[36]

The United States General Services Administration (GSA) has established a BIM program, stating:

> [t]he power of visualization, coordination, simulation and optimization from 3D, 4D, and BIM computer technologies allow GSA to more effectively meet customer, design, construction, and program requirements. GSA is committed to a strategic and incremental adoption of 3D, 4D and BIM technologies.[37]

At its core, BIM is a tool (composed of a number of software programs) that permits architects and other design professionals to combine and present their data collectively; its goal is to facilitate the collaborative process among the members of the design team. BIM generates a three-dimensional model that lets the team see not only how the building will look once construction is completed, but also how it will function. Since BIM can be used for many purposes, it is vital that the parties agree early on in the process what it will be used for with respect to their particular project. If it is to be used for construction purposes, it may require a different type (and level) of detail than when used to determine the upkeep and ongoing maintenance the building might require. It should also be noted that there are some BIM supplementary programs that are used in analyzing data generated by using the BIM process. While these programs are out of the architect's control, they could nonetheless end up driving design decisions. For example, if a supplemental program used to determine energy usage (based upon the BIM-generated model) shows that a particular window design may result in what the owner deems to be an unacceptable level of energy loss, the architect may be asked to come up with a new window design.

In these relatively early stages of BIM, architects still have a lot of questions they must address. For example, who will own the ultimate model? Who is responsible for any errors that crop up in the BIM process (which is by its nature collaborative)? Should the parties share the risk? Since the AIA assesses an architect's performance (i.e., standard of care) against those of architects "practicing in the same or similar locality *under the same or similar circumstances*" (emphasis added), if you use BIM, your performance may well be compared not simply to that of your peers but to other architects in the area who use BIM, which could be a much smaller set. What are the industry's "best practices" where BIM is concerned? And, since multiple parties presumably contribute to the end design, who then owns the copyright in that design? Will you, as the architect, retain the initial copyright and license others to create derivative works? While the AIA addresses some of these concerns in its Form E202 Standard Agreement for Integrated Projects (as does the AGC in its own series of documents), you (or your counsel) must make sure that your individual issues and concerns are addressed in whatever agreement you choose to use.

WHAT IS A TRADEMARK?

As stated earlier, a trademark is another form of intellectual property. It is a word, phrase, symbol, or design, or a combination of words, phrases, symbols, or designs, that identifies and distinguishes the source of the goods of one party from those of others. A service mark is the same as a trademark, except that it identifies and distinguishes the source of a service rather than a product. For example, Coca-Cola® identifies the source of a particular product (or line of products); H&R Block® identifies the source of a particular service. The idea of both kinds of marks is to protect the reputation for quality, the "goodwill," that a provider has created in its products or services. Architects and designers can have service marks or trademarks to protect their goodwill (or that of their entities) as the denoted providers of services—such as architecture or design—or goods—such as furniture, lighting fixtures or any one of a number of products.

Unlike copyright, trademarks must be registered to receive protection under federal law. While trademarks can be protected under both federal and state law, it is often preferable to register a trademark nationally through the United States Patent & Trademark Office (also known as the "USPTO"); such a registration also protects trademarks at the state level. (Some states also recognize trademarks without federal registration, but this is relatively weak protection.)

To register a trademark with the USPTO, you must first determine what "class" of goods or services you intend to provide under the mark. For example, architecture and furniture fall under two separate classes; if you want to use the same mark to provide both architectural services and sell furniture, you have to apply to register the trademark in both classes. The USPTO charges a fee for the application process, based on the number of classes in which you want to register the trademark. The trademark application process is primarily conducted online, through the USPTO's website, www.uspto.gov.

CAN ANY WORD OR SYMBOL BE TRADEMARKED?

No. As a general matter, a trademark cannot simply be a generic or descriptive term, since it is supposed to designate a specific source of goods. However, an otherwise weak or descriptive sounding mark can be entitled to protection under the trademark law where the provider of the good or service has built up a substantial amount of goodwill in the mark over the years.

The USPTO's "class" system exists because the trademark law focuses on how a mark is used in commerce—that is, how a consumer tends to recognize or ask for products. If a consumer is not likely to confuse two classes of goods—such as "LEXUS," for high-end automobiles and the identical-sounding "LEXIS," for legal research—then the USPTO is often willing to register identical or similar marks in those classes.

Because of the massive number of trademarks that are in use, you should do a search to see whether your proposed trademark is already in use or sounds or looks substantially similar to one that is. You can perform these searches through the USPTO website for free (in which case you'd discover only identical trademarks) or through one of the services that conducts trademark searches for a fee (but which search not just for trademarks that are identical to the one you want to register but also for those that look or sound similar).

Unlike copyright, which ultimately expires, the life of a trademark can be indefinite. To maintain a trademark registration, the USPTO requires periodic proof that the trademark is still actually being used in commerce. If a trademark is found to be "abandoned," the original owner's rights lapse and another individual or entity may then use or register the trademark.

Once a mark is registered, the owner must display the "®" symbol in connection with the mark, or, if such a symbol is not possible or desirable for marketing reasons, the owner may display the statement "Registered in the U.S. Patent and Trademark Office." The trademark law declares that if the owner fails to indicate that the trademark is registered and an infringement lawsuit arises, the trademark owner may not be awarded damages (unless the infringer actually had knowledge of the registration).

WHAT ARE THE PENALTIES FOR TRADEMARK INFRINGEMENT?

Just as a copyright can be infringed, so can a trademark. To rule that a trademark has been infringed, the court must find that consumers are likely to be confused as to the source of the goods or services. Again, as stated earlier in connection with how the "classes" work, the court (as well as the USPTO) looks to how the mark is actually used in commerce.

Just like the copyright law, the trademark law gives a court the power to restrain, or "enjoin," continuing infringement; destroy infringing articles; and award the trademark owner recovery of reasonable attorneys' fees. However, if a court finds that a trademark has been infringed, it can award the trademark owner not only the infringer's profits, and any financial damages the trademark owner may have suffered, but it may also treble those damages, a remedy unavailable under the copyright law.

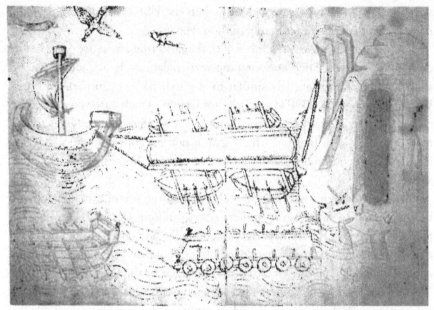

Reproduction of Il Badalone, Brunelleschi's boat design. Facsimile after Palato 766, fo. 40ʳ–41ʳ.

WHAT IS A PATENT?

A patent grants you the right to exclude others from making, using, offering for sale, or selling your invention in the United States or from importing your invention into the United States. Like trademarks, patents must be registered with the USPTO. To get patent protection for your invention, you must prove that it is both "novel" and "non-obvious." The USPTO does not simply accept your proof at face value; it conducts searches domestically and internationally to make sure your invention is worthy of protection under the patent law. Once granted, patent protection lasts for twenty years, making it a more limited monopoly than copyright.

The federal laws protect three types of patents. A *utility patent* protects a new and useful process, machine, article of manufacture, or composition of matter, or any new and useful improvement thereof. A *design patent* protects a new, original, and ornamental design for an article of manufacture. Finally, a *plant patent* protects a distinct and new variety of plant. In general terms, a utility patent protects the way an article is used and works, while a design patent protects the way an article looks. Unlike utility patents, a design patent lasts for only fourteen years.

While both design patent law and copyright law protect the esthetic features of articles, as stated earlier, the copyright law does not, generally, protect useful articles. By their very nature, design patents protect the ornamental features of a useful object. For example, a design patent could protect the look of a lighting fixture, which—unless the ornamental aspects could entirely be separated from the useful ones—would not ordinarily be protectable under copyright law.

While all protection under the intellectual property law is based upon the owner's being the first to create something, patent law is more stringent than copyright or trademark law in requiring proof of the time an invention was created. So, if you think you might want to seek patent protection one day, keep a record of when you first conceived of the invention and when you successfully completed it. You should also start the patent application process as soon as possible, in case someone else has also come up with the same invention or design.

WHAT ARE THE PENALTIES FOR PATENT INFRINGEMENT?

Claims for patent infringement can be made only after a patent is validly registered. However, once the application for the patent is submitted and pending review, some prepatent protection may be available. Under the patent law, in addition to reasonable attorneys' fees, the court may award the patent owner damages "adequate to compensate for the infringement, but in no event less than a reasonable royalty for the use made of the invention by the infringer, together with interest and costs as fixed by the court."[38]

In different times, the penalty for infringing upon a patent was considerably harsher. In 1421, the government of Florence awarded one of the world's first patents to Filippo Brunelleschi for a means of bringing goods up the usually unnavigable river Arno to the city (see oppposite). He demanded and was duly awarded legal protection for his invention, and was given the right for three years to burn any competitor's ship that incorporated his design. (Such attempts at self-help are currently frowned upon, at least in the United States.)

* * *

Intellectual property is an architect's stock in trade, and it needs to be protected accordingly. While contractual protection is always advisable, the law can provide protection even where the contract is silent. The intellectual property law does not protect everything an architect does, however. For example, an architect's ideas, no matter how valuable, do not have legal insulation from use by others; those ideas must be expressed in some tangible form before they are deemed protectable—and even then, an architect who claims that her design was infringed needs to prove that the alleged copy is "substantially similar" to her design. Whether trying to protect a design for a building, a fabric pattern, or an invention, the architect should (i) provide notice of his intent to protect his rights in his work product, and (ii) consult with an attorney about the best way in which to obtain such protection.

THREE

WHY DO I NEED INSURANCE?

"You can never have too much insurance!" "They won't sue you if they know you don't have insurance!" You are likely to hear both such contradictory pronouncements in the construction world. The first may cause you to pay unnecessary insurance fees, but the second could lead you down a very dangerous path. As any experienced lawyer will tell you, there are always people ready, willing, and able to sue for almost anything, regardless of the likelihood of ultimate success or the ability to collect on a judgment. And the openness of the American court system and ease of bringing arbitrations simply reinforce those propensities.

The decision to invest in appropriate types and amounts of insurance is a no-brainer. Given the increased complexity of construction, the expense of resisting claims, the risks to one's livelihood from an adverse result in a contested dispute, and the benefits of having the peace of mind from knowing that financial support and claims expertise back you up, you simply have to bite the bullet and do it. Every architect should carry insurance for professional liability, commercial general liability, workers' compensation (if you have employees), business office coverage, and automobile liability (for owned and non-owned autos). You should also consider other kinds of insurance, including employment practices liability insurance and, if you get involved in a large project involving potential exposure of millions of dollars, project insurance. We address each of these types of coverage in the discussion that follows. But first let's look at some definitions and consider a few basic facts about how insurance for design professionals works.

WHAT EXACTLY IS INSURANCE?

"Insurance" is shorthand for an agreement by which one party (the "insurer") promises to provide something of value for another party (the "insured") upon the occurrence in the future of some specified contingency. The thing of value is most often "indemnification," that is, making good any loss, damage, or liability incurred by the insured or by some third party who claims to have been harmed by the insured. In addition, the thing of value may include providing a defense in any proceedings brought by a third party for damages claimed to have been caused by the insured. In exchange for the promise to do these things in the future, the insurer receives payments in the present, often in installments over time, known as insurance "premiums."

The written agreement in which the insured's duty to pay premiums and the insurer's duty to provide value in the future is called the insurance "policy." The typical insurance policy for design professionals is as thick as a ream of paper and practically impossible for any human being untutored in the ways of insurance to read and understand. Such policies usually start with a cover sheet called the "declarations" that identifies the insured (you), the insurer (the insurance campany), the policy number, type of insurance, premium, and the effective and expiration dates of the policy. The declarations may not detail the specific risks you are protected against or how much money will be paid if protection under the policy is triggered. You may have to read on to a sheet buried in the stack of papers for a paragraph or set of sentences that actually specify the insurance coverage. From that you must go back into the definitions section to determine the actual scope of the policy and how the coverage will apply to you.

Insurance policies can be divided into two general categories: claims-made policies (sometimes referred to as "discovery policies") and occurrences policies. A claims-made policy indemnifies against all claims made during a specified period, regardless of when the incidents that gave rise to the claims occurred. In contrast, an occurrences policy indemnifies against claims based on the event occurring within the policy period, regardless of when the claims are made. As discussed in greater detail below, insurance that protects you against claims arising out of defects in your design of a structure is provided under a claims-made policy. In other words, provided the policy in force when the claim is asserted has prior acts coverage, the policy will cover that claim even if the claim relates to work done or an injury that occurred before the policy took effect. In contrast, general liability insurance that covers personal injury, fire, or possibly damage to property, is ordinarily occurrences coverage. This means the policy in force when the relevant event occurred provides the coverage, even if you no longer have that policy in force when the claim is asserted.

The typical insurance policy also contains pages known as "endorsements" that modify the scope of coverage by adding further benefits for the insured or placing limitations upon the kinds of risks for which indemnification is provided. Insurance is heavily regulated because its complexity creates the potential for fraud on customers and because it is in the public interest to be sure that resources are available to compensate for certain types of injuries. As a result, a number of the endorsements and other notices that appear in an insurance policy note that they are mandated by law or state regulation.

In addition to language stating how much you receive when coverage is triggered, you normally find a provision in the policy imposing a "deductible" or "self-insured retention." This is the amount of an otherwise-covered loss that is not payable under the policy and that you must pay before your insurer pays benefits. Sometimes the deductible kicks in with respect to payment for the legal expense in resisting a claim, and sometimes it applies only to the amount payable for the loss itself. In the latter case, the policy is said to provide "first dollar coverage" for defense costs. Where that exists, the amount payable for the loss may or may not be reduced by the amount the insurer pays for legal expense. Indeed, even where the deductible applies to defense costs, the overall payment for a loss may be reduced by the payments the insurance company makes for defense. How this is handled affects the amount of your premium so you should clearly understand it before you purchase the policy.

Every insurance policy details how to give "notice," that is, how to notify your insurer when a claim is or may be brought against you, requiring your insurer to defend you or ultimately pay insurance proceeds for a loss. Other than the act of obtaining the insurance policy and paying your premiums on time, *nothing you do in connection with your insurance is more important than providing timely notice.* You can lose the entire benefit of the policy and all the premiums you have paid by delaying notice. Be sure you understand the notice requirements of each policy when you get it. In this regard, your insurance broker is an important resource.

WHAT ROLE DO INSURANCE BROKERS PLAY?

There is a huge industry in the United States consisting entirely of intermediaries, or "brokers," between the companies that issue the insurance policies and the customers who buy them. Given the arcane language of insurance policies, the proliferation of complex definitions, and the general difficulty of simply reading the document your premium has paid for, it is no small wonder architects (like just about everybody else) ordinarily turn to an insurance broker for guidance. A number of insurance brokers specialize in the needs of design professionals and in guiding them through the process of selecting appropriate policies, negotiating the cost, and explaining the coverage. Later, when you need to invoke the benefits of a policy because a claim is made or an injury occurs, the broker receives and forwards your notice of claim to the insurance company and serves as your advocate in obtaining the benefits you bargained for if the insurance company balks.

You should be aware of two key documents that an insurance broker often issues when you obtain insurance coverage. The first is what is known as the "binder," sometimes called a "binding receipt" or a "binder slip." This is a memorandum or letter providing you with temporary coverage while your application for an insurance policy is being processed or while the formal policy is being prepared. The binder is rarely more than a page or two and provides only a minimal description of the terms of insurance. The broker sends it to you upon receipt of whatever premium deposit is required with the application. The binder states that the coverage it reflects remains subject to the insurance company's acceptance of the application and agreement to provide the requested policy. Therefore, if the application is denied, the binder has no effect. Its purpose is merely to establish an early start date for an insurance policy that in fact gets issued several days or weeks later.

The other document supplied by a broker is an "insurance certificate." This is a confirmation by your broker that the insurance company has issued a policy providing coverage of the kind specified on the document but does not detail the terms of your policy. You can show the certificate to owners, lenders, contractors, and public authorities to show that you have insurance. You should resist the temptation to treat the insurance certificate as an adequate substitute for the policy itself—it is not, and that can cause problems. For example, brokers occasionally issue a certificate even though the insurance carrier has not actually issued a policy. Or a valid insurance certificate exists, but the certificate fails to note a policy limitation, for example, that the insurance policy does not cover work in a certain locale.

Anyone who requests proof of your insurance and is sent a copy of your insurance certificate is called a "certificate holder." But a certificate holder is not afforded any coverage or rights under the policies listed on the certificate, and does not become an "Additional Named Insured" under any of the

Sample ACORD Certificate of Liability Insurance

policies listed on the certificate. A certificate holder is simply informed that you have secured the referenced policies, and that they are "in force." In the event that your policy is canceled, notification of cancellation is accordingly sent to a certificate holder.

Do not therefore treat the insurance certificate as an adequate substitute for the policy itself; it is not. In fact, if your broker offers to hold your policy for you so that you can avoid the inconvenience of having to read and file the complete, practically incomprehensible document, do not accept his offer. Get the complete policy, check it over, raise questions with the broker about anything you do not understand, and be sure to keep a copy in a place where you can readily retrieve it.

All insurance policies have a term so be sure to keep current and do not let any policies lapse. Your insurance policies are valuable assets of your professional practice. Guard them carefully, and have them ready to use when the time comes. The chances are, unfortunately, that it will come.

WHAT DOES PROFESSIONAL LIABILITY INSURANCE COVER?

At the top of your list of insurance policies to invest in is a policy protecting you against claims for professional liability—or, more simply stated, malpractice insurance. A professional liability policy covers you for claims for errors, omissions, and negligent acts in your professional practice. It does *not* cover you if your acts were intentionally wrongful, willful, or fraudulent. Professional liability policies also typically do not cover explicit warranties or guarantees that you make. So, as we advised in Chapter 1, do not "guarantee" that your plans are free from defects. The typical professional liability insurance policy somewhere in its many complex pages spells out the coverage available to you in terms something like the following, which is based on an actual policy:

> To pay on behalf of the insured all sums in excess of the deductible, subject to the policy limits of liability, which the insured shall become legally obligated to pay as damages and/or claim expenses as the result of claims first made against the insured during a policy year and first reported to the insurance company, in writing, during the policy year or within sixty (60) days after the end of the policy year and: (1) the claims arise out of a wrongful act; (2) such wrongful act must have been committed or alleged to have been committed subsequent to the Retroactive Date(s) stated in the policy; and (3) prior to the inception date of this policy, none of the insureds' directors, officers, principals, partners or insurance managers

knew or could have been reasonably expected that such wrong-ful act might give rise to a claim.[39]

Professional liability policies usually have a per-claim limit and an aggregate of coverage for the policy period. In other words, if you have a professional liability policy with a $1 million per claim/$2 million aggregate, you would have $1 million available to you to respond to a single claim and a total of $2 million to cover all claims during the policy period, which is generally one year. Be mindful that defense costs are often included in a policy's limit of liability and as such can reduce the amount available to pay damages.

A professional liability policy is a claims-made policy, covering claims asserted during the policy period. For example, if you work on a project for one year, and eighteen months after the project is completed a claim is made against your firm on that project, the policy in effect at the time the claim is made would apply to the claim. For that reason, it is critical that, as you continue to be in practice, you carry the appropriate professional liability insurance. If, for some reason, your policy lapses, a claim relating to an earlier project would not be covered. In addition, should you decide to give up the practice of architecture or your firm is merged into another firm, you should continue to carry insurance for at least several years after your firm has closed its doors, to cover claims arising out of your projects. This is known as "tail" coverage. There is no simple answer to how long the tail period should be, but it should at least cover the statutory period in your home state for claims by an owner against your firm for malpractice.

Each professional liability policy has a coverage period and a geographic coverage area. It is usually possible, for the right price, to get coverage for claims arising from acts before the coverage period began. This is known as "prior acts" coverage. If you have practiced for some period of time without coverage and are just now taking out insurance or if you are changing carriers, be sure to review with your broker how you are covered for claims arising from possible errors or omissions before the commencement date of the policy period that you are purchasing. This is necessary because the new policy does not cover any negligent act committed during a prior period when you did not have insurance. If you are changing insurers, you must make sure the new insurer provides coverage for your firm's prior acts.

As for the area of coverage, be sure that your policy covers you for claims wherever you are working. If your firm is working overseas, does the policy you have cover a claim arising there? Does your overseas client accept coverage by your carrier or must you also obtain coverage from a carrier based in or permitted to offer insurance in the foreign locale? You need answers to these questions when entering into a contract for overseas work. You do not want to sign an agreement for a foreign project with a set fee and learn later that you have to purchase additional insurance because your carrier does not cover you for a claim in that foreign country or because your client insists you get other insurance.

Professional liability insurance policies generally cover the firm and its owners and employees (including former owners and employees) for claims against them. As a licensed professional, you can be held personally liable for your own negligent acts, errors, and omissions in the practice of architecture. Setting up a professional corporation, a professional limited liability company, or a professional limited liability partnership does not in itself shield you from being sued personally for your own malpractice, but the firm's professional liability policy can provide the coverage that indemnifies you to the same extent as if you had a personal policy.

Nearly all professional liability insurance policies have a deductible and the policies also vary as to how they cover the expenses of handling a claim. The amount of a deductible, obviously, affects your premium. The claim expenses (principally the cost of attorneys) are part of a policy's limit of liability. Some policies provide "first dollar" defense, which means the total defense costs are covered from the start by the carrier, but the legal fees reduce the amount of available insurance. Most other policies provide a defense but your firm is responsible for paying the legal fees and expenses until the deductible is met, and if there is a settlement or judgment with respect to the claim, any remaining portion of the deductible is your responsibility. Most insurance companies work with selected counsel whom they have vetted and who are experienced in handling professional malpractice claims. At the same time, you are often able to request that your own regular outside counsel handle a claim. Different professional liability insurance companies approach the assignment of counsel differently.

As noted above, every insurance policy has a requirement that the insured give timely notice of claims, both actual and potential. Many architects are afraid that if they report potential claims to their insurance broker and carrier, their premiums will go up. Experience suggests that this worry is misplaced as many factors go into the calculation of your premium. You should always err on the side of reporting a potential claim. If you do not report it, and the matter matures into a real claim, the insurance company may take the position that you knew about it way back when, failed to report it, and have therefore lost coverage under the policy. You do not want to wake up one morning and find that the "minor" incident at the project you failed to report has become a claim, and your carrier is declining coverage for lack of notice. Here too rely on your broker for guidance as to when a claim or potential claim should be reported to the insurance company.

By reporting the potential claim you have placed the insurance company on notice, and if a real claim is made at some point, the company cannot decline coverage based on your failure to satisfy the notice requirement in the policy. You reap other benefits by promptly reporting potential claims. To begin with, some insurance carriers offer preclaim assistance at no cost to you. In addition, the carrier's designated representative works with your firm to address the possible claim and assists you in taking steps to mitigate the potential liability. Last, but certainly not least, reporting the claim brings peace of mind—you know you have done what is necessary to preserve your rights.

With regard to premiums for professional liability insurance, be sure that your broker fully understands the nature of your practice and that your application for insurance fully discloses information about your work. Some types of projects, such as condominiums, may impact your premiums. If you have not been doing condominium developments and are asked to do one, check with your broker to see what impact, if any, the new project will have on future premiums.

WHAT DOES COMMERCIAL GENERAL LIABILITY INSURANCE COVER?

Anyone operating a professional architecture practice should have general liability insurance for claims by third parties for bodily injury in your office, travel, and at the job site, as well as for property damage caused by the practice's nonprofessional negligence. This insurance also covers you for libel or slander claims but is often less expensive than professional liability insurance. General liability insurance does not usually cover claims of malpractice; however, when a claim or a potential claim for malpractice surfaces, you should discuss with your insurance broker whether you should report the claim to just the professional liability carrier or to both carriers.

Unlike professional liability insurance, commercial general liability insurance policies are occurrence-based policies and defense costs are not included in a policy's limit of liability. This means that the policy in effect at the time of the occurrence of the event giving rise to a claim covers that claim. For example, if one of your employees causes property damage at a project site and a claim is made three years after the project is finished, the policy in effect at the time of the property damage governs the claim.

WHAT DOES WORKERS' COMPENSATION INSURANCE COVER?

Workers' compensation insurance is mandated by every state, and the limits are set by the state. This insurance provides coverage for claims by people working for you who are injured while in your employ. A workers' compensation insurance policy can kick in so long as the injury arises in the course of employment during the policy period. With a few exceptions, if one of your employees is injured, he or she has no right to sue you for that injury but must obtain recovery from workers' compensation insurance provided by your firm. Unlike with professional liability insurance, there is no requirement that there be a finding of negligence.

If an employer intentionally causes an injury to a worker, the worker may, notwithstanding the worker compensation rules, be able to sue his or her employer. Furthermore, employers are not necessarily off the hook if the injured employee sues a third party who in turn claims over against the employer, thereby bringing the employer back into the case. Each state looks at workers' compensation insurance in its own way, so it is best to have your insurance broker explain how your state handles this type of insurance.

WHAT DOES COMMERCIAL (BUSINESS) AUTOMOBILE INSURANCE COVER?

If you use an automobile in your business, then you need to carry insurance on your owned, hired, or borrowed vehicles to cover claims. Automobile insurance covers you for injury to you or your employees while driving company-owned, leased, or rental cars, for injury to third parties, and for property damage to your vehicle or someone else's in an accident.

WHAT DOES BUSINESS OFFICE INSURANCE COVER?

If you have an office you should carry insurance to cover certain aspects of your office operations. You should carry property insurance so that if there is a fire or other casualty in your office and you need to rebuild your office, you have insurance proceeds to cover the costs. If you are leasing your office, your landlord in all likelihood has certain insurance requirements in your lease that obligate you to cover your own losses and perhaps damages to the building. Be sure to review the insurance provisions in your lease. If you fail to carry what is required, you are not only in breach of the lease, but you are potentially at great risk of owing huge sums of money to your landlord for damage.

Valuable papers insurance covers you for the cost to regenerate your work product should it be lost or destroyed. Some firms also carry what is known as fidelity bond insurance. This insurance covers you should one of your employees steal from you. For example, suppose you entrust one of your employees to deposit your client's checks into your firm's account. Instead the employee deposits the checks into his or a friend's account. Fidelity bond coverage helps you recover such a loss.

WHAT DOES EMPLOYMENT PRACTICES LIABILITY INSURANCE COVER?

Claims by employees for discrimination, sexual harassment, or wrongful termination are on the rise. Employment practices insurance provides your firm with coverage for these and other claims. (We discuss claims covered by this type of insurance in more detail in Chapter 6.) We would all like to think that our workplace is immune from such claims but employment practices claims arise even in the best of firms. All it takes is a hypersensitive employee or a really dumb manager or fellow employee, and you can get caught up in a discrimination or harassment lawsuit. This insurance, therefore, is worth considering.

WHAT DOES IT MEAN TO BE AN ADDITIONAL INSURED?

You are the architect on a new house and someone visiting the construction site is injured when the contractor's foreman drops a joist by accident. The injured person is going to sue, and it is quite possible the angry and upset individual will sue everybody he or she can find. After all, the more people in the mix of a lawsuit, the better the chance of a good recovery. For you, the architect, the last thing you want is to have to go to your insurance carrier for a defense. Since this was not your fault, wouldn't it be better if you could go to the contractor's insurance company for a defense? Being what is known as an "additional insured" on the contractor's policy makes this possible. Being identified on as many policies as possible as an additional insured is a cost-free way to get coverage in a multiparty project. If there is a claim against your firm and you are an additional insured on another party's insurance and that party caused the problem, then you have the right to go to that party's insurance company and seek to have that insurance company defend you and cover you for any liability.

It is critical that your firm be an additional insured on the contractor's general liability insurance policy in force during the time that the contractor is working on your project. This gives you the right to have the contractor's insurance company defend and pay any liability for a claim against your firm where the liability rests with the contractor.

Professional liability policies do not permit additional insureds since such coverage is intended for claims involving *professional* negligence. Accordingly, your client cannot be an additional insured on your professional liability policy. However, your client can be an additional insured on your commercial general liability and automobile policies. Clients often ask to be listed as an additional insured on those policies. This is an appropriate request that your commercial general liability and automobile insurance broker should be willing to accommodate.

Additional insured status is usually evidenced by the additional insured's being listed on the insurance certificate issued by the broker for the party offering the insurance. Although it is good to see the insurance certificate and have your firm's name listed as an additional insured on that form, the form may legally be meaningless if the insurance company itself has not issued an endorsement to the policy adding your firm as an additional insured. Unfortunately some insurance brokers on occasion issue insurance certificates listing additional insureds, but the insurance companies have no knowledge someone is added as an additional insured and disclaim coverage. Therefore, it is critical that you either ask the contractor directly or recommend to your client (the owner) that he or she get the contractor at the outset of the project to provide actual copies of the policies with the appropriate endorsements so you know the proper insurance is in place and that you are in fact covered.

WHAT INSURANCE SHOULD MY CONSULTANTS CARRY?

Your consultants must carry appropriate limits of insurance for the duration of the project and for whatever period of time you may be required by your client to carry insurance after the project is completed. Not all consultants need to have the same limits of insurance that you may be required by your client to carry. To the extent the owner seeks high limits for consultants, the matter must be addressed at the time you are negotiating your basic services agreement for the project. Be sure to obtain at least insurance certificates if not actual policies from your consultants and then make sure that during the project your consultant's insurance is always current.

WHAT IS PROJECT INSURANCE?

If you become involved in an extremely large project, after the euphoria has faded, take stock in your risks. If something goes wrong, you might face millions in claims. Sometimes the owner or developer decides that your practice policy limits are insufficient to cover such a large project and takes out an additional insurance policy at his or her own expense. Such a policy is known as "project insurance." It applies to a single project and may cover some or all of the design team members. You too can get project-specific insurance, but it covers many parties, is principally beneficial to the owner, and is often prohibitively expensive.

WHAT IS A WAIVER OF SUBROGATION?

Once an insurance company pays a claim it typically steps into the shoes of its insured and has the right to pursue any claim the insured could have asserted against a third party. In this situation, the insurance company is said to be "subrogated" to its insured's claims. The result is that payment on a claim does not end the potential for litigation. For example, a house under construction is destroyed by fire due to the architect's improper design of doors for fire stopping. Under a homeowner's policy, the insurance company may pay the owner the cost to rebuild the home. But under its right of subrogation, the insurance company has whatever claim the homeowner would have had against the architect.

The standard AIA owner/contractor agreements provide for both parties to waive their subrogation rights against architects to the extent claims are covered by property insurance. This contractually agreed to waiver prevents insurers for either the owner or the contractor from going after the architect for payment of a property damage claim.

HOW ARE MY PROFESSIONAL LIABILITY INSURANCE PREMIUMS CALCULATED?

Insurance premiums can be a significant expense for architecture firms, particularly newly established firms. Unfortunately, you most likely cannot find a definitive and simple explanation of how your premiums for professional liability insurance are calculated.

Your premium for professional liability insurance depends on many factors. One of the most important is your annual billings. Insurance companies look at your billings, perhaps taking a three-year average or maybe just one year. If you have a new firm you will most likely be asked to project your billings for the first year. The premium may also depend on the nature of your practice: Are you designing condominium developments? Only apartment interiors? Are you working overseas? What is your firm's claim history?

What you pay for professional liability insurance also depends on the size of your deductible and how the carrier handles the defense of your firm when a claim is made. Some insurance companies also offer discounts if you have certain provisions in your contract and have quality-control processes in place as the project progresses. Some companies may give a credit against your deductible if you have a dispute that gets resolved in mediation.

A broker acting on your behalf will most likely obtain several quotes for you when applying for insurance. Be sure to sit down with the broker to review these quotes and ask the following questions:

- How does the deductible work?
- Are there things I can do in my practice to take advantage of possible discounts from the carriers?
- How long have the different carriers been insuring architects, and are they financially stable?
- What is the reputation of each insurance company for claims management?
- Which insurance companies will permit me to retain counsel of my choosing if there is a dispute?

* * *

Understanding all of the ramifications of insurance is not easy, but working with your broker you need to make every effort to understand at least the basics of the coverages you and your firm need. You certainly do not want to be surprised some day after a claim is filed to learn you have a huge deductible that you knew nothing about. At least once a year, sit down with your broker, review your policies, tell the broker about any changes in your practice, and discuss whether changes should be made in any of your insurance policies. While insurance may seem like a minor item for an architect to consider in developing a practice or moving forward on an important new project, in reality, nothing can be more important. Legal exposure without the proper insurance can destroy your practice and your peace of mind. Don't let it happen to you.

FOUR

WHAT DO I NEED TO KNOW ABOUT GETTING PAID?

For the architect who wants to make a living from architecture, getting paid by the client warrants some attention. The contract you have with your client needs to spell out what your fee is, how it is calculated, and when it is due. Your contract should also address what happens when you are not paid on time: What are your remedies? Can you stop work? Can you file a lien? How do you start the dispute resolution process?

WHAT ARE THE DIFFERENT MEANS OF DETERMINING THE FRAMEWORK FOR COMPENSATION?

Architects generally have four ways of getting paid for their basic services: a fixed fee for the project, a percentage of construction cost, by the hour, or some combination of these options. Additional services are usually billed hourly or as a multiple of personnel expense. Whether you use an AIA form of agreement or your own letter agreement, you need to be very specific about the payment terms. When in the course of the project you will get paid can be a bone of contention in contract negotiations. Architects like to get paid as much as possible early in the project since the construction phase can drag on and on. On the other hand, your clients want the comfort of knowing that you will stick around to do your job because you are still owed a good part of your fee. Compromise is usually possible, but the issues have to be addressed head-on in negotiations.

Fixed Fee

If you are quoting a fixed fee, then you need to detail how that fee will be paid. One standard way is to allocate a percentage of the total fee to different phases of the project, such as schematic design, design development, construction documents, bidding and negotiation, and construction administration. But allocating fees to each phase can be contentious as owners prefer a large percentage in the construction phase while architects prefer more of the fee allocated to the design phases. You also need to specify whether the payments should be made monthly or at the end of each phase. (Remember that you incur most of your own costs, including your largest—employee compensation—at least monthly.)

Percentage of Construction Cost

If you are getting a percentage of the construction cost as a fee, then you need to define how the construction cost is calculated. Typically construction cost is defined as the cost of the work that you design or specify. A question then arises: what about work designed by consultants who are retained by others (such as the owner), but whose plans are part of your construction document set? Coordinating your work with these consultants can be time-consuming, and if you are not paid for any of the work that these consultants design, you may find yourself spending a great deal of time without being compensated.

    If your fee is a percentage of the cost of the work, then you need to establish in your agreement an estimated budget for the project against which your fee is initially calculated. Keep in mind that the construction cost will probably change during the design phase as plans for the project evolve, as well as during the construction phase as change orders occur. If you are being paid a percentage of the construction cost, then it is critical that you have a mechanism in your agreement to adjust your fee as the construction cost changes. In addition to the construction cost for billing purposes that is established in the initial agreement, you should have a provision stating that your fee will be recalculated whenever the construction cost is adjusted. This adjustment may occur when you or someone else does a cost estimate during the design development or construction document phase or when a contractor's bid is accepted. You should also stipulate that a final calculation be made at the end of the project when the total cost of the project is finally known. A provision incorporating these ideas might read as follows:

> For initial billings, the Architect's fee shall be ____ percent
> (___%) of $_____ which is the initial estimated Cost
> of the Work. When the contract for construction is awarded and
> then again at final completion of the Project, the Architect's fee
> shall be adjusted. If an additional fee is due the Architect, Owner
> shall pay the additional amount within _____ days after the
> adjustment in the Cost of the Work has been determined. If the
> Architect has been overpaid based upon the Cost of the Work
> the overpayment will be credited against future statements for
> services.

In situations where the construction cost is reduced, you will be paid
less going forward, but make it clear in the contract with your client that
you must still be paid for work that you have designed to the extent you
were designing to a higher budget. Your client's change of mind should not
be used to reduce your compensation for a previously agreed-upon design
for a bigger job.

Payment by the Hour

Some projects are billed on an hourly basis. Sometimes the agreement is
hourly without limitation and sometimes it is hourly with a cap of either a
set dollar amount or a percentage of the construction cost. Whatever the
arrangement, be sure to provide for at least annual increases in your rates if
you expect the project to last longer than one year. A sentence like the following covers the point:

> Hourly rates may be adjusted on or about the anniversary date of
> this Agreement, provided that the increases shall be consistent
> with the Architect's rates charged to its other clients.

Retainer Deposits

Whether you are billing on a percentage of construction cost, hourly, or a
fixed fee, try to get a retainer deposit at the beginning of a project. Typically
the goal is to maintain the deposit until your final invoice so that, in the event
that your client fails to pay along the way, you have at least some money to
apply to any outstanding invoice. Many owners object to this and want any
retainer deposit credited early on. It is simply a matter of negotiation.

WHAT HAPPENS IF MY CLIENT FAILS TO PAY?

Getting paid in full by clients is often an issue. As projects proceed, owners often see their costs going up—for whatever reason—and then try to reduce their costs somewhere else. Unfortunately, they often look to you to adjust your fee or to negotiate a reduction. Your agreement needs to specify that you can, with appropriate notice, suspend or terminate for nonpayment. A typical provision might read something like this:

> If the Owner fails to make payment to the Architect within _____ days, the Architect may suspend or terminate its services on seven (7) days' written notice.

The notice requirement for suspension or termination can be as short as a day to as long as you and your client may agree. Your agreement should also specify how quickly the owner is expected to pay you after receipt of your invoice. Commercial owners tend to pay later. Residential owners can be expected to pay sooner. But set a time frame and monitor it carefully. It is easy on an exciting, fast-paced project to lose track of your billing, what is owed, and how long it has been outstanding. All agreements should provide for interest on overdue payments.

Owners often reserve the right to withhold payment if they have a question about an invoice. If an owner wants this right included in the contract, you need to set a time frame within which your client must raise any objections in writing after receiving your invoice. Uncontested amounts of any invoice should be paid, and you should also reserve the right to stop work if the amount of unpaid fees in dispute goes above a certain amount, particularly where the owner is being unreasonable in withholding sums due to your office. A provision addressing this point might read as follows:

> In the event that the Owner disputes the Architect's invoice, Owner shall provide a written statement within _____ days of receipt of the Architect's invoice detailing reasons for objection to the Architect's invoice. In the event the aggregate amount of the Architect's invoices in dispute by Owner exceeds $_____, the Architect reserves the right to suspend services on _____ days' written notice.

WHAT IS A LIEN?

What can you do if the owner fails to pay after the project is complete or after the agreement has been terminated by you because the owner failed to perform? In many states, architects are permitted to file a lien against the property of their client, the owner. Ordinarily a lien is filed with the county clerk where the property is located. It puts anyone who is interested in buying the property on notice (assuming a title search is done) that there is a claim against the property. The lien amount is typically the amount of the outstanding fees. States have very strict requirements as to the timetable for filing a lien, so you need to check the time frame in the jurisdiction where your project is located. If you miss the deadline, which is usually a certain number of months after you last perform services on a project, you will not be able to use a lien to encourage or enforce payment.

If you do file a lien, it is valid for a set period of time. If no action is taken to enforce the lien or the owner takes no action to remove it, you have to renew the lien before its period of effectiveness expires. This time frame differs from state to state. To get paid through the means of a lien filing, you have to start what is known as a lien foreclosure proceeding, which is kind of a lawsuit against the owner. If the lawsuit proceeds to judgment in your favor and your client does not pay, you can force a sale of the property to create a fund from which you can be paid.

Many owners confronted with a lien go to court to post a bond. The owner often deposits cash or another security with a company that in turn posts a bond with the court. The bond is in the amount of the lien (plus a percentage mark up). By posting security with the court, the lien no longer remains a cloud on title of the property. This means the property can be sold free and clear of any claim under the lien. But the good news for you is that a bond provides funds to pay any judgment that might be awarded in a lien foreclosure proceeding.

Overall, it is critical to consult counsel if you are considering filing a lien. The requirements are particular to each state and the consequences for an improper filing can be very serious, as it could prevent the owner from selling a property and thereby expose you to a claim for damages.

Many owners before making payment to an architect will require a waiver of lien rights. By signing a waiver, an architect typically represents that he or she has been paid through a certain date and has no need to

A 167—Notice of mechanic's lien, affidavits of service, individual, partnership or corporation, New York City—to be filed with County Clerk. Lien Law §3 et seq 9-96.

Blumberg Excelsior, Inc.
Publisher, NYC 10013

NOTICE OF MECHANIC'S LIEN

To the Clerk of the County of .... and all others whom it may concern:

Please Take Notice, that ....

.... as lienor(s) have and claim a lien on the real property hereinafter described as follows:

(1) The names and residences of the lienor(s) are

....

being a (partnership) (corporation) composed of ....

whose business address is at
and whose principal place of business is at ....
(1a) The name and address of lienor's attorney, if any ....

(2) The owner of the real property is ....
and the interest of the owner as far as known to the lienor(s) is
(3) The name of the person by whom the lienor(s) was (were) employed is ....
The name of the person to whom the lienor(s) furnished or is (are) to furnish material or for whom the lienor(s) performed or is (are) to perform professional services is ....
The name of the person with whom the contract was made is ....
(4) The labor performed was

The material furnished was ....

The materials actually manufactured for but not delivered to the real property are ....

The agreed price and value of the labor performed is $ ....
The agreed price and value of the material furnished is $ ....
The agreed price and value of the material actually mfd. for but not delivered to the real prop. is $ ....
                                                      Total agreed price and value $ ....
(5) The amount unpaid to the lienor(s) for said labor performed is $ ....
The amount unpaid to the lienor(s) for said material furnished is $ ....
The amount unpaid to lienor(s) for material actually mfd. for but not delivered to the real prop. is $ ....
                                                      Total amount unpaid $ ....
The total amount claimed for which this lien is filed is $ ....
(6) The time when the first item of work was performed was ....
The time when the first item of material was furnished was ....
The time when the last item of work was performed was ....
The time when the last item of material was furnished was ....
(7) The property subject to the lien is situated in the Borough of .... County of ....
City of New York, on the .... side of .... feet and
.... inches .... of .... , being .... feet
and .... inches wide, front and rear by .... feet and .... inches deep on each side,
and known as Number ....

That said labor and materials were performed and furnished for and used in the improvement of the real property hereinbefore described. That 8 months (4 months if a single family dwelling) have not elapsed dating from the last item of work performed, or from the last items of materials furnished, or since the completion of the contract, or since the final performance of the work, or since the final furnishing of the materials for which this lien is claimed.

Dated

....
The name signed must be printed beneath

Sample Blumberg Form of Notice of Mechanic's Lien, page 1 of 4

Re: Project Name

        Affidavit made this _____ day of _____, 20____ to _____ ("Releasees") by _____ ("Releasor") for furnishing of work, labor, services, materials and/or equipment in connection with the construction project known and described as _____ (the "Project"), in consideration of having received final payment, which is acknowledged as being the final and total amount due or alleged due or owing from Releasees in connection with the Project, the receipt of which, by Releasor from Releasees, and payment thereof, is hereby acknowledged; the Releasor does hereby covenant and agree not to claim or file a mechanic's or other lien against the Project or any part thereof for materials and/or labor furnished to Releasees in connection with improvements to the Project and does so covenant in recognition of the fact that payment in full has been received for all work, labor, services and materials supplied by the Releasor up to and including the _____ day of _____ 20____, and Releasor, its successors, affiliates and assignees hereby release Releasees from any and all claims, liens, suits and causes of action arising out of the Project or the furnishing of work, labor, services, materials and equipment to or on behalf of Releasees.

        The Releasor hereby agrees to indemnify and hold the Releasees, their successors, affiliates and assignees harmless from any and all damages, costs, expenses, demands, suits, liens and legal fees, directly or indirectly relating to any claim for compensation by any other party for work which was performed or should have been performed by the Releasor and/or its agents or subcontractors and from and against any claims relating to any work, labor, services, materials and/or equipment allegedly furnished by the Releasor and/or its agents or subcontractors. The Releasor hereby certifies and warrants that it has fully paid for all work, labor, services, materials, and/or equipment provided to it in connection with the aforesaid Project.

        IN WITNESS WHEREOF, this Waiver, Release and Discharge has been executed this _____ day of _____, _____.

Sample Final Waiver and Release of Lien

enforce the right to be paid by filing a lien (see sample waiver of lien form on the preceding page).

WHAT IS MY LAST RESORT?

If you have not been paid and all reasonable efforts to get paid (including filing a lien) have failed, you can bring a claim under whatever dispute resolution provisions exist in the agreement (see Chapter 7).

* * *

In negotiating your agreement with your client, be sure to be explicit about how your fee will be calculated, when you expect to be paid and what will happen if you are not paid. Also be sure to understand what will happen if you are not paid: do you have a right to file a lien? Will you have to sue or is there a different means of dispute resolution in your agreement? Negotiating provisions that address fee issues in advance is neither easy nor fun, but you've got to do it or risk the possibility of ending up working for free.

FIVE

WHAT DO I NEED TO KNOW ABOUT FORMING AND ORGANIZING AN ARCHITECTURAL FIRM?

Great buildings are the product of the creativity of individuals, not bureaucracies. Why, then, would any architect want to form a company to carry out creative work? As it turns out, you may want to operate your practice through a legal entity for several reasons: to limit your personal exposure to legal liability, to organize and enforce your relationship with other members of your practice, to obtain health and pension benefits for yourself and employees, to pool your creative and financial resources with others, to persuade potential clients that you have the resources to handle their projects, to reduce your tax burden, and for other valuable purposes. This chapter provides guidance on how you can structure your practice to achieve these results.

WHAT FORM OF ENTITY SHOULD I HAVE?

One of the first things you need to do if you want to set up an architectural firm, either alone or with one or more other architects, is to consider the legal form of such a firm. The most common forms for a one-owner firm are a sole proprietorship, a corporation, and a limited liability company. Common forms for a firm with two or more owners are a partnership, a corporation, and a limited liability company. We review these forms, including pros and cons, below.

Sole Proprietorship

If you plan on being the sole owner of your firm, you could practice as a sole proprietor without creating a legal entity. A sole proprietorship is easy and inexpensive to set up. In many states, you just need to register the name of your firm with a government office. Some states require that the business name you use contain certain words, such as "architect" or "architecture" (for example, Joe Smith Architect) so check with your local board of architecture beforehand.

The tax treatment of a sole proprietorship is fairly simple. Except for possible local taxes (for example, an unincorporated business tax) no separate tax returns are required of your firm. The income of your firm is reflected in Schedule C to your personal income tax return (Form 1040) and Schedule SE for self-employment taxes (Social Security and Medicare), and is taxed at your individual tax rate.

Although a sole proprietorship is easy to form, it is not necessarily the best legal form for a one-person firm. As a sole proprietor, you are liable not only for any professional negligence (malpractice) but also for any other "tort" claims (including slip-and-fall claims) and contractual obligations (including your office lease). To avoid or minimize such liabilities other than for malpractice, you should consider setting up a legal entity such as a corporation or a limited liability company.

Corporation

A corporation is a distinct legal entity that provides limited liability to its owners and managers. The owners of a corporation are called shareholders. The corporation is managed by one or more directors and officers. You need to check the requirements in the state in which you want to form your corporation with respect to the form of the corporation. New York, for example, requires that architects who wish to practice in the form of a corporation set up a so-called professional service corporation (PC) or design professional service corporation (DPC). New Jersey allows architects to set up a general business corporation (GBC). New York permits architects to practice as owners of a GBC if the firm was incorporated before April 13, 1929.

As a shareholder of a corporation that practices architecture you have the advantage of generally not being personally liable for the obligations of the corporation, except for any negligence in work performed by you or any person under your direct supervision and control. To maintain the benefit of limited liability, you will need to follow certain corporate formalities, including holding regular meetings of the board of directors and officers or recording decisions made by unanimous written consents of shareholders or directors, and keeping corporate minutes of all meetings and written consents of resolutions of shareholders and board decisions. Additionally, you should make sure that your corporation has its own bank account and keep business and personal expenses separate. Otherwise, a creditor could try to "pierce the corporate veil" and hold you personally liable for the obligations of the corporation. Of course, if you personally guarantee an obligation of your corporation, such as a lease, you are personally liable under the guarantee, even though you practice through a corporation.

Forming a corporation is relatively easy. You only need file a certificate of incorporation with the secretary of state for the state in which you wish to form your corporation. Each state has its own requirements for incorporation. In some states, before your corporation can be formed you must get consent from the state's professional licensing authority. The licensing authority may have several requirements for the corporation, such as: (1) including the word "architecture" or "architect(s)" in the name of the firm, (2) stating that the purpose of the corporation is architecture and not a more general business purpose, and (3) requiring that all shareholders, directors, and officers be licensed in the state. In New York, for example, until January 2012, all shareholders, directors, and officers (except the secretary if the corporation has only one shareholder) had to be licensed architects. Now, less than 25 percent of a new entity called a design professional (service) corporation or D. P. C. can be owned by unlicensed individuals. In New Jersey, at least two-thirds of the shares of a GBC and all shares of a PC must be owned by architects licensed in New Jersey, and at least two-thirds of the directors of a GBC must be New Jersey–licensed architects. In California, at least one officer or employee of a GBC must be licensed in California and his or her name must be part of the firm's name. In Colorado, the practice of architecture must be under the direct supervision of an architect who is licensed in Colorado and who is an officer of the corporation. In Florida, the firm name of a PC must contain the words "professional association" or the abbreviation "P.A."

The licensing regulations periodically change, so before setting up a firm check with your counsel on the licensing requirements for owners. If you set up a firm with an ownership structure that does not comply with the state's requirements you may find yourself charged with practicing architecture improperly, with potential for civil (or even criminal) penalties.

After the corporation is formed, a designated person who signed the incorporation document (called the "incorporator") elects the first board of directors, which is responsible for the management of the corporation. (Shareholders elect subsequent directors.) The board consists of one or more directors. If the board has more than one director, the board usually takes action by vote of a majority of the directors (although a different percentage for certain major decisions may be provided for in the corporation's organizational documents). The first directors elect the first officers, including generally a president, secretary, and treasurer, who manage the corporation on a day-to-day basis. The first board of directors also adopts the bylaws of the corporation, which describe, among other things, the roles of the shareholders, directors, and officers. In general, one person may perform all officer and director functions. The first board of directors generally also votes to issue shares to the shareholder(s). The shareholders of the corporation need to have an agreement setting forth their rights and responsibilities. We address these issues in the section on agreements among owners.

Corporations are subject to federal, state, and local corporate income tax (unless they elect so-called Subchapter S status as described below) on any profits retained in the corporation, and must file federal, state, and local corporate income tax returns. As of 2012 the federal tax rates on taxable corporate income of business corporations are graduated, while personal service corporations such as PCs are taxed at a flat percentage of taxable income. Tax rates change from time to time as a result of tax legislation by Congress.

With certain exceptions described below, the shareholders pay income tax on any profits distributed to them in the form of dividends. This results in double taxation. As a shareholder of a corporation in which you also work, you can receive compensation in the form of a salary. The corporation can then deduct your salary as a business expense, thereby reducing the corporate income tax. But then you need to pay income and payroll taxes on your salary.

To avoid or minimize corporate income taxes, shareholders can elect a so-called Subchapter S status for the corporation. Such corporations (commonly referred to as "Sub S corporations") do not pay federal corporate income tax. They may also be exempt from state and local income taxes. Instead, as a shareholder of an S corporation, you pay income tax on your individual share of the income of the corporation, whether distributed or not, at your own personal income tax rate. As a shareholder of an S corporation, you receive an IRS Schedule K-1 that shows your share of the profits or losses. S corporations are subject to certain limitations, including that all shareholders (cannot be more than 100) must be U.S. citizens or residents and can have only one class of stock (but such entities can have voting and nonvoting shares). Also, payments to employees and corporate officers for services performed are considered wages, which are subject to federal payroll expenses (Social Security, Medicare, federal unemployment taxes as well as workers' compensation and statutory disability insurance costs) and federal income tax withholding.

The above tax description is subject to the shifting winds of public politics, and a major change in the federal or state taxation arrangements may make an alteration in the legal form of your practice entity appropriate. You should consult a tax adviser when forming your entity and periodically thereafter to assure both that you are complying with tax laws and that you are aware of changes and can make appropriate adjustments.

Limited Liability Company

Many architects choose to form a limited liability company (LLC) instead of a corporation or a partnership. In states that require architects to practice in the form of a professional service entity, such an entity is called a professional service limited liability company (PLLC). LLCs offer several advantages over sole proprietorships, corporations, and general partnerships.

First, an LLC combines the limited liability benefits of a corporation with the tax benefits of a sole proprietorship or partnership (discussed below). Like shareholders of a corporation, and unlike sole proprietorships or partners in a general partnership, the owners of an LLC (called "members") are not personally liable for the obligations of the LLC, except that architects who are members of an LLC are personally liable for negligence committed by themselves or any person under their direct supervision and control in their practice. Like a sole proprietorship or a partnership, the LLC is not subject to federal or state income tax (but may be subject to a local unincorporated business tax). This avoids double taxation. All LLC profits are taxed at the owners' individual income tax rates. An LLC with one owner is treated as a sole proprietorship for tax purposes. The sole owner includes the profits or losses on Schedule C to the owner's individual income tax return.

LLCs with more than one owner are taxed as partnerships and file a partnership tax return. Each year, the owners receive a Schedule K-1 from the LLC, which shows their share of profits and losses for the prior year. The owners of an LLC are taxed on the income allocated to them, not on any profit distributions to them. Since the owners of the LLC have to pay income tax on any profits, even if they are not distributed, the owners often provide for periodic distributions (or "draws") so they can pay their quarterly estimated income taxes. Although Sub S corporations also have the same benefit of tax flow-through treatment as LLCs, Sub S corporations are subject to certain ownership restrictions as described above (including that all shareholders must be U.S. citizens or residents), which do not apply to LLCs.

Second, LLCs can have a simpler management structure than corporations. LLCs are managed either by all or some of the members (member-managed LLC), or by one or more managers who are elected by the members (manager-managed LLC). There is no requirement to have a board of directors or officers, resulting in less corporate record-keeping than for corporations. Many states require that some or all of the members and managers be licensed architects.

Third, formation and organization of an LLC is even simpler than for a corporation. The LLC comes into existence upon the filing of a formation certificate with the secretary of state for the state in which the LLC is formed. Many states require prior consent by the state agency that licenses architects. The licensing authority may impose several licensing requirements on the owners of the LLC, similar to those for corporations as described earlier in this chapter. Some states may require that, after formation, the LLC publish notice of its existence in one or more local newspapers, which can be expensive. Following formation, the owners need to enter into an agreement, often called an "operating agreement," that addresses several issues, including management of the day-to-day operations of the firm, allocation of profits and losses to the owners, distribution of profits, and transfers of ownership interests (buy-sell arrangements). Since the operating agreement addresses who the managers and owners of the LLC will be and what the percentage of ownership interests will be, there is no need for additional documents for the election of the managers and the issuance of ownership interests.

Fourth, an LLC allows more flexibility in structuring profit and loss allocations than a corporation. As a shareholder in a corporation, any profit distributions (called "dividends") are in proportion to your percentage ownership. As a member of an LLC, however, you can receive a percentage of the profits that is different from your ownership interest (within certain guidelines established by the IRS). Also, the percentage of losses allocated to a member can be different not only from the percentage ownership but also from the percentage of profits allocated to that member. All this must be spelled out in the operating agreement.

Partnerships

Another option for an entity with two or more owners (in addition to a corporation and an LLC) is a partnership. Architects can form one of two basic forms of partnership: the general partnership (GP) and the limited liability partnership (LLP). LLPs are different from limited partnerships, which are often used for investment purposes. In a GP, all the partners are personally liable for all of the obligations of the GP, including malpractice by another partner and any contractual obligations of the firm such as an office lease. General partnerships have become less popular since the introduction of the LLP and the LLC. Similar to shareholders of a PC and members of an LLC, partners of an LLP are not personally liable for the obligations of the LLP, except they are personally liable for negligence committed by themselves or by any person under their direct supervision and control in their practice.

The profits of a partnership, whether a GP or an LLP, are taxed in the same manner as those of an LLC, as described above. Partnerships are managed by all or some of the partners.

A GP generally comes into existence upon agreement by the partners. Although no filing is typically required, partners usually file a certificate containing the name of the partnership with the county clerk's office. An LLP comes into existence upon the filing of a formation certificate with the secretary of state for the state in which the LLP is formed. Whether prior consent by a state licensing agency is required depends on the state in which the LLP is formed. In New York, for example, although such consent is required for the formation of an LLC, it is not required for the formation of an LLP, thereby reducing the time necessary to form the LLP. You should also check whether the state in which you want to form your LLP requires that you publish notice of the formation in one or more newspapers, which can be expensive.

The licensing authority may have several requirements for the partnership. These requirements are often similar to those for corporations, including certain licensing requirements for the owners of the firm as described earlier in this chapter. Following formation, the partners should enter into a partnership agreement that addresses issues similar to those in an operating agreement for an LLC (including management, allocation of profits and losses to the partners, distribution of profits, and transfers of partnership interests).

WHY DO I NEED A WRITTEN AGREEMENT WITH MY OTHER OWNERS?

If you decide to practice with one or more other architects, you really ought to operate under a formal, written agreement. Often the group wants to get started right away, everyone trusts everyone else (why else would you be going into business together?), and there's a shared vibe that the details of a written agreement can wait. Big mistake. Partnerships or limited liability companies sometimes do not work out. Perhaps certain partners cannot get along; one member generates more business and wants more money; a partner has a midlife crisis and decides to move to Hawaii to paint; a partner is suddenly permanently disabled. The parade of potential disruptions is really endless. In the absence of an agreement, any one of these scenarios can lead to contentious issues and bitter and time-consuming negotiations. Negotiating, at the beginning, an agreement among all partners, shareholders, or members goes a long way toward avoiding conflict and providing a road map should the firm have to go through a transition.

Sitting down to negotiate an agreement with your colleagues may also reveal some major differences in thinking about how the firm should be run. It's better to get those issues out in the open early on.

You may enter into an agreement with your colleagues and never have to look at it for years (although it is a good idea to look at any agreement at least every year). But if you do not have an agreement and an unexpected event occurs, you may regret not putting in the time initially to get an agreement in place.

Any agreement should address several issues, including decision making, allocation of profits and losses to the owners (if a partnership or LLC), distribution of profits, and transfers of ownership interests. Such an agreement is called a shareholders' agreement for a corporation, a partnership agreement for a GP or LLP, or an operating agreement for an LLC. For the sake of simplicity, we refer below to the shareholders' agreement, partnership agreement, and operating agreement collectively as the "owners' agreement."

Capital Contributions; Equity Interests

Each owner (whether a shareholder of a corporation, member of an LLC, or partner of a partnership) usually makes a capital contribution in exchange for his or her ownership interest. The capital contribution can be in the form of cash, property, or services. The law does not require any minimum capital amount. The owners' agreement should state the capital contributions by each of the owners and how many shares each shareholder owns or which percentage ownership each member or partner has.

Profit and Loss Allocations; Distributions

Profit distributions to shareholders of a corporation are in proportion to their percentage ownership. If the corporation is a Sub S corporation, any profits (and losses) are allocated to the shareholders, whether or not the profits are distributed to the shareholders.

If the firm is an LLC or partnership, then the owners can agree on an allocation of profits and losses different from (with certain limitations) the owners' percentage ownership interests. In other words, you can own 60 percent of an LLC or partnership, but receive 75 percent of the profits and be responsible for 55 percent of the losses. The owners' agreement should specify when profit distributions will be made and the percentage of ownership interests required to vote for such distributions. Many owners' agreements provide for distribution of quarterly profits to enable the owner to pay his or her quarterly estimated income taxes.

As an owner of a partnership or LLC, you have a capital account, which reflects your equity interest in the firm. Capital contributions by and allocations of profits to you increase your capital account; withdrawals of capital by and allocations of losses and distributions of profits to you decrease your capital account.

Buy-Sell Arrangement

The owners' agreement should state the terms under which an owner may withdraw from the firm voluntarily, including a transfer of such owner's interest in the firm back to the firm or the other owners. The owners' agreement must also provide under which circumstances an owner is required to transfer his or her ownership interest to the firm or the other owner(s) (such event is often referred to as a "triggering event"), and at what price. Such circumstances include death, permanent disability (to be defined in the agreement), employment termination (if the owner is an employee of a corporation) or expulsion by the other owners, bankruptcy, and loss of one's professional license. A "mandatory withdrawal" clause might read as follows:

> A Shareholder, or his or her estate as the case may be, shall be required to offer his or her Shares for sale to the Company upon the occurrence of any of the following events with respect to such Shareholder (each such event, a "Triggering Event"): (1) death; (2) disability pursuant to Section [____]; (3) the affirmative vote of Shareholders holding at least two-thirds of the Shares (excluding the Shareholder subject to expulsion); (4) a material breach of a Shareholder's obligations under this Agree-

ment; (5) such Shareholder becoming incompetent; (6) such Shareholder being adjudicated a bankrupt or entering into an assignment for the benefit of creditors, or upon the appointment of a receiver to administer his or her interest in the Company, or such interest being seized by a creditor prior to the appointment of a successor to the Shareholder; (7) such Shareholder becoming legally disqualified to practice architecture within the State of New York; (8) conviction of, or plea of nolo contendere to, a felony or crime involving a moral turpitude; or (9) employment termination. Upon the occurrence of one or more of the events mentioned in (1) through (9) with respect to a Shareholder, the Company shall purchase such Shareholder's Shares at a purchase price to be determined pursuant to Section [_____] of this Agreement.

The agreement should define when an owner would be deemed permanently disabled so as to trigger the buyout provisions. For example, the agreement could provide that an owner be deemed permanently disabled after having been unable to work due to disability for 90 consecutive days or 180 days in any 365-day period. A clause defining disability might read as follows:

> If a Shareholder shall become physically or mentally disabled so as to be unable to perform his or her responsibilities, and continues to be disabled for a continuous period exceeding 90 consecutive days or 180 days during any twelve-month period, then the Company or the Other Shareholders may cause a resignation of such disabled Shareholder from the Company by sending a notice in writing to the disabled Shareholder or to his or her representative, thereby causing a Triggering Event.

The agreement could provide for a reduction in profit sharing or compensation during a disability period as follows:

> During the first 60 days of disability, the disabled Shareholder shall continue to receive his or her salary; during the next 60 days, he or she shall receive 50% of his or her salary; and during the following 60 days, he or she will receive 25% of his or her salary. If the disabled Shareholder is covered by disability

insurance, any insurance proceeds shall be deducted from his or her salary.

The owners should also consider whether an owner could be expelled from the firm by the other owners, under what circumstances (for example, for "cause" such as theft, fraud, gross misconduct, breach of a material obligation under the owners' agreement, or upon a vote of a certain percentage of owners even without cause) and the ownership interest percentage required for a vote on expulsion. This can be a sensitive issue; it's better to work it out at the beginning when everyone is getting along.

In the event of withdrawal of a member, the agreement should state what the purchase price for the owner's interest is or by which method it will be determined at some later date. Since you hope the value of the firm increases over the years, it may make more sense to provide for a method by which the purchase price is calculated at the time of the buyout rather than set a fixed price in advance.

You can use several methods to determine the value of an owner's interest, including the following: first, the agreement could provide that a withdrawing member is entitled to his or her share (percentage ownership interest) of a multiple of the firm's average earnings during the prior three years. Second, the agreement could provide that the owner is entitled to his or her share of the accounts receivable when collected by the firm, minus expenses. Third, the value could be based on the book value of the firm, which equals the firm's assets minus the liabilities at a certain point in time. Since the book value is often lower than the actual value of the firm, this method is not used frequently by architectural firms.

Fourth, if the firm is a partnership or LLC, the agreement could provide that the purchase price is the value of the owner's capital account. The value of a capital account of an owner of an LLC or partnership is (1) the amount of the owner's capital account as of the last day of the previous fiscal year for the LLC or partnership, (2) increased by any capital contributions by, and allocations of profits to, the owner during the current year, and (3) decreased by any withdrawals of capital by and allocations of losses and distributions of profits to the owner during the current year. The owners' agreement should provide whether profits to be allocated to a member's capital account are calculated on an accrual basis or on a cash basis.

If the capital account is calculated on an accrual basis, then the agreement could provide that the profits of the firm would include for the current fiscal year any fees billed and received by the firm, plus any fees billed and outstanding (accounts receivable). Subtracted from this sum would be any invoices received and paid by the firm and any invoices received and unpaid (accounts payable) in the current fiscal year. The agreement should also address whether work-in-progress and expenses that have not yet been invoiced should be included in an accrual-based valuation.

If, on the other hand, the capital account is valued on a cash basis, then the profits of the firm consist only of any fees received by the firm, minus any invoices paid by the firm during the current year. Valuation on a cash basis does not include accounts receivable, accounts payable, work-in-progress, or expenses incurred but not yet invoiced.

Fifth, you can also leave the determination of the purchase price to a valuation expert. That expert could be given free rein to determine the buyout price or could be instructed to follow certain guidelines and include certain items in the calculation.

You should provide in the owners' agreement the date as of which the value is to be determined (for example, last day of the fiscal quarter, month, or year immediately preceding the triggering event) and whether different valuations will be used depending on the circumstances of the buyout. For example, the agreement could provide that if an owner of an LLC or partnership leaves voluntarily, the purchase price for his or her interest is the value of his or her capital account calculated on an accrual basis, but when he or she is expelled from the firm for cause, he or she receives the value of the capital account on a cash basis. A valuation clause for an LLC might read as follows:

> The purchase price that shall be payable upon the sale of a Membership Interest caused by a Triggering Event shall be equal to the value of the capital account of the Member whose Membership Interest is to be transferred (the "Transferring Member"), minus any unfunded amounts (i.e., unpaid capital contribution obligations) which amount shall include the Member's share of net profits or net losses of the Company through the date of transfer, calculated on an accrual basis; provided, however, that in the event of expulsion of the Member for Cause, the amount shall be calculated on a cash basis. The term "Cause" shall mean one or more of the following events: (1) act of fraud or embezzlement against the Company, (2) misappropriation of the Company's assets for personal gain, (3) conviction of, or guilty plea concerning, any felony, or (4) inability to perform

material duties as a result of any addiction to alcohol or controlled substances, other than medication prescribed by a duly licensed physician.

The owners' agreement should also provide the payment terms for any buyout of an owner. Although a departing owner may favor a lump-sum payment, a payment in installments over a number of years is often preferable for the firm to minimize its financial burden.

It may make sense for the firm or the other owners to obtain life insurance on each of the owners to fund a buyout upon death of an owner. The owners' agreement should then detail what happens should insurance proceeds amount to more or less than the purchase price. For example, the agreement could provide that when the proceeds are less than the purchase price, the difference is paid by the firm or the remaining owners in installments; when the proceeds exceed the purchase price, the excess proceeds are paid to the firm. The agreement could provide for a life insurance trust arrangement whereby a trustee collects the proceeds and pays them to the estate of the deceased member in exchange for the deceased owner's interest. As a result of such an arrangement, the insurance proceeds do not become part of the firm's assets and therefore subject to claims by the firm's creditors. A life insurance clause might read as follows:

> The Company may decide to obtain insurance insuring the lives of each of the Shareholders, the proceeds of which shall be used to purchase the Shares of a deceased Shareholder. If the Company decides to obtain life insurance, the life insurance policies shall name a Trustee (the "Trustee") as the beneficiary, pursuant to the terms of a trust agreement among the Company, the Trustee, and the Shareholders. In the event of the death of a Shareholder, the Company shall promptly notify the insurance carrier, which shall pay the proceeds of the policy insuring such deceased Shareholder to the Trustee, who shall pay the proceeds to the estate of the deceased Shareholder. If the amount of the proceeds is less than the purchase price that is payable upon a sale of the Shares of the deceased Shareholder, then the Company shall pay the balance of the purchase price to the estate of the deceased Shareholder over a period of five (5) years. In the event the proceeds exceed the purchase price, the excess amount shall be paid to the Company.

Management

The owners' agreement usually contains provisions concerning management of the firm. If the firm is a corporation, management decisions are made by the directors (by majority vote) and executed by the officers. If the firm is a partnership or LLC, then the firm is managed by a majority of the owners unless the owners' agreement provides for management by one or more designated owners ("managing partners" or "managing members"). To protect minority owners, the agreement can provide that certain major business decisions may be made only by vote of a supermajority such as two-thirds of all owners. Such decisions could include admission of additional owners, distribution of profits, a sale or merger of the firm, incurring certain loans, and certain other similar developments.

Confidentiality

The owners should consider requiring that all nonpublic information about the firm, client lists and matters under consideration with clients or prospective clients, including responses to requests for proposals, designs, and other documents regarding the firm's projects, be kept confidential. Upon withdrawal from the firm an owner should be required to return all firm property, including all documents, computer software and hardware, and client and prospect data bases that are the property of the firm. If a firm owner wants to be able to use some of his or her drawings or photographs or renderings of projects to show future employers or clients, the owners should provide for such in the owners' agreement to avoid disputes later. A confidentiality clause might read as follows:

> All information, knowledge, or data of a confidential or proprietary nature of or pertaining to the Company that is not generally known in the profession of architecture, including, without limitation, all such information, knowledge, and data concerning marketing, clients' and prospective clients' lists, and Company operations and finances (collectively "Confidential Information"), shall be kept secret and confidential by each Shareholder at all times during and after the end of his or her relationship with the Company, and shall not be used or divulged by them outside the scope of such relationship, except as required by law or court order

or as the Company's Board of Directors may otherwise expressly authorize in writing. The provisions of this Section shall not apply to any Confidential Information that, after the date of this Agreement, becomes publicly known under circumstances involving no breach of this Agreement.

Noncompetition/Solicitation

The owners' agreement often includes provisions restricting a former owner, after withdrawal from the firm, from competing with the firm (a "noncompete clause") and/or soliciting the firm's clients and employees for a certain period of time, for example, twelve months (a "nonsolicitation clause"). Those restrictions must be reasonable in terms of geographic area and duration. A noncompete clause can be more difficult to enforce than a nonsolicitation restriction (and is unenforceable in some states, such as California). An owner who wishes to be able to continue to provide services to clients whom he or she brought to the firm should ask for an exception to the nonsolicitation provision for such clients. A nonsolicitation clause might read as follows:

> A Shareholder shall not, during the period he or she is a shareholder and for a period of twelve (12) months following thereafter (the "Restriction Period"), in any way, directly or indirectly, for himself or herself or on behalf of any other person, firm, or company, (a) solicit any person who has been an employee of the Company on the effective date of transfer of the Shareholder's Shares or during the Restriction Period, or (b) solicit or provide services to any current or prospective clients except for clients he or she has introduced to the Company. A "client" means any individual or entity for which the Company has performed services at any time during a period of two (2) years prior to the effective date of transfer of Shares or during the Restriction Period. A "prospective client" means any person with whom there have been substantive discussions with any employee of the Company at any time within one (1) year preceding the effective date of transfer of his or her Shares or during the Restriction Period concerning the possibility of the Company rendering services to such person.

Dispute Resolution

The owners' agreement should include a clause that addresses how to resolve disputes among owners. Such a clause could provide for litigation in the federal or state courts in the city where the firm is based. As an alternative, owners may prefer arbitration instead of court proceedings to resolve disputes other than those that involve nonsolicitation, noncompete, or confidentiality covenants. We discuss the considerations involved in deciding on an appropriate forum for dispute resolution more fully in Chapter 7.

CAN I PRACTICE ARCHITECTURE WITH OTHER PROFESSIONS?

If you wish to combine the practice of architecture with one or more other design professions or services in one firm you need to check the requirements of the state in which your firm is based. In New York, for example, architecture may be combined with landscape architecture, engineering, and/or land surveying, provided that at least one shareholder, director, or officer is licensed and registered to practice each profession, and the firm name includes each of the professions practiced by the firm (for example, Joe Smith Architecture and Landscape Architecture P.C.). A New York architectural firm may also offer interior design services that fall under the definition of "architecture." In New Jersey, a GBC may combine architecture, landscape architecture, engineering, and planning ("closely allied professionals") if (1) at least two-thirds of the directors are licensed architects and closely allied professionals; (2) at least one director is a licensed architect; (3) two-thirds of the shares are owned by licensed architects or closely allied professionals; and (4) a minimum of 20 percent of the shares are owned by licensed architects.

WHAT DO I NEED TO KNOW ABOUT PRACTICING IN OTHER STATES?

If your firm wishes to work on a project in a state other than the state in which your firm has its office, you and your firm need to comply with any license and registration requirements of the foreign state's board of architecture. (See Chapter 9.) Such licensing requirements often also apply to merely "offering" to provide architectural services to a potential client in such states although what constitutes "offering" architectural services depends on interpretations in each individual state. California, for example, regards entering into negotiations with a potential client for a project in California as "offering" to provide architectural services, requiring participation of a California-licensed architect. In Texas, on the other hand, you do not need to have a Texas license to enter into discussions with a potential client. Likewise, in New York, an out-of-state architect does not need to be licensed in New York to conduct interviews with prospective clients. That architect, however, must tell the potential client that he or she is not licensed in New York but will be licensed and will have complied with New York requirements for out-of-state firms when the potential client retains his or her firm.

In addition to complying with licensing and registration requirements of another state's board of architecture, your firm may also need to comply with any registration requirements of that state's secretary of state before your firm can "do business" in that state. Before proceeding with any additional registration requirements, first determine whether your proposed activities in that state rise to the level of "doing business." Different states have different policies on this issue, but as a general matter a firm that contracts for design work in another state on a project that requires the firm's employees to make periodic and regular visits to that state may safely assume the firm is "doing business" in that state for registration purposes. Performing design work in a state and never visiting the locale where the project is located may be a different situation altogether.

Registration with the Secretary of State

Let's assume your firm needs to register with the secretary of state in another state. Now you must address the requirements for such registration. A few states do not allow certain out-of-state firms to practice in their state at all because of the legal form of those firms. California, for example, does not allow a firm organized as an out-of-state professional corporation (PC) to practice in that state. It does, however, allow out-of-state firms organized as general business corporations to practice in California, provided they meet certain requirements. Likewise, New Jersey does not allow an out-of-state PC or PLLC to practice in that state, but allows an out-of-state general business corporation or LLC, provided it meets certain licensing requirements for its owners and directors (for example, two-thirds of the directors must be architects licensed in New Jersey, and two-thirds of the shares must be owned by New Jersey–licensed architects). New York, on the other hand, requires that the out-of-state firm be a PC or PLLC instead of a general business corporation or LLC.

If a firm wishes to practice in another state but is not allowed to practice in that state in its current legal form, the owners must consider forming a new legal entity that meets the requirements of that state. When considering a project in another state make sure to determine whether you need to establish a new firm in that state. Doing so is an additional expense, but failure to create the proper firm structure may get you into trouble with the authorities and prevent you from collecting unpaid fees.

Not only must a firm meet any out-of-state requirements concerning its legal form of entity but it also must meet that state's licensing requirements for owners, managers, and/or employees, which can be quite onerous. For example, New York requires that all owners, directors, and officers of an out-of-state professional corporation be licensed in the state of incorporation of the firm, and all architects who render services in New York and at least one shareholder, director, or officer be licensed in New York; if the out-of-state firm is a professional LLC, then all owners of the LLC must be licensed in both the state of formation and New York. Nevada requires two-thirds of the ownership of an out-of-state firm to be held by Nevada-licensed architects.

Here are a few other quirky examples. Connecticut requires that all shareholders and the chief executive officer of a professional corporation (or two-thirds of the ownership and the chief executive officer of the corporation in the case of a general business corporation) and the professionals providing services in Connecticut be licensed as architects in that state. West Virginia and Wyoming, on the other hand, require only the architect or landscape architect in charge of the project to be licensed in that state (he or she does not need to be a shareholder, director, or officer). Colorado requires not only that a majority of the directors and officers be licensed in Colorado but also that the architect in charge of the Colorado project be licensed in Colorado and be an officer of the firm.

These kinds of variations exist in other states as well, so you should consult with counsel to check on the particular requirements of a state. For more on licensing requirements, see Chapter 9.

Registration with the Board of Architecture

In addition to registration with the secretary of state, when you have an out-of-state project your firm may need to register with the board governing architecture in the other state. As of 2011, states that required registration with their board of architecture included: Arkansas, Connecticut, Florida, Montana, Maryland, Pennsylvania, South Carolina, and Virginia. States that did not require such registration included: California, Georgia, Utah, Hawaii, Texas, West Virginia, and Wyoming. The law in this area is subject to change, so be sure to check the requirements before beginning an out-of-state project.

To further complicate the issue, not all boards of architecture have the same requirements. For example, the board of architecture and landscape architecture of Virginia (called the Virginia Department of Professional and Occupational Regulations) requires that the firm include in its by-laws that (1) nonlicensed individuals do not have a say in any matter affecting the practice of the firm requiring professional expertise or considered professional practice, and that (2) the firm's activities are limited to rendering the services of architects and/or landscape architects.

Failure to Register

What are the consequences of failing to meet the requirements of a particular state for registration with the secretary of state or board of architecture? To begin with, if your firm is doing business in another state without registration with the secretary of state for that state, you may be prevented from bringing an action there to collect unpaid fees. Although you may be able to register at a later time, you may still be prevented from bringing the action after registration if the statute of limitations has expired.

In addition, failure to register could certainly impact your ability to obtain public projects in the state, especially those projects awarded after competitions or requests for proposals. Your firm may win the design competition or make the strongest bid, but failure to comply with the state's requirements may cause your firm to lose the project anyway. Although noncompliance is unlikely to have a negative impact on the status of an architectural firm in the firm's home state and on the professional licenses of the firm's principals, there is enough uncertainty to warrant complying with out-of-state registration requirements.

WHAT DO I NEED TO KNOW ABOUT EXPANDING OWNERSHIP OF MY FIRM OR MERGING MY PRACTICE?

If you are an owner of a firm and wish to add one or more owners, you should do so by providing an offer letter to the new owner and having the new owner sign the owners' agreement. Your offer letter should address whether the new owner needs to pay for his or her ownership interest, and if so, how much. The new owner is subject to income tax on any difference between the value of the ownership interest and the purchase price ("buy-in price"). Many owners prefer to pay the buy-in price in installments.

Architectural firms can merge with one another, or one architectural firm can acquire another. Such a transaction is often done in the form of an asset purchase in which the selling firm sells and transfers to the acquiring firm all or a substantial portion of its assets, including office furniture and equipment, the office lease, existing contracts with clients and other third-parties (to the extent transferable), business files, accounts receivable, and cash on hand or in bank accounts. Often it is necessary to obtain consent from third parties, including clients and the landlord, to permit the transfer of certain assets. The acquiring firm should make sure that the asset purchase agreement provides that the acquiring firm does not assume any liabilities of the selling firm except specific liabilities the acquiring firm may agree to assume. The buyer should also make sure the seller has obtained professional liability insurance that covers claims for at least three years in the future. For a discussion of the types of insurance an architectural firm should have, see Chapter 3.

An asset purchase agreement typically includes (1) payment terms, (2) description of assets to be transferred, (3) representations and warranties by the selling firm and acquiring firm, (4) conditions that must be met before the transaction closes (the "conditions precedent"), (5) obligations that must be complied with (the "covenants"), and (6) indemnification provisions (whereby the selling firm agrees to indemnify and hold harmless the acquiring firm for any liabilities arising before the transfer).

The seller may be asked to give a representation like the following in an asset purchase agreement:

> Seller has good and marketable title to all its assets and interests in assets, whether real, personal, mixed, tangible, and intangible (the "Property"). The Property is free and clear of restrictions on or conditions to transfer or assignment, and free and clear of any encumbrance, and with respect to which no default exists. Neither Seller nor Shareholders have heretofore obligated Seller to dispose of or assign any of the Property, and they have not disposed of any of its assets or the Property other than immaterial dispositions in the normal course of business since [date]. The Property consists of all of the property and assets, including

without limitation, all real and personal property, tangible and intangible property and rights, used in any manner by the Seller in its Practice. Shareholders have no right, title, or interest of any nature in any of the Property other than that of Shareholders in the Seller.

An indemnification provision might read as follows:

Seller and Shareholders, jointly and severally, agree to defend and indemnify Buyer, its shareholders, officers, directors, agents, and employees (as used in this Section, the "Buyer Indemnitees"), against, and to hold each of them harmless from all actions, claims, suits, losses, liabilities, costs, damages, and expenses (including but not limited to reasonable attorney's fees including those fees necessary to enforce its rights to indemnification hereunder) ("Damages") arising from or resulting by reason of: (a) any adverse and inaccurate representation made by or on behalf of Seller in this Agreement or any certificate or other document delivered pursuant hereto; (b) the breach of any of the warranties or agreements made by or on behalf of Seller in this Agreement or of any certificate or other document delivered pursuant hereto; (c) the breach or default in the performance by Seller of any of the obligations to be performed by it hereunder; (d) any claim by any person that Buyer is liable for obligations of Seller not expressly assumed by Buyer; or (e) the ownership or operation of the Practice prior to the Closing Date.

* * *

Operating your practice through a legal entity offers you many benefits, including limited liability (except for malpractice). What the best form of the entity is (corporation, limited liability company, or limited liability partnership) depends on a number of considerations, including tax factors. If you operate your practice through a legal entity with other owners, you should have an owners' agreement which addresses how the firm is managed, how profits are allocated and distributed to the owners, and when and how an owner may or must transfer his or her ownership interest. If you wish to combine the practice of architecture with one or more other design professions, you should check your state's requirements as to which design professions can be combined in one firm and what the ownership requirements are. If your firm wishes to work on a project in another state, you need to check whether your firm complies with that state's requirements for the legal structure of out-of-state firms and the licensing of its owners. If you wish to expand your firm, you can do so by adding owners or acquiring or merging with another firm. Since each state has its own particular requirements regarding the practice of architecture through a legal entity, you should discuss with your attorney and your accountant the best way to structure and operate your practice.

SIX

WHAT EMPLOYMENT ISSUES DO I FACE AS AN ARCHITECT?

Except for small solo practices, architects must use the services of others to help with the work, administer the office, and pay and issue bills. In short, you end up having employees. This chapter outlines some of the legal issues that come up at the various stages of the employment relationship, from the hiring process through termination. For the most part, our discussion is aimed at architects as employers. Architects can also be employees, and some of this material is also helpful in understanding their concerns.

Employment has become increasingly regulated, with a diverse array of laws and regulations at the federal, state, and local levels. Given the geographical variations, complexity and frequent changes of the applicable rules, the following discussion is necessarily no more than an attempt to call your attention to some of the recurring issues. You can get a lot of useful information from the websites of government agencies, and some of those are mentioned below. However, as you begin hiring others to work with you, you should get professional advice from a local lawyer or human resource expert addressing your specific situation.

WHAT DO I NEED TO KNOW ABOUT HIRING?

The Difference Between Employees and Independent Contractors

One of the decisions you make as an employer is whether you should hire an "employee" or in the alternative an "independent contractor" for a particular job. As a business owner, you need to understand the legal distinction between these categories of service providers, because that distinction determines many of your duties. For example, a business is generally required to withhold payroll taxes for employees, withhold and pay social security and Medicare contributions for employees, and pay unemployment taxes for employees. But these requirements do not apply if the workers are independent contractors. In addition, some federal antidiscrimination laws apply only to employees (although state and local anti-discrimination laws cover both in some cases). A mistake in classification that results, for example, in failure to withhold payroll taxes for a worker who should have been classified as an employee can result in fines and penalties for the employer.

Not surprisingly, the difference between employees and independent contractors turns mainly on the extent of the employer's control over the worker and the work: more employer control for employees, more independence for independent contractors. The IRS advises that all facts relating to the degree of independence must be weighed, and that the relevant facts generally fall into three categories:

1. *Degree of behavioral control.* Who controls how the work is done? A worker is likely to be an employee when the employer has the right to control what the worker does to perform the job and how he or she does it. If the employer does not have control over a worker's methods, the worker is more likely to be classified as an independent contractor.
2. *Degree of financial control.* Who controls the business aspects of the worker's job? A worker is likely to be classified as an independent contractor when he or she puts money into the work performed and is not reimbursed for expenses, has the opportunity for both economic gains *and* losses through employment, and provides his or her services to more than one employer.
3. *Type of relationship.* How do the parties treat the relationship? A worker's receipt of employee benefits such as insurance, pensions, vacation, or sick pay weighs in favor of classification as an employee.

The IRS stresses that no single fact is conclusive, and, in some cases, an analysis of all the facts does not produce a clear-cut answer. In those cases, an employer may ask the IRS for a determination by filing IRS Form SS-8, "Determination of Worker Status for Purposes of Federal Employment Taxes and Income Tax Withholding." A response from the IRS can take several months, but the form itself outlines many of the relevant factors, and filling it out may help you to make your own determination.

How the Discrimination Laws Apply to the Hiring Process

We are all generally familiar with the fact that the law prohibits discrimination in hiring, and how important it is to be an "equal opportunity employer." But this simple phrase carries with it a multitude of not-so-simple requirements. Understanding the details of all the requirements would practically necessitate giving up architecture to practice law. Still, you as an employer should know at least what characteristics are protected from discrimination by the laws that apply to your practice.

Some federal antidiscrimination laws do not apply to very small employers. For example, Title VII of the Civil Rights Act of 1964, a federal law that prohibits discrimination on the basis of race, color, religion, gender, and national origin, covers only businesses with fifteen or more employees. However, many state and local governments have their own antidiscrimination laws that reach smaller employers. The best approach is to assume that your business is covered by antidiscrimination laws of some sort. Generally, these laws prohibit refusing to hire (or taking other discriminatory action against an employee) based on race, color, sex (including pregnancy), age, national origin, religion, creed, or military status. They also usually prohibit discrimination because of disability, if the applicant can perform the job with reasonable accommodation. What constitutes a reasonable accommodation depends on specifics such as the job duties, the nature and cost of the accommodation, and how the requested accommodation would affect the workplace.

Some states and localities have additional (and sometimes unusual) discrimination prohibitions. New York City law, for example, prohibits discrimination based on marital and partnership status, sexual orientation, or status as a victim of domestic violence or stalking. New York State even has a law that prohibits discrimination based on legal nonwork recreational activity. New York, recently joined by the federal government, also outlaws discrimination based on genetic predisposition. Connecticut law specifically protects persons with mental impairment or learning disabilities. The websites of the US Equal Employment Opportunity Commission and your state and local antidiscrimination agencies are a good place to look for general information on the prohibitions that would apply to your business.

Once you have a list of the discrimination prohibitions in your community, remember to update your list periodically and to keep it in mind throughout the hiring process. Some states (New York is one) expressly prohibit employers from asking questions on application forms or in interviews that would elicit information about protected characteristics. Even if the law of your state does not directly prohibit such questions, it is better to avoid them and thus avoid the suggestion that the information would play a part in your hiring decision. Below are some examples (by no means exhaustive) of the kinds of questions that should not be asked:

- *Age*: "How old are you?" "Are you close to retirement age?" "When did you attend high school/college?"
- *Criminal history*: "Have you ever been arrested?" (You may ask about criminal convictions if they may have special relevance to the job a candidate is applying for; for example, an employee might ask applicants for a bookkeeping position if they have ever been convicted of embezzlement.)
- *Health/disability*: "Do you have any medical conditions or disabilities?" "Have you ever had a drug or alcohol problem?" "Do you have or have you ever had cancer?" (If the job has certain physical requirements, you may ask the applicant if he or she can perform the required tasks.)
- *Marital/family status*: "Are you single?" "Do you prefer to be called Mrs. or Miss?" "What does your spouse do for a living?"
- *Military status*: "Did you serve in the military?" "Are you in the reserves?"
- *National origin/citizenship*: "Where do you come from?" "What kind of name is that?" (It is permissible, indeed required by federal law, to ask if the applicant is legally authorized to work in the United States.)
- *Race*: "What race are you?" "Do you belong to the NAACP?"
- *Religion*: "What religion are you?" "Do you observe any religious holidays?" (If the position requires specific working hours, you may state the position's working hours and ask if the applicant can work on that schedule.)
- *Sex*: "Are you pregnant or do you plan on becoming pregnant?" "Would your husband approve of your taking this job?" "Do you find it difficult being a man or woman in this profession?"
- *Sexual orientation*: "Are you gay?" "Do you date men or women?" "Do you ever go to the Stonewall Bar (or other nightspots known to cater to gays)?" "Who do you live with?"

- *Workers' compensation:* "Have you ever filed for or received work-ers' compensation benefits?"

The Advantages of a Written Employment Contract

Binding employment contracts, specifying in writing the terms and condi-tions of a job, are not generally required by law. However, some states have laws requiring a written agreement for particular jobs or terms. In New York, for example, commission salespeople and sales representatives are entitled to a written agreement specifying how their commissions are calculated. More-over, it is common, if not customary, for high-level executives to have detailed employment agreements. Thus, you may be required, as a practical matter, to offer a written agreement to someone you want to hire at that level. But, for the most part, you have a choice whether to offer a written contract.

A well-drafted and comprehensive agreement provides certainty to both employer and employee and thus tends to reduce the likelihood of disputes. On the other hand, certainty reduces flexibility, and particular terms may limit the rights of one side or the other. You have to decide on a case-by-case basis whether to offer a contract and what terms to include. In some cases, policies applicable to all employees can be covered in an employee handbook, making it unnecessary to include those terms in an individual agreement. (See below for a discussion on handbooks.) If your employees are members of a union (rare in architecture firms but common in public agencies), the policies are stated in a collective bargaining agreement. (We do not address labor union questions here.)

Ordinarily, an employment contract should address job duration, ter-mination restrictions, duties, compensation, benefits, restrictive covenants, intellectual property, and dispute resolution. We discuss each briefly below.

Duration. From a legal perspective, this is the most important term in any employment contract. In many states, if there are no explicit contractual restrictions on termination and if the agreement does not specify a par-ticular duration, it can be terminated "at will" by either party. Thus, if the contract does not have a stated duration, an employee who agreed to accept a particular job at a particular salary can walk out without consequences if he or she finds another job; likewise, the employer can fire the employee if he or she finds someone who is willing to do the job for less or is otherwise preferable for some other nonillegal reason. At-will employment is the stan-dard practice for most nonexecutive, nonpartnership staff positions among architects.

On the other hand, if the agreement is for a specific length of time, such as one year, the premature termination of the relationship by one party may entitle the other to recover damages. Note, however, that neither party to such a contract can compel the other to continue the employment unwillingly for the stated period. The employee can always leave, and the employer can always send the employee packing, even if there is time left on the contract. An employer who terminates early, though, is ordinarily obligated to pay the contract balance if the employee cannot find another comparable job. It is less common that the early departing employee has to pay the employer.

Termination restrictions. Generally, employers prefer to retain as much flexibility as possible to terminate the employment relationship at will. A typical offer letter from an architectural firm to a prospective employee is explicit on at-will status or is silent on the term of employment, which in most states means it is at will. As an employer, you are best advised to avoid ambiguity by having any written agreement with your employee state that it does not limit the right of either party to terminate the relationship at will, for any reason or no reason at all. Usually, at least two weeks' notice of termination is specified. If you are a job applicant, you should consider asking for a specific term of employment and have it confirmed in writing, although many employers deny the request.

Position and duties. To allow for flexibility, the description of the position and duties should be general and provide that the employee perform any additional tasks and duties you may assign consistent with the employee's qualifications. (An applicant, however, may want a list of specific duties to provide clear notice of what lies ahead and to protect from involuntary reassignments.)

Compensation. Compensation arrangements vary tremendously in structure and complexity and many aspects are regulated by state and federal laws. In general, if the contract is time-limited, you can simply specify the agreed-upon salary or other compensation and the frequency of payment. For agreements of unlimited duration, you should specify the "initial" salary. You can be specific about when and how adjustments are determined, but employers generally prefer to maintain some flexibility by saying something general, like "subject to adjustments as determined by management in its discretion from time to time."

Depending on where you practice, there may be legal restrictions on payment of bonuses to your employees. Be sure to check whether your state permits a licensed architect to share his profits with a nonlicensed employee.

A bonus based on the employee's own performance rather than the firm's profits is considered wages in some states, like New York and New Jersey, and nonpayment of wages may subject the business (and possibly you personally) to penalties. To retain the flexibility to pay a bonus without any guarantee, the best approach is to specify that management has sole discretion over whether a bonus is paid and the amount. As a retention incentive, you may want to specify that a bonus is paid only if employment continues through the bonus payout date, even if the employee was employed for the entire bonus year.

Benefits. The federal Employee Retirement Income Security Act (ERISA) regulates retirement plans and benefit programs. Among other things, it contains requirements for administration of benefit plans and imposes certain restrictions on offering benefits to some employees that are not available to all. The details are beyond the scope of this book, but the issue can best be managed in an employment agreement by stating simply that benefits are available in accordance with the firm's plan's and policies.

Restrictive covenants. Contract provisions designed to protect the employer from unfair competition by the employee after leaving employment are very common and are an important motivation for employers to use employment agreements. The most common provisions restrict departing employees from using or disclosing confidential information, working for a competitor, or soliciting firm clients or employees. To the extent these restrictions go beyond what the law requires anyway, they are enforceable only if the employer gives something of value in return, called "consideration." If you include the restrictions in an initial employment agreement, it is clear that you have given something in exchange, that is, employment.

Even if the restrictions are part of the initial employment agreement, they may not be enforceable. The law varies widely from state to state. Courts generally enforce confidentiality provisions restricting an employee's disclosure of an employer's trade secrets, client lists, and intellectual property. In addition to these general prohibitions, you may want to specifically prohibit disclosure of architectural drawings, proposals, and designs.

Limitations on a departing employee's ability to work for competitors are more difficult to enforce. Some states, like California, rarely enforce any restrictions on future employment. Others, like New York, enforce restrictions that are "reasonable" under the particular circumstances. New York courts look at the scope of the restrictions, including the time period, the geographical reach, and the industry coverage to determine whether the restrictions are reasonable to protect legitimate business interests. If restrictions are overly broad, some courts throw them out entirely. Other courts may be willing to "blue pencil," that is, narrow the restrictions and enforce what they consider reasonable.

Given the complications, your best bet, if you want to include restrictive covenants in your agreements with employees, is to consult an attorney who is familiar with the laws of your state.

Ownership of intellectual property. Designs and proposals are the foundation of your business. It is thus critical to be clear at the outset of the employment relationship that all designs, sketches, blueprints, proposals, and the like that are developed or created during employment belong to the firm, not to the employee. You should require all prospective employees to sign an agreement to this effect as a condition of employment, even if you do not have a more comprehensive employment agreement. The agreement should also provide that the employee must assign to the firm all of his or her rights to intellectual property created while employed by you and cooperate with the firm in obtaining copyright, trademark, or patent protection.

Dispute resolution. We devote Chapter 7 of this book to claims and dispute resolution. Although that chapter does not specifically address disputes with employees, the same principles apply. It is to the employer's advantage to decide in advance how disputes with employees are resolved and cover this issue in an initial agreement with new employees. Everyone benefits by addressing workplace disputes internally and resolving them promptly. Policies and procedures for internal dispute resolution may be handled in an employment handbook rather than in an employment agreement, as discussed below.

Disputes that cannot be resolved internally have to be resolved in court in the absence of an agreement on another forum. The litigation process in both state and federal courts is inevitably time-consuming and expensive. It is also public, and to most employers the prospect of airing internal disputes with employees in a public setting open to casual observers as well as the media is exceedingly distasteful. Because arbitration is generally cheaper and less time-consuming than court litigation (although not always) and because arbitration is a confidential process, employers generally prefer arbitration to resolve disputes with employees. If this is your view, you should include a requirement to arbitrate all disputes in your employment agreements. If you do not use a comprehensive employment agreement, you should require all new employees to sign a separate arbitration agreement as a condition of employment.

The Paperwork For New Employers

The Small Business Administration has a website (www.sba.gov) with lots of helpful information including a list of "10 Steps to Hiring Your First Employee." We summarize the 10 steps here:

1. *Get an Employer Identification Number.* Before you hire anyone, you need to get an employer identification number, also called an employer tax ID or EIN. The IRS issues EINs. You can apply online at www.irs.gov.
2. *Prepare to withhold taxes.* For every employee, you must obtain and submit an IRS Form W-4 withholding exemption certificate upon employment and annually report on Form W-2 wages and taxes withheld.
3. *Fill out Employee Eligibility Verification (Form I-9).* Under federal law, you must complete this form within three days of hiring to record that you have checked the specified documentation to verify that your employee is authorized to work in this country. You must keep the form on file.
4. *Register with state new hire reporting system.* Federal law requires employers to report new hires within twenty days. Search for "new hire reporting" on the Web to find your state's procedure.
5. *Obtain workers' compensation insurance.* Check with your state's workers' compensation insurance program.
6. *Register for unemployment insurance tax (if required).* Check with your state's tax agency.
7. *Obtain disability insurance (if required).* A few states require employers to provide insurance coverage for lost wages due to disability. New York, California, and New Jersey are among them.
8. *Obtain and display required posters.* Some laws require postings by employers to alert employees of their rights. You can usually find out what is required and print out the postings from the federal and state labor agency websites.
9. *File your business taxes.* As an employer who pays wages, you must file quarterly IRS Form 941 and IRS Form 940.
10. *Keep informed.* Workplace requirements change frequently. Check with your legal or human resources adviser at least once a year.

WHAT WORKPLACE ISSUES SHOULD I BE AWARE OF?
Preventing Discrimination and Harassment

The law imposes an obligation on employers not to discriminate against employees based on protected characteristics such as race, gender, religion, and national origin. (See the discussion of various protected characteristics above.) The prohibitions against discrimination apply to all workplace decisions, not just hiring and firing. This means that you have to be sure that protected characteristics do not enter into decisions regarding compensation, assignments, work schedules, promotions, benefits, or any other terms or conditions of employment. To ensure that legitimate factors like work performance, qualifications, and seniority drive these decisions, require that more than one manager or senior professional concur on any adverse employment action and that the reasons be documented. Since work performance is often the most important factor, you should have a regular process for assessing and documenting employees' performance. Those assessments must be complete and honest, should be communicated to the employee, and should be filed for future reference.

Some employment lawyers who primarily represent management advise that an employee's file should not include written reports critical of employees when they are prepared in contemplation of dismissal. The worry is that negative reports can lead to defamation claims and complicate cases involving claims of wrongful dismissal. We do not share this view. We believe honest and accurate evaluations are appropriate at any time. Having a practice of documenting positive and negative evaluations in the long run helps more often than it hinders, although there may be exceptions in individual cases.

In addition to prohibiting discriminatory decision making, the anti-discrimination laws require employers to protect employees from workplace harassment and hostile working environments based on protected characteristics. Long gone are the days when employers could afford to tolerate ethnic jokes or sexist remarks as harmless fun. As an employer, your firm is responsible for any discrimination or harassment by managers and supervisors affecting the employees they supervise. The firm is also responsible for taking steps to prevent discriminatory harassment among coworkers and hostility in the workplace toward workers with protected characteristics.

As an employer you can take several steps to combat workplace discrimination and harassment. First, your firm should prominently post and distribute to all employees a clear written statement prohibiting discrimination and harassment and should prominently encourage respect for others in the workplace. An equal employment opportunity poster is required by federal law for businesses holding federally assisted construction contracts and may be required by your state's law as well. You can usually print the required postings from the website of your local antidiscrimination agency.

The firm should also develop procedures for employee complaints about discrimination or harassment, should distribute the procedures to all employees through a handbook or by posting, and should encourage employees to use them. The procedures should require employees to report discriminatory harassment or hostility by coworkers to their supervisors, and should provide another avenue for employees to complain about misconduct by supervisors. If an employee complains, the firm must conduct a prompt and thorough investigation and take appropriate action based on the findings. Finally, the firm should hold periodic training sessions to educate employees about the firm's antidiscrimination policies and the firm's lack of tolerance for violations. If consistently followed, these steps may provide the firm with a defense to a claim of workplace harassment or a hostile work environment. More important, they discourage misconduct from occurring in the first place.

Combating Illegal Retaliation

The antidiscrimination laws discussed above prohibit not only discrimination itself but also retaliation against an employee for complaining about discrimination or assisting in a discrimination investigation, proceeding, or hearing. Retaliation complaints by employees under the antidiscrimination laws have risen dramatically in recent years and should be a serious concern for every employer. An employer who penalizes an employee in any way for a good faith complaint of discrimination, even if there was no discrimination in fact, risks liability to the employee. Damages payable to the employee can include not only lost wages but also compensation for emotional distress, punitive damages, and attorneys' fees.

Other laws protect employees who report or complain about workplace illegality. New York, for example, prohibits retaliation against any employee who complains about or reports any violation of New York's labor laws or any workplace activity that threatens public health or safety. Federal laws protect employees who report fraud by employers in connection with federal government contracts, and those laws also provide financial incentives for employees to make such reports. There are many more so-called whistle-blower laws not catalogued here. Since the laws vary by location, size and nature of business, you should consult your local attorney to identify the ones that apply to you.

Retaliation in the workplace can be discouraged and retaliation claims blunted by taking steps like those outlined above for preventing discrimination. Have a clear, written policy against retaliation, and distribute it to everyone. Have a procedure for employees to make complaints, encourage them to use it constructively, and take their complaints seriously. Train all supervisors and employees generally on actions that could be viewed as retaliatory. Most important, if an employee makes a complaint, warn all supervisors and coworkers who know about the complaint that retaliation is prohibited and take steps to make sure that any subsequent decisions regarding the complaining employee are justified by objective, legitimate factors.

Wage and Hour Restrictions

A complex, and by no means seamless, web of federal and state laws governs work hours and pay practices. At the federal level, most of these laws are administered by the United States Department of Labor (DOL). The DOL has a comprehensive website with a great deal of useful information, including a "Small Business Resource Center." Most states also have labor laws and state agencies to administer them, and most of those state agencies have helpful websites.

We cannot possibly cover all the applicable regulations here, but touch on a few. Among the most important are the minimum wage and overtime pay requirements of the federal Fair Labor Standards Act (FLSA). The FLSA applies to most employers with $500,000 or more in gross revenue, and also applies to smaller employers if they do business interstate. It requires payment of a minimum wage to all employees except those who work in jobs that fall within specific exemptions. FLSA also requires covered employers to pay nonexempt employees overtime pay at one and one-half times their regular rate of pay for all hours worked in excess of forty hours per week. If your firm is covered by FLSA, you must display a poster explaining the basic FLSA requirements in a prominent place. (This poster, as well as comprehensive information on all DOL posting requirements, is available on the DOL website: www.dol.gov.)

The FLSA's requirements are a floor: they do not override state laws that are more favorable for workers. For example, if the minimum wage in your state is greater than that prescribed by FLSA, you have to pay nonexempt workers at the higher state rate. Or if your state requires overtime pay for a worker who is exempt under the FLSA, you have to pay the overtime.

As an employer, you need to have at least a general understanding of the exemptions from wage and hour laws. The exemptions from the FLSA are listed and described on the DOL website. The exemptions most likely to be relevant at an architectural firm are the exemptions for professional, executive, and administrative employees and computer professionals. Employees falling within these defined categories are exempt from both overtime pay and minimum wage requirements, provided they earn a salary exceeding a specified minimum. Here are the general qualifications for these exemptions:

- *Professional employees.* This is the most important exemption for your firm, since architects working in their field generally qualify as exempt learned professional employees. The learned professional exemption applies to employees whose work requires advanced, intellectual learning that is customarily acquired from a prolonged course of specialized instruction and requires the exercise of discretion. The creative professional exemption applies to employees whose work requires invention, imagination, originality, or talent in a recognized creative or artistic field, and generally covers graphic designers and interior designers.
- *Executive employees.* An exempt executive's main duties must consist of managing the firm or a specific department of the firm. The executive must regularly supervise at least two full-time workers and have the authority to hire and fire or have significant input into hiring and firing decisions.
- *Administrative employees.* The main duties of an exempt administrative employee must be nonmanual or office work and involve exercise of discretion and independent judgment on significant matters.
- *Computer professionals.* This exemption applies to skilled computer professionals like software engineers, systems analysts, and programmers, not to people who merely use computers or repair hardware. In your practice, you might employ someone in this category to adapt or design a computer system for your specific needs.

The DOL construes the exemptions narrowly, so if you have any doubt whether an exemption applies you should consult the DOL's Wage and Hour Division office for your area. Penalties for noncompliance can be very costly, including double back pay for an underpaid employee.

In addition to minimum wage and overtime requirements, the FLSA also contains the Equal Pay Act (EPA). The EPA prohibits unequal pay based on gender. It requires equal pay for "substantially equal" work, unless the pay disparity results from a seniority system, a merit system, a payment system based on work quantity or quality, or other factors other than gender. Some states have their own equal pay laws that may be stricter than the federal rules. Be sure to check your local and state labor agency websites and consult with a local attorney for other applicable wage and hour restrictions.

Injuries at Work

All states in the United States have some form of workers' compensation scheme and require most employers to purchase insurance to cover medical expenses of employees injured at work. Each state has its own system and its own governing board to oversee the system. In most states, it is illegal to retaliate against an employee for reporting an injury at work or for filing a workers' compensation claim. Your local attorney and the website of your state workers' compensation board provide details on the system in your state and the rules that apply to you.

Leaves of Absence

Employee leaves of absence present management challenges for every business, but especially for smaller employers with fewer employees to cover for those who are absent. Some leave requirements, like those imposed by the federal Family and Medical Leave Act—the FMLA—apply only to larger employers. Others apply to all employers, regardless of size. It is important to know which ones apply to your firm.

- *Family and medical leave.* The federal FMLA applies only to employers with fifty or more employees. (If your firm is too small to be covered by the federal law, be sure to find out whether your state has a similar law reaching smaller employers.) Covered employers must allow eligible employees to take a total of twelve weeks of unpaid leave during any twelve-month period.

Employees may choose to substitute (or may be required by your policy to substitute) any available paid leave for all or part of the unpaid leave. The leave may be taken in one twelve-week period, in several shorter leaves for different reasons, or intermittently as a reduced work schedule.

An employee is eligible for federal FMLA leave if he or she has worked for you for at least twelve months (not necessarily consecutively), has worked at least 1,250 hours during the immediately preceding twelve months, has a qualifying reason for taking leave, and gives appropriate notice of intent to take leave. Qualifying reasons for FMLA leave include the birth or adoption of a child; the need to care for a child, spouse, or parent with a serious health condition; the employee's own serious health condition; the need to care for a spouse, child, or parent injured in military service; and exigent circumstances caused by the deployment or impending deployment of a child, spouse, or parent in military service. If the need for leave is foreseeable, you may require up to thirty days' notice from the employee. You may also ask for medical certification, and should use the DOL model medical certification form (available at www.dol.gov).

At the conclusion of FMLA leave, the employee must be reinstated in his or her former position or an equivalent position, unless the employee cannot perform the essential functions of the job; the employee would have been transferred or terminated from that position if he or she had not taken leave for an unrelated reason such as a reduction in force or company restructuring; or the employee is a highly paid "key" employee, the employee was so informed at the outset of the leave, and reinstatement would cause severe economic injury to the business.

- *Military leave.* In contrast to the FMLA, the Uniformed Services Employment and Reemployment Rights Act (USERRA) applies to all employers—regardless of size. The USERRA allows employees to reclaim their civilian jobs after absences for military service. Moreover, it requires that the returning employee be reinstated with the same seniority and other rights and the same benefits he or she would have received if he or she had not taken military leave. Thus, an employee's military leave time counts as work time for purposes of calculating eligibility for other benefits such as FMLA leave.

- *Sick leave and maternity leave.* Federal law does not require employers to provide paid sick leave and requires unpaid sick leave only for employers covered by the FMLA. A few localities require that employers provide sick leave; San Francisco, Washington DC, and Milwaukee are among them. Even if not required, most employers give some sick leave in the interest of employee morale and retention. If you provide sick leave, you must do so evenhandedly—to men and women, older workers and younger, and regardless of the particular illness. Federal law requires that pregnancy and related conditions be treated the same way as other temporary medical conditions. For example, if you give up to four weeks of paid sick leave for other medical conditions, you must give up to four weeks of paid leave for childbirth.
- *Jury duty leave.* Federal law requires employers regardless of size to give time off to employees to serve on a federal jury, but it does not require paid leave. Most states also require leave to serve on a state jury. Some state laws include payment requirements. In New York, for example, an employer of ten or more employees must pay an employee at least $40 per day during jury duty leave.

Performance Reviews

Performance reviews are not required by law, and most employers would rather not have to do them. As noted above, some people argue that employers should never give formal performance reviews because they often are poorly thought out and fail to provide accurate and fair assessments. But honest feedback undoubtedly benefits both employees and employers. It gives employees a chance to learn and improve, and it gives employers a solid basis for making decisions about compensation, promotions, and layoffs. As mentioned earlier, every employer should formally review each employee's performance at least annually. Here are some "musts" for performance reviews.

Reviews must be honest. This is critical. You never want to be in a situation where you need to fire a poorly performing employee but find no mention of poor performance—or even areas in need of improvement—in previous evaluations. This happens more often than you might think, because supervisors are afraid of confrontation or too busy to make a thoughtful assessment. Overreliance on employee self-evaluations can contribute to the problem by allowing busy managers to add a few hasty comments, if any, to what usually turns out to be just a list of the employee's accomplishments. Unless you are going to pair employee self-evaluations with face-to-face discussions and carefully written comments by supervisors that focus on accomplishments, shortcomings, and future goals, they are not as valuable as employer evaluations. It is better for the supervisor to prepare the evaluation and give the employee an opportunity to respond. Training sessions with a good human resource professional often help supervisors produce more useful evaluations. Reducing the number of employees each supervisor must review and encouraging supervisors to keep a diary during the review period can also improve the quality of your firm's performance evaluations.

Reviews must be objective and evenhanded. The idea is to prevent personal biases or discriminatory or retaliatory motives from infecting the evaluation process. Your goal should be to apply the same standards to everyone who does similar work. The best way to do this is to decide on the standards in advance, looking not at the individuals but at the categories of workers your business employs. For example, an architectural firm may employ licensed architects, designers, and clerical workers. You should identify the qualities and skills you believe are important for each and evaluate all the employees in that category on the same set of qualities and skills. Obviously, you should tailor comments to particular employees and situations as well.

Reviews must be documented. The right kind of documentation—a standardized evaluation form—helps you achieve the first two "musts." Do not underestimate the value of a good form. It makes evaluations easier, more evenhanded, and more useful. It should list the qualities and skills you have identified as important and ask for a rating and for specific comments. The form should also provide separate spaces designated for comments on strengths, areas for improvement, and general comments and recommendations. An example of a generic evaluation form is included in this book, but you should adapt it to include the qualities you believe are important for your employees.

Reviews must be communicated to employees accurately. This is often difficult for managers. Again, training can help. So can the evaluation form. If the written evaluation is clear and direct, the discussion is likely to be also. Both the positives and the negatives should be discussed, in balanced, nonjudgmental language. The employee should be invited to comment. Indeed, the best review sessions are constructive conversations that result in concrete steps and optimism about moving forward and improving the employment relationship.

Office Performance Appraisal

Employee Name: _____ Job Title: _____

Date of Hire:_____ Department:_____ Supervisor: _____

Annual Review ☐   90 day Review ☐   Review Period: From _____ To _____

_____

SECTION I - Review the employee's performance by checking the most appropriate box in each category based on the time on the job. Write specific example's supporting each rating.

Job / Technical Knowledge:
☐ Outstanding ☐ Exceeds Expectations ☐ Meets Expectations ☐ Improvement Needed
☐ Unsatisfactory
Possesses and demonstrates a thorough understanding and working knowledge of all phases of the job; including the various techniques and skills necessary for efficient completion of all tasks. Remains up to date on changes /trends in technical knowledge related to job. Understands the impact of his/her job function on other functions/departments and business.

Specific Examples / Comments: _____
_____

Problem Solving and Decision Making:
☐ Outstanding ☐ Exceeds Expectations ☐ Meets Expectations ☐ Improvement Needed
☐ Unsatisfactory
Demonstrates ability to make sound and proper decisions by; defining the issue, diagnosing the problem; analyzing the cause(s) and drawing on professional expertise, internal external resources to make recommendation or solutions with minimal negative effect on departmental /company goals and employee relations. Employee demonstrates willingness to take ownership and responsibility for decisions made.

Specific Examples / Comments: _____
_____

Planning and Organization:
☐ Outstanding ☐ Exceeds Expectations ☐ Meets Expectations ☐ Improvement Needed
☐ Unsatisfactory
Plans effectively to produce required volume to meet production / dept. goal utilizes appropri-ate resources; meets or exceeds deadlines without jeopardizing quality; seeks opportunities to increase productivity and/or eliminate waste; able to re-prioritize as required to meet new/changing demands. Carries out work assignments and tasks within budget.

Specific Examples / Comments: _____
_____

Communication - Verbal and Written:
☐ Outstanding ☐ Exceeds Expectations ☐ Meets Expectations ☐ Improvement Needed
☐ Unsatisfactory
Demonstrates clear effective communication (includes; listening, nonverbal communication and lan-guage) in individual and group settings (all levels, internal and external). Keeps manager/supervisor, associates and subordinates fully informed on work/project status and problems. Provides accurate concise written communication to support scope of assignments.

Specific Examples / Coments: _____
_____

Interpersonal Skills / Teamwork:
☐ Outstanding ☐ Exceeds Expectations ☐ Meets Expectations ☐ Improvement Needed

Sample Office Performance Appraisal

Self Management Skills:

☐ Outstanding ☐ Exceeds Expectations ☐ Meets Expectations ☐ Improvement Needed
☐ Unsatisfactory
factory Displays confidence and remains in control when handling difficult or new situation's. Demonstrates adaptability and flexibility when handling change. Demonstrates a sense of cooperativeness by remaining open and positive when receiving direction or constructive feedback.

Specific Examples / Comments: _____
_____

Section II - Results of Goals and Objectives (established at prior review)

Goal/Objective: _____

Result: _____

Goal/Objective: _____

Result: _____

Goal/Objective: _____

Result: _____

Section III - Accomplishments and Contributions:

Section IV - Performance Summary:

RATE OVERALL PERFORMANCE (include Managers / Supervisors Addendum if applicable)
☐ Outstanding ☐ Exceeds Expectations ☐ Meets Expectations ☐ Improvement Needed
☐ Unsatisfactory

Section V - Goals and Objectives (for new review period):
1. _____

2. _____

3. _____

4. _____

Employee's Comments: _____
—

_____

Discussed/reviewed with employee on: _____ Follow up requested/desired: ☐ YES ☐ NO

Manager/Supervisor Signature: _____ Date: _____

Sample Office Performance Appraisal, continued

Employee Handbooks

Employee handbooks are very useful to ensure that your policies are communicated clearly and consistently to all employees. Like employment agreements (and some employers use them as a substitute for employment agreements), handbooks help to reduce disputes by making sure employer expectations are understood. The drawbacks are that once you have a handbook, you have to follow it and you have to update it regularly to incorporate changes in your policies and in the law.

Your handbook should be tailored to your business, its size, its policies, and the governing law. You may want to include these topics, among others:

- Termination and resignation policies and procedures
- Antidiscrimination, antiretaliation, and antiharassment policies
- Confidentiality requirements
- Policies regarding company property and ownership of work product
- Policies regarding work hours and schedules
- Document retention requirements
- Moonlighting restrictions
- Vacation and leave policies
- Performance review procedures
- Use of company computers and electronic messaging
- Social media policies
- Procedures for dispute resolution
- Employee benefits

Every employee should be given a copy of the handbook upon hiring and should be asked to sign a statement acknowledging receipt and agreeing to abide by its provisions. Every supervisor should be required to review the handbook annually. Your handbook should be your first reference for resolving questions about workplace conduct or policies.

WHAT CAN I DO TO AVOID LITIGATION IF I HAVE TO TERMINATE EMPLOYEES?

No one likes to fire employees, but it is sometimes necessary. In our litigious society this unpleasant task has become even more distasteful because it inevitably raises the specter of litigation. Employment claims have sky-rocketed over the past twenty-five years and now occupy a large percentage of court dockets nationwide. The federal Equal Employment Opportunity Commission (EEOC), which reviews federal discrimination and retaliation claims, receives nearly 100,000 new claims every year. In this environment, you must do everything you can to avoid litigation.

Know the Legal Restrictions on Employment Termination That Apply to Your Firm

Ideally, you have consulted a local attorney and learned the most important prohibitions before you hire your first employee. The prohibitions on discrimination and retaliation that apply to hiring and workplace decision making also apply to firing. As discussed above, some prohibitions apply everywhere, for example, against race and sex discrimination. Others vary from state to state and even from one locality to another. Consult the website of your local antidiscrimination agency for details. You should understand whether your state is an "employment-at-will" state. If so, you can terminate an employment relationship for any reason (or no reason) as long as the termination is not specifically prohibited by law (for example, because it is discriminatory). Other states have less well-defined prohibitions against "wrongful" termination. In those states, it is especially important to consult a local attorney to get a general understanding of the restrictions that apply to you. In addition to restrictions imposed by law, you need to be aware of any restrictions imposed by employment contracts and your own policies. If your handbook states that the firm has a policy of progressive discipline you should follow that policy and any other termination policies and procedures you have adopted.

Terminating an Employee on the Spot for Serious Misconduct

The situations where immediate termination is necessary are very rare, but can arise. Criminal behavior in the workplace, like threatening violence at work or being caught red-handed stealing company or coworker property, must be met with prompt and firm action. In those cases, you should consider calling law enforcement authorities immediately to safeguard other employees and yourself. Speak with the offending employee only in the presence of a witness. Tell the employee clearly and calmly that you are terminating his or her employment, retrieve any firm property (especially employee ID, credit card, building keys, laptop, cell phone, and passes), and have the employee escorted from the building. Immediately remove his or her access to firm e-mail and computer systems.

Terminating an Employee under Other Circumstances

Most termination decisions should be made only after careful review and deliberation, not in anger or haste. Speak to all the employee's supervisors and review the personnel file. Make sure that you can articulate an objective reason for the termination even if the law does not require you to give a reason. And make sure that the employee's record supports it. This is when the work of preparing honest performance evaluations on a regular basis pays off. Countless cases have been lost by employers who claimed they fired an employee for poor performance despite positive performance evaluations in the employee's file. On the other hand, a clearly documented record of past problems is the best defense against an employee's claim of wrongful termination.

Consider offering some severance pay in exchange for a release if the reason for termination is not misconduct and if your firm can afford it. Even if you have done everything right, a bitter employee can still sue, but a signed general release will put a prompt end to virtually all cases. Most employers are willing to pay something for that peace of mind. Have your legal advisor prepare a release and severance agreement for you, at least the first time. You may want to include additional protections beyond the release, and your advisor can help you decide which ones you need. In addition to a release of all potential claims, severance agreements often include non-disclosure and confidentiality restrictions, limits on solicitation of co-workers and clients, and prohibitions on disparagement.

Preparing a Letter Explaining the Status of Pay and Benefits

After you make the termination decision and decide on severance pay, decide on a termination date and figure out what other pay and benefits the employee will be entitled to upon termination. You should prepare a letter to give to the employee following termination that explains the status of all pay and benefits. Generally, the employee has a right to be paid through the date of termination and to receive payment for all accrued but unused vacation. Under the Consolidated Omnibus Budget Reconciliation Act of 1980, called COBRA, and similar state laws, the employee may be entitled to continue as a member of the firm's medical plan for a period of time (generally 18 months) if he pays the premium. Other benefits, like life insurance, may have to be transitioned, and your letter to the employee should make that clear and give information on how to do it.

Meeting with the Employee

Although not required, a face-to-face meeting is far preferable to any other method for informing the affected employee of your termination decision. Arrange for someone else to be present with you during the meeting. The person who handles the human resource function in your office would be the best choice, but anyone who does not have a personal relationship (friendly or unfriendly) with the employee being terminated can serve as your witness. Immediately before the meeting, or during it, cut off the employee's access to firm e-mail and computers.

Deliver the news in a direct, non-judgmental manner. Do not detail the reasons, but be prepared to give a simple and honest answer if the employee asks why. Give the employee the letter you've prepared and then briefly explain the pay and benefits she is entitled to, including eligibility for unem-ployment compensation, if it would be available, and any severance you have decided to offer in exchange for a release. If you are offering severance, give the employee the severance agreement to review at home. If the employee is over 40 years old, you must give him at least 21 days to consider it and seven days after he signs it to revoke. Most employers give all employees regardless of age several weeks to think about whether they want to sign.

Finally, ask the employee to turn in his or her keys, credit cards and any other firm property, and wish him or her well.

Group Layoffs

Hopefully, you never face the need to downsize your practice, but economic developments beyond any individual's control have in recent years required many architects to lay off groups of employees. For group layoffs consult your legal adviser well in advance. The federal WARN Act and some state laws require employers to give advance warning of group layoffs and may impose other restrictions. Whether your firm has to comply with these laws generally depends on the size of the firm and the number of employees to be laid off. Before implementing group layoffs, you should have a professional review the EEO characteristics of the group selected for downsizing to ensure that the layoff decisions appear to have been made in an objective, evenhanded manner. Your adviser can also assist you in preparing age statistics that you must disclose in connection with obtaining releases from older employees.

* * *

Do not let the complications of employment law discourage you. If you want to expand your practice, at some point you have no choice but to become an employer. Many resources are available to help you through the maze of laws and regulations. The government agency websites referred to above provide a wealth of helpful information for free. Your state and local departments of labor may also answer questions by phone. But one of the best investments you can make in the growth of your practice is to consult a knowledgeable local employment lawyer or human resource specialist when you begin hiring and from time to time as your firm grows. They can help you institute employment practices and procedures at the outset that not only comply with the law but also will save you time, money, and aggravation in the future, freeing you to enjoy the practice of architecture.

SEVEN

HOW DO CONSTRUCTION DISPUTES GET RESOLVED?

In construction, to paraphrase Lincoln, you can't please all the people all the time. Building and design work breeds disputes like a swamp breeds mosquitoes. Some of this may be inevitable—a lot of participants can be involved in construction situations, and there are a lot of opportunities for things to go wrong. Owners become emotionally caught up in their projects. Contractors are often independent entrepreneurs who may bring outsized personalities to the job. The interests of the players are not perfectly aligned. The dynamics of getting selected to do the work may lead to underestimation of cost. Trade custom sometimes includes sharp practice and a lack of candor. And there is plenty of room for honest misunderstandings; details may be inadvertently overlooked; inattention may be interpreted as acquiescence. Nor can one overlook some people's disinclination to part with their money even after they have promised to pay.

The architect must be prepared for the possibility of disputes and the resulting claims. The likely adversaries are to some extent predictable. Owners battle with the general contractors over (among other things) delays, defective workmanship, work not in accordance with specifications, failure to perform specified work, and charges for extra work done outside the contract or the original specifications. Contractors battle with subcontractors over the same sorts of thing. Municipal building inspectors issue stop-work orders for alleged violations that everyone else disputes. Workers sustain personal injuries ranging from trivial to devastating, and either they or (in the worst cases) their estates bring claims for damages. Providers of labor, services, and materials sue to get paid. The architect is not immune. You, too, may need to sue for compensation. You, too, may be on the receiving end of a claim, be it for nonpayment, violation of code, responsibility for personal injury or property damage, or professional malpractice.

No matter how diligent and competent you are and irrespective of whether you're regularly and repeatedly in the right on every issue, as an architect you face the potential for a host of possible claims every time you ply your trade in the real world. As a threshold matter, to practice real-world architecture you *must* have appropriate insurance coverage (see Chapter 3). But you must also be able to recognize and deal directly with claims yourself.

WHAT DOES A CONSTRUCTION CLAIM LOOK LIKE?

Some claims announce themselves with trumpets; others sneak up behind you and kick you in the seat. To be a street-smart architect, you need to know how to respond to the former and anticipate the latter before the soreness sets in. The loudly asserted claim arrives in no uncertain terms. You have just told the general contractor and his carpentry subcontractor that half a football field's length of wall was installed a foot off spec and must be completely torn down and repositioned. The general contractor's project manager, the owner of the sub, and three carpenters are shouting at you in unison that the drawings were unclear, the demolition and rebuilding will be an extra cost, and the cost should come out of your hide. The owner is silently weeping ten feet away. Other claims are obvious in other ways. They come in an e-mail from your client, her neighbor, a contractor, or the Department of Buildings. Or they come in a white envelope with jagged green borders bearing "certified mail" insignia and the return address of a prominent law firm. Or they're delivered by a young man with a backpack and a bicycle helmet who turns out to be a process server.

Less obvious claim situations come from many possible directions but do not escape the sharp eye of an experienced architect. Consider the contractor who begins to ask for progress payments or advances without customary documentation because "he hasn't had time and has to pay the subs"; the owner who signed a dozen change orders behind your back because he toured the premises with his designer and "she had some ideas"; the subcontractor who casually mentions his employee twisted his ankle as he climbed off the scaffold, but "no worries—he's covered by our workers' comp"; the neighbor who, peeking around the construction wall, observes meekly, "I didn't realize our houses were going to be this close"; and an infinite number of other possible scenarios. Like most normal human beings, you will be mightily tempted to ignore these telltale hints of trouble. A voice inside you counsels, Let the sleeping dog lie. The inner advice may actually be right. But do not trust your immediate inclination to accept it. You are expected to have your professional antennae up, to be the intellect and the conscience of the project. That means being alert to indicators that something is amiss and, if so, to identify the issues or to refer the matter to someone who can. The claim could very well end up including you.

Every claim can be analyzed in terms of the particular issues it presents. Where the claim is overt, that is, in the form of a demand letter or an outright lawsuit, at least some of the main issues are obvious. A suit or demand for money raises the immediate issue of whether the money is owed for the work supposedly done or the injury supposedly sustained. A claim for remedial work raises the immediate issue of whether the original work was done improperly and whether the proposed fix is appropriate. Where the claim is simply implicit from circumstances, identifying the issues may require more searching thought. For example, the contractor mentioned above who is looking for advance payments could actually be planning a premature departure from the job with more money in hand than he is entitled to, leaving you, the architect, holding the bag. The owner with the change orders may later hold you responsible for work that was outside your control. The subcontractor and the neighbor may be alerting you to problems with site safety and surveying, respectively.

WHAT IS MEANT BY THE TERM "CLAIM"?

Every dispute involves a claim in one or both of two very different senses. The term "claim" may simply mean an assertion of some fact or right that is open to dispute. Alternatively, it may mean the aggregate of facts that generate a recognized right enforceable in our legal system. In the first sense a claim is a mere announcement and not necessarily enforceable or even believable; in the second it is the essence of being enforceable and believable—it's the law. Disputes often involve the process by which a claim in the first sense becomes a claim in the second sense—in other words, the process by which a mere assertion becomes a legally recognized right that the claimant can take to the bank. The rest of this chapter addresses the various ways in which this is done or resisted.

WHEN DO I NEED TO GET A LAWYER INVOLVED?

When an issue emerges that is, or could be, the subject of a dispute, an architect must answer a threshold question: Do I need a lawyer? Dealing with claims often requires specialized knowledge. Just as architects have been trained and licensed to know about designing buildings, lawyers are trained and licensed to know about dealing with disputes. The license requirement in both professions derives from the legislature's awareness that real harm can result from people who engage in such activity without the requisite background and qualifications.

As a general proposition, where the dispute has not advanced to a demand for money, or where there is no injury to person or property, or where there is no risk of a claim of malpractice, a lawyer's assistance may not be necessary. If, however, any of these factors is present, legal guidance is in order. Here are a few examples of claim situations that may warrant legal advice:

- An assertion by the owner that the architect has committed malpractice.
- A stop-work order by the authorities based on the charge that the project violates zoning limitations on size or height of structure.
- A complaint by an adjoining property owner that the structure crosses the property line, backed up by a survey.
- The general contractor walking off the job after the architect rejects payment requisitions because of noncompliance with design specifications.
- The building inspector's refusal to issue a certificate of occupancy because of alleged code violations.
- A written charge from the state's professional certification body that the architect has been operating without a required license.
- The occurrence of a serious injury to a worker on the project resulting from a structural collapse.
- A dispute between the owner and a contractor over whether costly changes are required, arguably occasioned by issues with the architect's drawings.
- An owner's termination of the project just prior to completion with a substantial part of the architect's bills still unpaid.
- Receipt of a demand for arbitration naming the architect as a respondent in an American Arbitration Association arbitration.

- Receipt of a summons and complaint naming the architect as a defendant in a civil action in court.

WHAT ARE THE FIRST STEPS IN ADDRESSING A CLAIM?

Regardless of whether you consult a lawyer, some basic procedures apply when you have a claim or find yourself facing a claim. If *you* have the claim and want it to be honored by the person you have the claim against, you should start by making a record. This means putting the claim in writing in a manner that would be customary under the circumstances. For example, if the claim is for payment by an owner, and you customarily send your bills by mail, prepare a statement showing the date and amount of all unpaid bills, and transmit it by mail with a cover letter that declares explicitly:

> Enclosed is my statement showing the unpaid bills for my work on your project. You currently owe my firm $36,523.42 for fees and disbursements incurred as of the end of last February, all of which should have been paid by May as provided in our AIA agreement. Please make that payment promptly so that I can continue to work toward timely completion of the job and not have to invoke the enforcement provisions of the agreement.

If you customarily e-mail the addressee, including for billing, e-mail the message instead of using standard mail. The important thing is to have a record of what you said and proof that it was actually conveyed. Use of the reply confirmation feature for e-mails is helpful in that regard. If you transmit the written communication of the claim by mail, you might send it by certified mail with a return receipt requested or by an overnight service that provides tracking and evidence of delivery.

Even when your claim arises from an issue other than nonpayment, you should still make a record of the claim by written communication. The practice of architecture can yield all kinds of grievances besides unpaid bills. A claim may result from someone's (usually an owner's or successor architect's) wrongful use of your copyrighted drawings after you have left the job. A former employee may abscond with your confidential client lists or other proprietary information. You and your partner may have basic disagreements on how to run the firm. Your landlord may fail to keep the office premises in good order or fix the leak in the ceiling. If ordinary conversation cannot cure the problem, assert your claim in writing so the record is clear as to what your view of the dispute is, and the date is fixed as to when you finally found it necessary to articulate the claim.

Have someone review the writing and comment on whether it clearly describes the grievance. The reviewer should be loyal to you and capable of preserving confidences. The logical person for the job may be a lawyer—indeed, the point at which you feel it necessary to assert the claim is often the time to consult a lawyer, even if he or she remains in the background. The claim should be stated concisely and diplomatically. Keep your emotions in check. Your goal is to resolve the grievance if possible; name-calling does not further that objective.

WHAT SHOULD I DO WHEN THE CLAIM IS AGAINST ME?

Where a claim is made *against you*, you should also make a record by written communication in response. Otherwise your failure to object may mistakenly be construed as an admission that the claim is correct. Indeed, in some situations such as where a bill is sent that is not promptly objected to, a court or arbitrator may view it as an admission of liability. And while an oral reply might seem sufficient, it does not create a clear record of what your position is. However, before making that record, be sure you know the facts. Read the relevant documents and make the appropriate inquiry to people who know the facts (and, ideally, will not immediately report to the claimant about your conversation).

If you take notes, be careful what you write down, since it potentially could be produced to an adversary if the dispute goes to formal proceedings. Based on the facts, try to evaluate your exposure in a worst-case scenario. That is, consider the possibility that a tribunal would believe the claimant and not you, and assess how much money you might have to pay or the implications of doing (or not doing) what the claimant demands. If the risk to you is significant or unclear, now is the time to consult a lawyer, even before sending your written response to the claim.

WHY IS IT CRITICAL TO SAVE MY RECORDS?

Be sure to *save all records* relevant to any claim, regardless of whether you are asserting it or it is asserted against you. It's a simple task that can become critically important if and when formal proceedings begin. A case can be lost simply because key records were absentmindedly thrown away or deleted. Preserve copies of all bills and correspondence. Download e-mails and text messages and save them on an appropriate medium. Sometimes the documentation may be voluminous, and were it not for the claim you would have disposed of it in the ordinary course of business. Resist the temptation to do so until the claim is resolved or until an authoritative voice —your lawyer, an arbitrator, or a judge—tells you it's okay.

Every architectural practice should have a written document retention policy. The professional licensing authority in your state is likely to have requirements concerning how long you must keep copies of signed plans and other important construction documents. Discuss with your tax adviser how long you should keep copies of your tax returns and other financial records (usually for at least five years after you file your returns). Be sure those time frames are referred to in your own written policy (and adhered to). In addition, think about the kinds of documents you and your staff generate, and project into the future why you might need to refer to them.

Every state has statutes of limitations for professional malpractice claims. A statute of limitations defines the time period within which a claim can be asserted. Find out from an attorney what the relevant limitations periods are, and be sure your written policy requires that documents you might want to rely on (or that adversaries might want to see) are maintained until at least a year after the longest such limitation period ends. Having the document retention policy in writing is especially important for dealing with claims that arise long after the work has ended and where the claimant is demanding to see documents from many years ago that were thrown away in the interim. It will be obvious from the written policy that you disposed of the documents in the ordinary course of business, not to avoid scrutiny.

WHAT ARE THE MAIN DISPUTE RESOLUTION VEHICLES?

After you have taken the first steps in addressing a dispute, you need to find a means to resolve it. Both informal and formal vehicles exist for dispute resolution. The availability of *formal vehicles* may be limited because of the provisions in a governing agreement. Such provisions may mandate the use of one particular vehicle, or a series of vehicles, and categorically exclude any other formal mechanism of dispute resolution. An *informal approach*, however, is always a possibility, with or without the guidance of a lawyer.

Formal vehicles for resolving claims include nonbinding decision making by someone chosen by both sides of the dispute, formal mediation, arbitration, and litigation in court or before a governmental agency. Where the dispute is with a governmental agency itself, the agency may provide a procedure for having the claim dealt with in-house first, followed by the possibility of an appeal to a court if you don't like the result. We address all of these vehicles in greater detail below.

HOW ARE DISPUTES RESOLVED INFORMALLY?

What could be more sensible, cost-effective, and satisfying than resolving a claim without resorting to formal procedures? Yet, surprisingly, some players in the construction process ignore this obvious step and rush to court or arbitration out of emotion or tactics. Perhaps it is for this reason that some contracts provide for a cooling-off period, directing the parties to confer after notice of a claim is given and to attempt to reach a negotiated solution. Regardless of whether the parties' agreement requires it, however, common sense suggests that discussing the problem and seeking out common ground are generally preferable to a time-consuming, money-hemorrhaging fight.

The essence of informal dispute resolution is *negotiation*, the process by which two or more parties engage in bargaining with the objective of reaching an agreement. You can approach negotiation in various ways. One method is for the parties to exchange letters, starting with the claimant's describing the grievance in detail, answered by the responding party's point-by-point reply. Another method is to have a face-to-face meeting, either by the parties themselves or through intermediaries. Use of go-betweens often facilitates resolution because emotions are kept in check, and the representatives are able to make and respond to offers while having the ability to go back to their principal before rejecting a proposal. Having someone other than a lawyer serve the intermediary function is sometimes desirable, because it reduces the appearance of hostility, avoids legal arguments, and keeps the cost down. Of course, depending on the extent of the claim, you might prefer to have a lawyer handle the negotiation, which may result in the other side bringing in a lawyer, too—or vice versa. This is not necessarily a bad option as long as both sides appoint the right lawyers, that is, experienced professionals who are diplomatic and practical rather than attack dogs. There are plenty of lawyers in both categories. Careful vetting allows you to select the right one (a subject discussed in Chapter 10 below).

HOW CAN MONETARY CLAIMS BE RESOLVED INFORMALLY?

Applying a few time-honored techniques can enhance the effectiveness of informal negotiation and the likelihood of a successful result. If you have a claim for payment of money, you should begin the process by making a demand for a specified sum. That "opener" should be formulated with compromise in mind. Presumably the parties are informally negotiating because they know formal dispute resolution brings added expenses, uncertainty in result, and diversion of valuable time and resources. So as the claimant, you already anticipate getting less, and the respondent anticipates paying more, than what each believes to be just. Whether the initial demand should be substantially greater than the amount that would be acceptable, or whether it should be very close to that amount ("take it or leave it"), is a matter of judgment and factual context. Informal negotiation is more art than science, and experience from prior situations can be a big help.

The party against whom the claim is asserted should respond to the initial demand by making a counteroffer. The considerations that guide the amount of the counteroffer are similar to those that guide the amount of the initial demand. Sometimes the goal is to bring the process to a rapid conclusion with a take-it-or-leave-it figure. Sometimes it is to create a floor that the claimant must approach for any prospect of resolution. And sometimes it becomes the next step in an elaborate back-and-forth dance in which the parties' offers get closer and closer until they meet somewhere in the middle. One thing, however, remains a constant in the informal negotiation of a claim for money: there must be an initial demand and a counteroffer for the process to achieve a result. A lot of talk about who's right, who's wrong, and why gets you nowhere.

HOW CAN NON-MONETARY CLAIMS BE RESOLVED INFORMALLY?

Informal dispute resolution may also work for claims that do not simply seek payment of money. Almost any claim an architect may get caught up in can potentially benefit from negotiation, including disputes between partners; employer-employee issues; claims based on covenants restricting the post-employment acts of departing staff members; claims for copyright infringement, plagiarism, and other unfair use of intellectual property; breaches of contract terms involving nonmonetary terms; claims by neighboring owners for encroachment on their property; claims by local authorities for violation of zoning ordinances or building codes; and other areas of dispute where the claimant's objective is not just to get paid.

Applying some basic techniques can lead to an informal resolution of many nonmonetary claims. First, before engaging with the other side, define the issue. Determine what the main source of contention is and what alternative course of action could make it go away. If these critical items of information are unclear, investigate. It may even make sense in some instances to ask the other side. For example, if the claim comes from a building inspector, sit down with the official and get chapter and verse on what's wrong and supposedly needed to get the job back on track. If you believe your partner may be moonlighting in violation of the partnership agreement, bite the bullet and ask him or her for particulars. Whether to seek out information directly from the other side is a judgment call. If you are uncertain, ask the advice of an experienced colleague or a lawyer.

Second, having defined the issue and reached a view on what outcome or range of possible outcomes would be acceptable, map out potential compromises. Discuss them with a trusted adviser before approaching the other disputant. Have the adviser argue the other side's position and develop an appropriate response that is constructive but does not concede the other side's position. Where, for instance, an owner and her new architect are using your drawings in violation of your copyright, arguing that you were discharged for "failure to supervise the contractor," you need not protest that you had no duty to supervise (although your objection would be correct). Instead, you might respond, "no one contests your right to replace me with another architect for whatever reason you wish, and even if the reason might be unfounded. At the same time, however, my copyright in the drawings continues after termination of our relationship, so we have to work out mutually acceptable conditions for your continued use of those drawings." Where an owner complains that your drawings were negligent and demands that they be reworked for free and that you should pay for the contractor's extra charges, you should resist the temptation to be combative. Informal resolution would be better served by developing a diplomatic response such as, "our disagreement on this issue should not delay completing your project. I'm prepared to compromise as follows [etc.]."

Third, once you have developed your ideas about possible compromises, have an informal discussion with the other disputant, preferably in person rather than by telephone. Confirm that the discussion is off-the-record. Listen to the arguments of the other side. Be respectful and diplomatic even if you think the position presented to you is baseless. Try to find and articulate points of agreement. There are almost always such shared points, and the more of them you can come up with, the better the context for reaching agreement on the disputed points. Minimize the discussion of who's right and who's wrong. Direct the discussion to ways to resolve the controversy. If the other disputant makes a "final, nonnegotiable" offer, don't reject it out of hand. Ask for additional time to reflect on it and the situation as a whole. Look for creative solutions, ideas about what you might be able to give the other side in exchange for getting what you want. That's why the process is often referred to as "bargaining."

SHOULD DISPUTE RESOLUTIONS BE DOCUMENTED?

Generally speaking, it's a good idea to confirm in writing the successful resolution of a monetary or nonmonetary claim. When you reach agreement with the other side, immediately list all the key elements in a memorandum, date it, and have all parties initial the list. Be sure to think about and include, where appropriate, mechanisms to assure compliance with the terms of the deal. For example, if the agreement settles a payment dispute by allowing reimbursement over time in installments, have the paying party sign a promissory note listing the dates and amounts of the future payments. If the agreement prohibits someone from using your proprietary information, you may want to require payment of specified damages if the person does not comply. Such documentation is best handled by a lawyer. If the agreement is not written carefully, disputes can arise from the interpretation of the agreement itself. Just because you resolved a claim informally does not mean it shouldn't be documented carefully.

WHAT ARE THE MAIN TYPES OF FORMAL CLAIMS RESOLUTION?

Formal procedures for the resolution of disputes are divided into two categories, nonbinding and binding. The difference lies in whether the process results in a directive *compelling* some act or abstention for the benefit of one side against the other. A nonbinding procedure does not compel a result against the will of any of the participating parties; a binding procedure does.

The three main categories of formal procedure are mediation, which is non-binding, and arbitration and litigation, whose results are binding.

HOW DOES MEDIATION WORK?

Mediation is the common, formal, nonbinding claims resolution procedure in which a neutral third-party attempts to facilitate settlement of the dispute by conferring with the parties jointly and in separate "caucuses." It is similar to informal negotiation using a single middleman, a bit like the shuttle diplomacy that State Department officials sometimes perform in international controversies. But it contrasts with informal negotiation in being governed by a set of ground rules. A mediation cannot get off the ground if the parties fail to follow the rules.

Under commonly used forms of owner/architect contracts, such as those developed by the AIA, engaging in mediation is a precondition to binding dispute resolution, such as a lawsuit. As the 2007 B101 Agreement puts it, in language of medieval resonance (but which lawyers consider modern lawspeak):

> *Any claim, dispute or other matter in question arising out of or relating to this Agreement shall be subject to mediation as a condition precedent to binding dispute resolution.* (B101, Article 8.2.1)

Under this contractual requirement, only if the parties cannot work it out in mediation may they carry their dispute forward into arbitration or court.

The parties to a dispute do not need to have a contractual requirement to invoke the mediation process. Claims can arise where the disputants do not have a contract between them, for example, where the claim involves an adjoining property holder, a governmental agency, or even a contractor or a worker on the job. If informal negotiation fails to result in a resolution, the parties may voluntarily submit the claim to mediation by locating a mediator acceptable to both sides, with a reputation for effectiveness in settling cases. Organizations such as the American Arbitration Association (AAA), Chartered Institute of Arbitrators, International Chamber of Commerce (ICC), JAMS, and many others in every state and in most industrialized countries administer voluntary mediations under their own rules or provide lists of mediators who can set up an ad hoc mediation. The mediator can instead be an acquaintance of one or both sides who has the trust of the parties and agrees to proceed in accordance with the ground rules developed specifically for that particular dispute.

Mediation Agreements

Mediations share several characteristics, no matter what the context. First, mediations begin with an agreement to mediate (except where a dispute is already in court and a judge compels mediation). The agreement may be a provision in a pre-existing contract between an owner and the architect, or arrived at voluntarily after the dispute surfaces. Most arbitration forums, such as the AAA, have a standard form of agreement. Second, the parties are subject to strict confidentiality. What is said during mediation may not be used in subsequent binding proceedings if the claim is not settled. In addition, certain principles associated with "due process" are thrown to the winds in mediation. For example, the normal practice in a court case that prohibits the judge from hearing arguments privately from one side is abandoned in mediation. So-called ex parte communications with the mediator are an integral element of the process because they help the mediator come up with ideas for bridging the gap between the disputants' positions.

The Role of the Mediator

Another characteristic common to all mediations is that the mediator does not issue a decision declaring one side right and the other wrong. The sole function of the mediator is to facilitate a resolution. That may involve the mediator's giving an opinion to one side or the other about the merits of a party's position. This is normally done privately with the party whose position is being criticized and not shared with the other party. It constitutes an attempt to inject "realism," the view of an objective outsider, which might cause a party to rethink a position and lead to compromise. Finally, the mediation comes to a binding result only if both parties agree upon it and reduce it to writing in an enforceable settlement agreement—the same kind of agreement that can result from informal negotiation (discussed above).

Mediation Procedures

The procedures followed in mediation are relatively uniform no matter who the mediator is or what organization is administering it. After the parties sign the mediation agreement and agree on the forum, the mediator schedules a meeting. The mediator often requests some form of documentation to familiarize himself or herself with the issues prior to a meeting with the disputants. Such documents may include correspondence, bills, drawings, or other materials relevant to the claim. The mediator may also request position papers from both sides to become acquainted with competing takes on the facts and the applicable law and/or have telephone conferences with each side to ask questions and start sounding out possibilities for compromise. The shuttle diplomacy may actually begin even before the first meeting. The mediator typically insists that people with authority to settle the dispute be present at the actual mediation or, if not possible, be available by phone.

At the face-to-face session, usually held at the mediator's workplace or at an attorney's office, the mediator reminds the disputants that he is a facilitator, not a decision maker, and that everything said is confidential and cannot be used later in binding adversarial proceedings. Each party then usually states its view. Where attorneys are engaged, they may present the statement, but clients usually make the statement, which personalizes the claim or response.

After the opening remarks, the mediator ordinarily meets separately with each side. It is common in such shuttle diplomacy sessions for the mediator to ask for clarification of facts or legal positions, offer an independent evaluation of the strengths and weaknesses of the parties' arguments, probe alternative approaches to compromise, and develop offers to convey to the other side. This back-and-forth process can last for hours. Renewed joint sessions, outbursts by one side or the other, and noisy walkouts may ensue. Ultimately, these are followed by a return to dialogue, or an adjournment to permit further exploration of relevant facts or to provide an opportunity for the parties to reflect on how the discussions have developed. Sometimes a mediation results in dispute resolution on the first day. Other times the mediation leads to a stretch of time during which the mediator continues to facilitate discussions both by telephone and in person, with a successful resolution finally achieved after an extended period of cajoling.

How an Unsuccessful Mediation Can Resolve a Dispute

This may seem intuitively unlikely, but a mediation that fails in the short term to achieve a final settlement of the claim may nevertheless turn out to be constructive. The work of the mediator in getting the disputants to talk out their opposing positions and consider alternative solutions may provide a basis for subsequent negotiation and resolution without the mediator's further involvement. The parties can always continue to talk, either directly or through their attorneys, and sometimes the mediator is called upon at a later point to help develop a solution to remaining obstacles to settlement. This can occur over the telephone or even by reconvening another mediation session. The process does not really end until the fat lady sings, which may only happen when the dispute is settled or resolved in arbitration or litigation. Mediation has the potential to work magic, bringing bitterly antagonistic parties together and creating through discussion and creative thinking solutions to disputes that previously seemed intractable.

Using Administrative Process as a Means to Achieve Nonbinding Dispute Resolution

While mediation is the most common vehicle for formal, nonbinding dispute resolution, administrative procedures in government agencies can, under some circumstances, serve a similar function. Many such agencies require that issues involving their jurisdiction be presented for determination by an administrative law judge or agency tribunal before an aggrieved party can go to court or commence arbitration. The process is known broadly as the duty to "exhaust administrative remedies," and the courts and arbitrators generally enforce it. This means that a claimant who fails to bring a claim before the agency for resolution is not permitted to pursue the claim elsewhere and is sent back to the agency to satisfy the exhaustion of remedies requirement. In a sense, this parallels the requirement in many architect/owner agreements and construction contracts that the parties proceed to mediation before they undertake binding dispute resolution.

Sometimes the government agency's exhaustion of remedies requirement is pro forma. For example, if you have an employee who asserts a claim of race or sex discrimination under the Civil Rights laws, the employee is required to submit a charge of discrimination to the U.S. Equal Employment Opportunity Commission (EEOC) or equivalent state human rights agency before a court considers the charge. The agency rarely takes any formal action against the employer, and after six months pass, the employee is permitted to proceed in court. But during the interim, the agency on an informal, nonbinding basis may attempt to achieve an amicable settlement of the dispute.

In other instances, the agency may carry on an actual adjudicative proceeding and issue a decision resolving the dispute, but the decision is not binding on a court or arbitration panel that subsequently hears the same dispute after the exhaustion of administrative remedies. Typical examples an architect might encounter include an administrative appeal from a building department or zoning board decision limiting the size or design of a structure. Such a ruling often leads to negotiations with the agency and a compromise result. In the absence of such a resolution, the party aggrieved by the ruling is generally free to challenge it in a court. Sometimes the court has the power to completely reconsider the issue, rendering the agency ruling in effect nonbinding. On other occasions, however, the court may defer to the expertise of the agency and overturn its ruling only if it is clearly in violation of the applicable law.

Because agencies differ in the extent to which their administrative rulings receive deference from a court or arbitration panel, you should know beforehand how binding the administrative ruling will be and what is expected of you. Sometimes you must prepare for an administrative hearing as if you were involved in a court trial. In other instances, the hearings are largely an invitation to negotiate a settlement. In either case, where exhaustion of administrative remedies is a requirement, you must take it seriously. And be on the lookout for ways in which the requirement can be used as a vehicle for voluntary resolution of the dispute.

HOW DOES ARBITRATION WORK?

Arbitration is a method of formal claim resolution involving one or more neutral decision makers, jointly selected or accepted by the disputing parties, to whom the dispute is presented for a binding decision. It's another alternative to going to court (thus the term "alternative dispute resolution" or ADR). This resolution method has the benefit of using as arbitrators industry experts familiar with relevant practices and circumstances. The construction industry has long resolved disputes by arbitration because unfamiliar terminology and complex issues can make cases related to construction or design issues unsuitable for juries or overburdened judges.

As of 2007, the standard AIA forms for architect's contracts use a check-the-box approach to dispute resolution. The parties can select "arbitration," "litigation," or "other" as the dispute resolution procedure. (In contrast, the AIA forms for construction contracts provide only for arbitration.) Moreover, those forms prescribe arbitration as the final step in a series of procedures beginning with the requirement that the architect or another designated decision maker make an initial nonbinding judgment on the dispute, followed by mediation, and ultimately arbitration.

While in theory arbitration is supposed to be more informal and streamlined than a court proceeding, it does not always work that way. Arbitration can involve arcane legal elements and court proceedings (such as a request for an injunction or a ruling on scope of arbitration). Parties are no less in need of legal representation in arbitration than they are when they walk into a courthouse. Avoiding court by agreeing to arbitration does not, alas, mean you can avoid engaging a lawyer.

Arbitration Agreements

The parties to a business relationship, such as an architect and an owner, ordinarily can only proceed with arbitration if they have previously entered into an agreement to do so. Most often the agreement is reached long before any dispute arises and is outlined in a clause ("arbitration clause") in the document that establishes the basic underlying professional engagement. Even in the absence of such a clause, and even after a dispute emerges, the parties can sign a separate contract known as a "submission agreement" to permit the dispute to be resolved through the medium of arbitration. Like mediation, arbitration cannot proceed without a signed agreement. And in the absence of that agreement, parties have to seek their remedies in court.

The fact that you cannot have an arbitration without a contract is important not just for the legitimacy of the procedure (and the enforceability of its result) but also for virtually every other aspect of the process. You can control all the major components of an arbitration proceeding through carefully chosen language in the parties' agreement to arbitrate. For example, construction arbitration can be administered by any of several available organizations, and the parties can specify in the contract which organization runs the show. While the AAA is spelled out in standard AIA contracts, the parties are free to choose another organization or leave administration entirely to the arbitrators themselves. You can also specify which issues are subject to arbitration and which must be resolved in court. One issue often preserved for judicial decision is the threshold question of whether a particular kind of dispute is covered by the arbitration clause ("arbitrability"). The contract can make clear who decides the issue of arbitrability—a court or the arbitrators.

Arbitration Procedures

The rules governing an arbitration proceeding are intentionally simple and encourage speed and informality. The AAA and other arbitration forums have their own sets of rules that establish applicable procedures. Ordinarily you begin an arbitration by filing case-opening forms with the administrative office of the tribunal and paying a filing fee in accordance with a fee schedule. The claimant (or the tribunal administrator if the rules so provide) delivers to the adversary a formal demand for arbitration form, complete with a statement of claim that describes the factual basis for the dispute. The adversary then has a set period of time in which to respond. The response, when delivered, may include counterclaims and also bring other parties who similarly have signed arbitration agreements into the case. Sometimes participants in a project who ought to be part of the arbitration cannot be compelled to participate either because they are not subject to an enforceable arbitration agreement or because an applicable agreement between two of the other parties expressly prohibits joinder of additional parties. This means that they may have to be dealt with in court, unless they can be persuaded to agree voluntarily to join in the arbitration.

The AIA, recognizing the benefits of having a dispute resolution proceeding include all parties involved in the dispute, provides in its owner/architect and owner/contractor agreements for consolidation proceedings or joinder of parties under certain circumstances:

> *Either party, at its sole discretion, may consolidate an arbitration conducted under this Agreement with any other arbitration to which it is a party provided that (1) the arbitration agreement governing the other arbitration permits consolidation; (2) the arbitrations to be consolidated substantially involve common questions of law or fact; and (3) the arbitrations employ materially similar procedural rules and methods for selecting arbitrator(s).* (B101, Article 8.3.4.1)
>
> *Either party, at its sole discretion, may include by joinder persons or entities substantially involved in a common question of law or fact whose presence is required if complete relief is to be accorded in arbitration, provided that the party sought to be joined consents in writing to such joinder. Consent to arbitration involving an additional person or entity shall not constitute consent to arbitration of any claim, dispute or other matter in question not described in the written consent.* (B101, Article 8.3.4.2)

Selecting the Arbitrator(s)

After the opening papers are filed, a list of proposed arbitrators and the procedure for selection is provided to both sides. The number of arbitrators ordinarily depends on the amount of money at stake. A single arbitrator usually handles smaller claims while a panel of three arbitrators usually handles larger claims. The rationale is obvious—the parties must pay the arbitrators, so the cost should be kept in reasonable proportion to the amount at stake. Here again, however, the terms of the contract providing for arbitration govern, and the parties may by their agreement expand or reduce the number of arbitrators from the default provided for in the rules.

In most construction-related arbitrations, both sides get a say in selecting the arbitrator(s). In some arbitration forums, each side selects its own arbitrator and those two arbitrators then meet to select the third arbitrator. In other forums the tribunal administrator circulates a list of prospective candidates, together with biographical information, for review by each side. The parties may suggest removal of certain candidates from the list because of a suspected conflict of interest. If the objection has merit, the arbitration organization strikes the name from the list. Similarly, candidates are required to disclose relationships with the parties; failure to disclose a conflict of interest can at a later point result in invalidation of an arbitration award. How the lists are dealt with differs from tribunal to tribunal. Some require each party to rank the candidates listed for selection. Others simply require a line-through for each rejected candidate. The administrator then reviews the parties' lists and selects the arbitrators based upon the names acceptable to both sides. Where there is no overlap of acceptable candidates, the rules may permit the tribunal administrator to make an arbitrary selection from a stable of candidates not previously presented on the list, and each such selection must be accepted unless a conflict of interest can be shown. In the case of a three-arbitrator panel, either the tribunal administrator or the panel (not the parties) designates which of the selected arbitrators is to serve as chair.

The Initial Conference

Once the arbitrator(s) are selected, a prehearing telephone conference is scheduled at which the parties' attorneys confer with the arbitration panel to discuss disclosure of information and scheduling of hearings. The arbitrators typically require exchange of documents relevant to the issues identified in the statement of claim and response. Another disclosure device called a "deposition" may be permitted under exceptional circumstances. A deposition involves taking testimony from a witness, which is recorded and transcribed by a qualified stenographer, prior to the arbitration hearing. The deposition can be used at the hearing and gives the opposing side a preview of what will be presented. The parties ordinarily must disclose whether they plan to rely on expert testimony. If so, an expert report and potentially a deposition of the expert may be required.

Hearings and Award

Arbitration hearings involve testimony by witnesses and presentation of exhibits much like a trial in court except under less formal conditions. Instead of a courtroom, for example, the hearing is usually held in a private conference room with the arbitrators at the head of the table. After all the evidence is presented, the arbitrators may ask for closing statements from the attorneys or for a posthearing "brief" (that is, written submission) from each side recapitulating their arguments. At that point, the proceedings are declared to be "closed," and the arbitrators are given a specified time period under the rules of the forum within which to issue their decision. That decision, known as the arbitration "award," may provide detailed reasons for the arbitrators' decision (referred to as a "reasoned award"), or it may just summarize the ultimate award without giving any reasons. The parties by agreement are free to specify whether they want a reasoned or a summary award.

HOW DO I ENFORCE A FAVORABLE ARBITRATION AWARD?

The issuance of an award does not end the proceedings. Construction industry arbitrators have no power to order a sheriff or other law enforcement official to pry money out of a judgment debtor's bank account or sell off the loser's property. To enforce the award, you must present it to a court for "confirmation" and have it converted into a judgment, which can then be enforced as if it were the result of a court case. In recent years, the process of getting a court to confirm an arbitration award has become very close to having it rubberstamp the arbitrators' decision. The United States Supreme Court has repeatedly expressed its enthusiasm for arbitration (it reduces the judicial workload), and several of the Court's decisions under Chief Justice John G. Roberts have made it clear that very little can be done to keep an award from being confirmed. Awards are generally not appealable and are not overturned unless the arbitrators reached a result beyond the scope of the arbitration, are corrupt, or failed to disclose a conflict of interest. Arbitration is supposed to be about efficiency and economy—you get one bite at the apple, and that's it.

HOW DOES LITIGATION WORK?

This brings us to the final and perhaps most familiar vehicle for resolving construction-related disputes: taking the fight to court. Civil litigation involves an elaborate set of procedures within the precincts of the world-renowned American judicial system. The distinguishing feature of dispute-resolution using the courts is the emphasis on procedural fairness. At every step along the way the disputing parties must give notice to one another concerning what they want the court to consider, when it will be considered, and what the deadline is for objecting. Everything is strung out over lengthy intervals of time (except in special urgent situations, for example, where a temporary restraining order (TRO) is sought to maintain the status quo while the court is considering the issues). Following the correct procedure is often a prerequisite to having your claim or defense even considered on the merits. This is known as "due process;" it is the pride and joy of the judicial system, and a source of endless frustration for litigants.

The Court System

The United States has a system of courts that have different powers to provide different kinds of redress for different kinds of claims, as well as to consider appeals from the rulings of lower courts. The two court regimes in this country, federal and state, operate in parallel. The vast majority of cases are heard in the state courts. Federal courts only entertain disputes that arise under the U.S. Constitution or federal statutes or involve opponents who are not from the same state, a basis for jurisdiction known as "diversity of citizenship." The theory is that the federal courts are more remote from local politics and favoritism than the state courts so that an out-of-state litigant gets a fairer shake in the federal court.

Courts handle both criminal and civil matters, the former being prosecuted by the government against wrongdoing that the legislatures have labeled "criminal," the latter being pursued under a congeries of laws that are not criminal in nature. Architects mostly encounter civil litigation. In other words, the claims to be resolved concern demands for money ("damages") or requests to stop or, in rare instances, compel some activity (known as "injunctive relief"). Sometimes, however, architects find themselves caught up in criminal proceedings. The filing of false documents with public authorities, acting as an architect without proper licensing, being involved in improper payments to suppliers or inspectors, or making misrepresentations can all give rise to criminal liability. But for the most part the interface between architecture and litigation is on the civil side of the courts' dockets, so that is the primary focus here.

The Two Main Conditions for Court Action

To obtain redress in court, the claimant (usually known as the "plaintiff") must first show that his or her claim meets two criteria: (a) it is recognized by statute or common-law principles ("states a claim") and (b) the court has the power ("jurisdiction") to rule on that kind of claim. The plaintiff must demonstrate in the initial papers submitted to the court that both criteria are satisfied, an exercise that requires specialized legal knowledge. Although construction litigation is often complex and warrants representation by a litigation lawyer, an individual may represent himself or herself "pro se." An entity such as a corporation, however, must be represented by an attorney in court.

Pleadings

An elaborate set of procedural rules governs the sequence of events in any litigation, regardless of the court. The plaintiff states his or her claims in a civil "complaint" filed with the court and delivered to ("served upon") the adversary. The adversary ("defendant") replies with an "answer" to the claims, asserting defenses, and, where appropriate, alleging counterclaims against the plaintiff and cross-claims against co-defendants. The plaintiff generally serves a "reply" to any counterclaims, and co-defendants may be required to serve their own answers to cross-claims. The complaint, answer, reply, and certain other case opening documents are traditionally known as the "pleadings," terminology that reminds one of the ancient origins of this otherwise very modern activity.

Parties

Multiple parties can be joined in the case through either the pleadings or requests to the court for permission. Litigation is much more flexible than arbitration in allowing all relevant participants within reach of the court's jurisdiction to be brought together for resolution of the dispute in a single forum. This is because, unlike arbitration, a party needn't agree to be brought into a civil litigation. Indeed, an arbitration may proceed with only some of the relevant parties, making it necessary to start a parallel court case against the other parties who did not agree to arbitration.

Pretrial Proceedings.

After the complaint, answer, and reply are filed and served, the parties engage in pretrial proceedings, which may include some or all of the following activities:

- "Discovery," including disclosure of relevant documents, responding to written questions ("interrogatories"), and the taking of depositions under oath before a court reporter in the lawyers' offices
- Pretrial conferences in court at which deadlines for various procedures are set and the judge resolves disagreements over how the case should proceed
- Requests (known as "motions") to the judge for orders affecting the progress of the case, for example, to extend or limit discovery, modify the schedule of activities, narrow or expand the subjects at issue, or even dismiss the case
- Retention of expert witnesses who address technical construction issues relevant to the claims, and who often write up a report and appear for a deposition by the adversary

Discovery

In litigation involving construction issues, discovery can be time-consuming, sometimes dragging on for years. Since most court cases settle during or after discovery, this stage of the process is the one you are most likely to experience firsthand. The other side may demand that you track down every relevant scrap of paper, including drafts and drawings. (The importance of careful record keeping, mentioned previously, cannot be overstated; litigation is where adherence to a careful document retention policy can pay huge dividends.) You may have to download and transfer onto CDs electronically stored data such as e-mails. Even metadata (the computer information that describes formatting, changes in text, and dates of preparation) have to be preserved and potentially produced to the opponent (who will have to do the same thing with his or her material for your benefit). Failure to carry out this mind-numbing and burdensome work can result in "sanctions" from the court that may include fines or orders disadvantaging you in the case.

Certain specific material is exempt from discovery. The parties are entitled only to disclosure of information "relevant" to the issues in the case or "calculated to lead to the discovery of admissible evidence." Since some courts take a broad view of relevance, your attorney can help you gauge the proper scope of document demands. Even relevant information may be insulated from discovery, however, if it is "privileged." Examples of privileged material include attorney/client communications, so-called work product of the lawyers or those acting under their instructions (which in some instances may be you after a litigation has begun), and communications with certain other categories of professionals such as physicians, psychologists, and clergy, and between spouses. If you become involved in a construction dispute, file your written communications with your attorney separately to simplify locating and protecting the privileged documents in the event you later have to respond to a request for document disclosure.

The big shift from work done on paper to work done electronically in some ways creates additional discovery burdens (for example, organizing and producing the huge volume of e-mails in almost any project). On the other hand, the changeover to electronic drafting of construction plans and paperless record keeping can actually be beneficial when you are collecting information for a court case. It is in every architect's interest to develop well-designed information storage systems, if only as a matter of professionalism and sound practice management. An added benefit is that it simplifies the process of finding and organizing information for discovery and can save you time and money when you find yourself caught up in litigation.

A few more words are in order about depositions. Everyone involved in a construction project tends to get dragged in if a lawsuit results. They all end up having to engage lawyers, many paid for by insurance carriers. Each party gets questioned in turn by the lawyers for all the other parties. It can be hard to schedule depositions because all the lawyers' schedules have to be consulted, so the process can drag on for months. The scope of questioning can be very broad—anything that could lead to admissible evidence is fair game, and the lawyers are not permitted to instruct the witnesses to refrain from answering unless privileged information is improperly being sought. Between preparing for depositions and locating documents for disclosure, an architect who has commenced or been dragged into litigation rapidly regrets the situation. This is one of the major reasons why the AIA owner/architect contracts provide the parties with the option of selecting arbitration instead of litigation. Sometimes, unfortunately, there is no way out of it short of settlement or a full-blown trial unless the case gets stopped by a "dispositive motion."

Dispositive Motions

There are two main types of such motion, whereby a party asks the court for an order ending the case quickly without a trial. First, early in the case a defendant can make a motion to dismiss the complaint on the ground that there is no recognizable basis for the plaintiff to succeed even if everything the plaintiff charges is true. Second, later in the case, either plaintiff or defendant can make a motion for so-called summary judgment in his or her favor. In a plaintiff's summary judgment motion, the plaintiff claims that there is no defense to her claims and therefore judgment should be entered awarding the relief sought in the complaint (typically damages). A defendant's summary judgment motion claims the opposite, namely, that the facts show no merit in the plaintiff's claims so they should be dismissed. The court has to determine whether there is any "issue of fact" that could affect the outcome and that would require weighing the credibility of witnesses. In the absence of such an issue, the court grants the motion in favor of the party with the overwhelmingly stronger position. If, on the other hand, an important issue of fact emerges, the case is directed to trial.

Trials

The trial is the procedure in which the court examines the evidence and reaches its findings of what the key facts actually are. Every claim must have legal and factual support. The trial enables the court to determine whether such support was adequately demonstrated. Deciding questions of law is exclusively the province of the judge. Deciding questions of fact is exclusively the province of the fact finder, which in a jury trial is the jury while in a trial without a jury (bench trial) is simply the judge. The facts in the case are presented through so-called admissible evidence, which may include testimony by knowledgeable witnesses and experts and submission of relevant documents. The fact finder may also examine tangible things, such as equipment that is brought into the courtroom, and may make a visit to the work site. Evidence is "admissible" if it satisfies certain standards of reliability that the courts have developed over the years. Not every item of evidence meets those standards, which means that certain facts are not permitted to be considered by the fact finder. (Arbitration tends to be less fussy than litigation over the admissibility of evidence.)

The Result of the Trial

The ultimate decision when the fact finder is a jury is called the "verdict," while a judge's determination is usually called a "decision after trial." The verdict or decision after trial may be subject to post-trial motions to reverse or modify the result. The verdict or decision is then translated into the final result of the case, called a "judgment." This states how much money the plaintiff is entitled to, or finds for the defendant by dismissing the plaintiff's claims and possibly granting the counterclaim (if there is one) against the plaintiff, or arrives at a mixture of determinations. Where there are multiple parties, the judgment may have a number of elements (for example, requiring different parties to pay different amounts based on different percentages of fault) and can be quite complicated. As we mentioned in the discussion of arbitration, the complexity of construction cases is often better addressed by a panel of expert arbitrators than by a judge or jury in court.

If the judgment calls for payment of money, it is enforceable with the assistance of a public officer such as a marshal or sheriff, who is authorized by law to seize bank accounts or sell the judgment debtor's property after certain other due process proceedings take place. A nonmonetary judgment that prohibits or requires certain action is enforceable by the court's power to hold the disobedient party in contempt. Contempt of court may result in fines, arrest, and a stay in the local jail.

WHAT ARE APPEALS?

Unlike most arbitration situations, in civil litigation a party who has lost on some point in the trial court may seek reversal or modification of that ruling in an appellate court. The theory is that due process is not fully served unless there is at least one opportunity to test the initial decision maker's ruling in another tribunal that can serve as a check against error or bias. Different jurisdictions have different rules that determine at what stage of the case an appeal can be made. The federal courts and some state courts permit appeals to be taken only from an order or judgment issued at the end of the lower court proceeding. Other state courts are more lenient and allow appeals from virtually any ruling on a significant aspect of the case. The latter approach assures that errors early in the case are addressed promptly so that procedures that might not otherwise be appropriate are avoided in the lower court. On the other hand, appeals in the middle of a lower court proceeding (known as "interlocutory appeals") delay the ultimate resolution of the case and burden the appellate courts. Thus, both approaches can have benefits as well as disadvantages.

In the federal system and in most states, the appeal from the trial court is taken to an intermediate court of appeals. A panel of three to five judges reads the papers and testimony and, in many instances, hears oral argument on the appeal before issuing a written decision. When the decision is rendered, the possibility of a further appeal to the highest court in the jurisdiction remains—the U.S. Supreme Court for federal matters, the state's highest court (in many states also called a "Supreme Court") in state matters. The requirements for obtaining an audience in the highest court are usually stringent, and in the case of the U. S. Supreme Court highly subjective. Public policy considerations are often paramount. As a practical matter, litigants must be prepared to accept the opportunity of only one level of appeal except in unusual cases that satisfy the criteria for further consideration.

* * *

As we said at the beginning of this chapter, disputes go with the territory in construction. Any architect who wants to see the product of his or her creativity translated into a building in the real world must come to grips with all that construction entails, including the near inevitability of disputes. Many disputes can be avoided simply by being alert to the possibility that they can occur and turn into a big mess. Thus, being aware of regulatory requirements, focusing on detail in written agreements and drawings, carefully recording what is said during meetings with the client and the construction team, and maintaining complete and well-organized records can help you head off disputes before they happen and protect you when they erupt. Good human relations on the job and a conciliatory attitude toward difficult participants in the process can also reduce the likelihood of claims being asserted.

But sometimes all the conciliation in the world cannot prevent the filing of arbitrations and lawsuits. Sure, you did not decide to become an architect to get into fights; had that been your objective, you would have become a boxer, or a lawyer. Nevertheless, you should approach each new job know-ing that disputes may arise. Deciding beforehand how you want any possible dispute to be handled, whether mediation and then arbitration should be required, whether you would prefer to be in court, what limitations on rem-edies you will insist upon—this kind of preparation can make the dark side of an architect's role at least manageable, if not fun, and can go a long way toward assuring that an ugly dispute does not sidetrack your career.

EIGHT

I MAY HAVE COMMITTED MALPRACTICE:
WHAT IS MY LEGAL EXPOSURE?

For many Americans, the term "law" conjures up two unpleasant images—handcuffs and loss of money. This book does not devote much space to the former. Except in the area of performing professional services without a license (see Chapter 9), which can be a violation of penal law, architecture does not generally subject its practitioners to criminal law risks materially different from those faced by the rest of society. The principle that you should not slug the contractor or strangle the client is legal advice of general application. But when it comes to money, and particularly protecting it from claims in civil proceedings, architects face special, heightened risks, sometimes referred to as "legal exposure."

Legal exposure consists of two components, potential "liability" and potential "damages." To be held "liable" for a legal claim asserted by another person means simply to be found responsible for the circumstances that led to that person's grievance. Having so-called liability, however, does not always mean you have to pay lots of money. In many situations you could be held liable, but for various reasons not have to pay money. It could be because the claimant was not hurt badly enough to warrant compensation. Or it could be that someone else was even more liable or had the duty to make payment. Codefendants are in the former category, insurance companies in the latter.

The term "damages" stands for the money that a dispute resolution tribunal—a court or arbitration panel—orders to be paid based on a person's liability. Damages is a complicated area of the law, but it is important for an architect to be generally familiar with its broad outlines. Much of the following discussion addresses the various kinds of liability and damages, where they come from, and how to try to avoid them.

UNDER WHAT SORTS OF LAWS CAN SOMEONE SUE ME FOR DAMAGES?

The Common Law

The primary source of law governing potential civil liability and the calculation of damages for architects, as for most people, is the "common law"—a kind of legal bedrock of ever-evolving judge-made "case law" dating back to the Middle Ages. The fundamental governing principle of the common law is "stare decisis," which means following the same reasoning used in deciding similar or analogous cases in the past. The common law itself consists of the gradually evolving reasoning expounded by judges in their published decisions (often called "opinions"). Judges' opinions explain how they are following the spirit of precedents in deciding a particular new case, or why changed or different circumstances now require a different result.

Statutes (laws enacted by legislatures) and regulations (rules promulgated by government agencies under authority delegated to them by statutes) may modify, add to, or overrule the common law on a given point. Parties also may to some extent choose by contract to govern their own relationships by different rules. But the common law principle of stare decisis applies even to the way courts interpret statutes and contract provisions; thus, in the legal world, once courts have interpreted a statute or contract provision, it means what the courts have said it means, regardless of what the words of the statute or contract themselves may seem to say.

State supreme courts are the ultimate authority for the common law. Other state courts follow their own prior reasoning and that of higher-level courts in the same state. A federal court, barring some particular reason for doing otherwise in a particular case, applies the common law of the state where it is located, although federal courts have often made creative and influential contributions of their own in doing so. Where there has been no case with similar facts in a state, judges may follow the reasoning of courts from other states rather than try to reinvent the wheel. Nevertheless, differences in the common law evolve from one state to the next regarding who owes what legal duties to whom.

Contract versus Tort

Under the common law, someone can sue you and win damages only if you breach some "duty" you owe to that person and the breach causes some "injury" to that person. The courts recognize and enforce two basic kinds of common law duties in civil lawsuits: contract duties and tort duties. Contract

Aerial view of the Hartford Civic Center's sports arena rooftop, which collapsed under the weight of snow and rain, Jan. 18, 1978 during the early morning hours. No injuries were reported. (AP Photo/Bob Child).

duties arise from promises that people voluntarily or implicitly make to one another, which the courts interpret and enforce subject to general principles of contract law (for example, each party must get something out of the deal, and certain kinds of promises have to be in writing). Tort duties arise from rules that the courts impose on people to enforce particular interests of society in general, such as freedom from the danger of personal injury or property damage. There is a kind of middle ground between tort and contract referred to as "quasi-contract" or "unjust enrichment." For example, you present a contract to a client. The agreement is never signed but both you and your client proceed and follow the unsigned contract terms. A dispute arises and you sue for your fee. You cannot sue on the contract since it was not signed. Yet you performed work for the client, who made some payments in accordance with the proposed contract and benefited from your services. Your claim would be premised on the unsigned agreement and that the owner was unjustly enriched by your services. The damages in this middle ground are often measured much like contract damages.

A tort, or "tortious act," is an act of wrongdoing for which the law requires the wrongdoer, or "tortfeasor," to pay damages to the person injured. A tort duty in turn is a legal duty to refrain from, or take care to avoid, inflicting a particular kind of injury in a particular way on a particular category of person. For example, you have a tort duty to refrain from smashing the windshield of someone else's car deliberately (an intentional tort), as well as a tort duty to take care (a "duty of care") not to collide with someone else's car accidentally (a negligent tort). A negligence action (that is, a lawsuit for negligence) can exist only if the defendant owes the plaintiff a duty of care.

Determining whether a duty of care exists, and who owes a duty of care to whom, is a matter of public policy as judged by the courts in expounding the common law or interpreting statutes and regulations. Courts in different states differ slightly in their assessment of the nature of the duty of care that an architect owes. They differ even more so in their assessment of the "ambit" of that duty, that is, to how wide a circle of persons you owe a duty to avoid causing different kinds of harm.

The Professional Standard of Care

In an oft-quoted decision, the Minnesota Supreme Court explained the nature of a professional's duty of care as follows:

> Architects, doctors, engineers, attorneys, and others deal in some-
> what inexact sciences and are continually called upon to exercise
> their skilled judgment in order to anticipate and provide for random
> factors which are incapable of precise measurement. . . . Because of
> the inescapable possibility of error which inheres in these services,
> the law has traditionally required, not perfect results, but rather the
> exercise of that skill and judgment which can be reasonably expected
> from similarly situated professionals.[40]

This means that, unless it is glaringly obvious, someone who wants to prove in court that you were negligent as an architect normally needs another architect to testify as an expert witness that your work fell short of the normal standard of care, diligence, skill, and judgment that other architects commonly exercise.

Compliance with this standard of care is both a tort duty and an implied term of your contract with your client. Indeed, professional malpractice insurance policies generally do not provide coverage for breaching any higher standard of performance promised by the architect. Thus, you should not to agree to any contract language that implies that you will render a higher level of performance than others in the profession ordinarily render (for example, that your work will conform to the highest standards of the profession).

To fall short of this standard is professional malpractice, a hybrid legal animal that has aspects of both negligence and breach of contract. Accordingly, some states hold that a client can sue a negligent professional either for breach of contract or for negligence, or both. Other states maintain that it depends on the nature of the damage suffered. Some states treat malpractice like a breach of contract for some purposes and like a tort for others. Others refuse to entertain a negligence lawsuit where a contract exists between the parties.

Whether a given act constitutes a breach of contract or a tort is an important distinction. It can affect such things as how many years someone has to bring a claim (the statute of limitations); whether or not contractual limitations on liability apply (such as clauses waiving "consequential" damages and clauses limiting the amount of damages to the architect's fee or insurance coverage); whether arbitration clauses apply; whether the defendant can obtain payment for all or part of the damages from others whose actions may have contributed to the harm done; and what kinds of damages are available (for example, all that foreseeably resulted from a tortious act or, in a breach of contract case, only those the parties reasonably contemplated when they signed the contract).

Generally speaking (and subject in many states to exceptions for professionals), breaching a contract is not in itself a tort, regardless of whether the breach is negligent or intentional. On the other hand, if your breach of contract causes collateral damage to someone else, that may turn it into a tort. The mere fact that you may be engaged in performing a service under a contract does not change or reduce any duty of care you owe others in the vicinity of danger of your activity. You and your client cannot eliminate by a contract between yourselves any preexisting duty of care that either of you owes to third parties.

By entering into a contract with a property owner that requires you to, say, supervise excavation work, you may place yourself in such a relation to another party (say, an owner of adjacent property) that the law imposes on you a tort duty to avoid causing injury to the other party (say, from the undermining of a building on his property).

Other Sources of Civil Liability

In addition to liability for failure to conform to the professional standard of care under common law, architects may face civil liability for violations of statutes or regulations issued pursuant to statutes.

Some statutory or regulatory violations are relevant to whether you complied with the professional standard of care as an architect. Failure to follow a code provision or regulatory requirement, such as a building code provision or zoning regulation, is usually considered professional negligence "per se"—meaning there is no need for lawyers, expert witnesses, and jurors to debate whether you complied with the professional standard of care; the statute or regulation itself establishes the standard. The same may be said of violations of professional rules of conduct.

Other statutes and regulations are relevant to the business aspects, if not necessarily to the strictly architectural aspects, of practice as an architect. These include licensing, corporate, employment, tax, and copyright laws addressed in other chapters in the book.

Other potential sources of common law civil liability on the business side of the practice of architecture are breach of contract and deliberate fraud (as opposed to negligent misrepresentation—a more common claim in the strictly professional context, as discussed below).

Breach of contract and fraud unrelated to the provision of architectural services are beyond the scope of this chapter. In general, however, reneging on your contractual obligations exposes you to liability for damages calculated on the basis of the other party's lost "benefit of the bargain"—for example, the extra cost to the other party of paying someone else to do what you promised to do. In similarly general terms, deliberately lying to someone exposes you to damages based on the extra cost the other party incurs as a result of relying on what you told them. People allege breach of contract and fraud in all sorts of different contexts.

We focus the rest of this chapter on typical liability scenarios involving the performance of architectural services *per se*.

WHAT SORTS OF THINGS CAN I BE SUED FOR?

Personal Injury and Property Damage

All courts recognize and enforce a duty of care to others to avoid causing death, personal injury, or property damage to them. Thus, design professionals owe a duty of care to all persons who may foreseeably suffer these kinds of physical consequences if the designer makes a mistake. Failure to act in accordance with the architect's duty of care may give rise to liability and damages.

If your mistake causes a building or some component of it to collapse or fall onto a passerby or a parked car, or if someone is injured because you omitted some safety feature required by a building code provision, such as a handrail or means of egress or a fire-rated partition required at a particular type of location, you could be held liable to pay damages to the injured person and family members or to the owner of the parked car.

The damages in a personal injury case may include such things as medical expenses, pain and suffering, past loss of income and loss of future earning capacity, impairment of lifestyle, and loss of consortium.

The statute of limitations (the time frame in which lawsuits can be brought) does not begin running for such a claim until the injury or property damage occurs, so design professionals sometimes face such claims many years after finishing work on the project in question, although many states have "statutes of repose" that set an outside limit on how many years after a project someone can sue an architect.

Design professionals sometimes face personal injury claims from workers injured during the building project itself. Such claims are based on the legal "theory" that the defendant negligently supervised the construction. A worker can prove this type of case not only by showing that a supervisor actually did something, or gave some direction, that helped cause the accident, but also by simply showing that the defendant had authority to supervise the worksite (whether or not he or she actually did so) and that some safety precaution that could have prevented the accident was missing.

For this reason, architects' contracts usually disclaim any responsibility for, or control over, construction means and methods and safety precautions. They refer to the architect making "visits" to the site rather than inspections, and specify that this is only for the purpose of determining the progress of the work and compliance of the final product with design intent or the contract documents, and they do not give the architect authority to stop the work (refer to Chapter 1 for more details on architects' agreements).

Courts have interpreted this kind of language favorably to architects in alleged "supervision" cases. Some states even have statutes that expressly shield design professionals from liability for worker injuries provided they do not actually supervise the work or assume contractual responsibility for safety. Thus, you should refrain from saying you are "supervising" the work, and carefully document the limited number and duration and the nonsupervisory purpose of site visits, as well as the limited nature of any communications with anyone at the site. However, you can still be held liable if you actually observe or know about a dangerous condition or practice at a jobsite and fail to warn about it, in the event that condition or practice later causes an injury through acts or inaction of another person.

In one area in particular, you have a primary responsibility to warn of dangerous conditions. That is your responsibility to indicate on the plans any preexisting conditions at the building site that pose a danger to safety, such as buried utility lines or hazardous materials that you learn or should have learned about (for example, because they appear in publicly filed documents). Those dangerous conditions were caused by somebody or something other than you, but you must act affirmatively to disclose them. In one California case, the architect knew of the existence of a buried electrical line but did not ascertain the location or indicate the existence of the line on the plans. Instead, the architect merely wrote a letter to the project owner stating that it existed and that he had not determined the location. A worker later struck the buried line with a jack hammer and died. The appellate court's published opinion in the case calls the architect's failure to indicate the presence of the buried line on the plans "the paradigm case of an architect's negligence."[41]

Getting Blamed for Breaches of Duty by Others

You can find yourself held liable for breaches of duty as to matters that are not primarily your responsibility. For example, one way that you can become exposed to liability for a project worker's personal injury or for property damage caused by others on a construction project is by neglecting insurance-related obligations. Failure to procure insurance that a contract requires you to procure may result in liability for breach of the contract requirement. The damages for that breach equal the amount of the loss that the insurance would have covered. In this way, you could end up being held liable to pay for all the damages caused by someone else's mistake.

You should make certain to procure any insurance coverage your contract with the owner or anyone else requires you to procure (see Chapter 3). Just as important, if charged with responsibility for verifying contractors' and subcontractors' insurance coverage, you should insist on receiving copies of the actual insurance policies and endorsements and checking them for conformity to the contractual requirements. Otherwise you may wind up being held liable for any lapse.

It may later emerge that one of the parties' insurance brokers actually failed to procure the coverage stated in the party's insurance certificate or failed to obtain an additional insured endorsement listed on the certificate. If the broker is not an agent of the insurance carrier, the issuance of such a certificate is not binding on the carrier, and the certificate may be of no value except to support a lawsuit against the broker by the broker's client. Of all the ways to end up paying for someone else's mistake, this one should be scrupulously avoided. Make sure you receive the actual policy and endorsements rather than just the certificate.

Spreading the Blame

With so many participants in the construction process, disputes inevitably arise over who is responsible when something goes wrong or someone gets hurt. The law recognizes a variety of ways to spread the blame so that damages are allocated to more than one person involved. For example, because of the all-too-common insurance procurement situation described above, parties routinely assert claims against each other for failure to procure contractually required insurance in boilerplate fashion when, as often happens in injured worker and property damage cases, everyone involved in the project gets dragged into the lawsuit. The defendants all assert "cross-claims" against each other and "third-party claims" against additional parties whom the original plaintiff may have overlooked. The defending parties use these legal devices to shift the liability onto each others' shoulders.

The most common mechanisms parties use to shift, share, or spread responsibility for damages are by asserting entitlement to "indemnification" or "contribution" from their codefendants, or apportionment of the damages among the defendants based on their respective share of the blame. Attorneys assert these kinds of claims as a matter of routine and in a purely speculative fashion at the outset of a lawsuit, because they have to file pleadings in court staking out their positions early in the case and before all the facts have been sorted out.

Indemnification

The legal concept of "indemnification" or "indemnity" means that another person has responsibility for liability and damages a claimant has attributed to you. The law provides for both contractual and common law indemnity.

You can create contractual indemnity by including language providing for it in your owner/architect contract. Try to include in such contracts provisions that indemnify you for various kinds of liability, such as liability to a worker for any injury caused by the worker's employer. Workers' compensation laws prevent an injured worker from suing his own employer in most cases, but these laws do not prevent the worker from suing other parties involved in the project. Such other parties, however, are generally barred by the same laws from making claims against the injured worker's employer (even if the employer played the main role in causing the injury) *unless* the employer has agreed in its contract to *indemnify the other parties* against such claims. Therefore, you should seek to have the owner agree in your contract to indemnify you for any claim by a third party that does not arise from your negligence. You should also ask the owner to include you as an indemnified party in his agreement with the contractor.

The common law also recognizes a right to indemnification for participants in construction, even in the absence of a contractual provision. But the scope of common law indemnity is much narrower than contractual indemnity. Where, for example, an owner is held liable for some kind of non-action, sometimes referred to as "passive negligence," another participant in the project who was actually negligent in causing the harm or injury is held by the common law to have a duty to indemnify the owner. If, however, the owner is found to have been even slightly at fault (or his or her fault was only slightly active rather than strictly passive), the owner forfeits all right to indemnity under the common law—even if the other party was far more to blame. A contract provision can preempt the common law limitation by permitting indemnification even if the construction participant is slightly at fault.

Contribution

If you do not have the protection of contractual or common law indemnity, you still may be able to obtain "contribution" from the other party. Contribution is the duty of a party to a lawsuit to pay part of the overall damages. In most states the duty to make contribution is created by statute, though interpretation of the statute may vary slightly from state to state. For example, in many (but not all) states, if one party (such as a negligent contractor) causes a worker to fall but another party somehow then exacerbates the injury (for example, you, as a result of a negligent design or specification), contribution by the contractor to the damages you must pay may be limited or even unavailable.

For these reasons, it is worth repeating how important it is to negotiate for a contractual right to be indemnified in anticipation of personal injury to a worker on the project. It is rare that the architect is primarily responsible but not rare at all for the architect to be sued anyway. In some states where such provisions are restricted by statute, you can skirt the issue by requiring the contractors to name you as an additional insured on their own insurance (refer to Chapter 3). Because of the complex and varying interplay among the different states' indemnity and workers' compensation statutes and their case law construing these statutes, the appropriate contractual protection for this issue varies from state to state.

WHAT ARE "ECONOMIC LOSSES"?

Architects may face two broad categories of damages—damages for tangible harm such as personal injury and property damage (discussed above), and damages for "economic loss." The latter category is intangible but it can be huge.

Economic losses fall into two basic categories: costs to correct or repair (or inadequate value), and cost overruns. These kinds of losses can arise both in tort and breach of contract situations depending upon which state's law governs.

Costs to Correct or Repair

Costs to correct or repair are the usual measure of economic loss recoverable by an owner for building defects. Where the cost to correct would be so great compared to any resulting benefit that it would be economically wasteful to correct the defect, courts sometimes instead award to the owner the difference in value between the building as built and the building as it was supposed to be built. Costs to correct or repair may result from:

- *design errors or omissions* (for example, failure to provide adequate flashing details leading to later leaks in the building; or erroneous zoning calculations leading to an order from the building department to demolish part of a completed building which exceeds height restrictions).
- *negligent approval of shop drawings or submittals* (the lead engineer involved in the infamous collapse of the Kansas City Hyatt Regency Hotel skywalks lost his license primarily for that).
- *negligent testing, investigation, surveying, or reporting* (for example, inadequate subsurface investigation leading to damage to buried utilities, or excessive settling of the building after completion, or a

negligent investigation that leads to the need to demolish part of a
structure that encroaches on neighboring property).

• *negligent inspection of a contractors' work* (leading to failure to discover defects that are more costly to correct at some later date).

Cost Overruns

Cost overruns may result from faulty estimation of the time or materials
required to complete a project awarded to a contractor on a cost-of-the-work-
plus-a-fixed-fee basis. In that situation, a design professional who provided
the estimate may be liable to the owner for damages. The courts calculate
cost overruns in various ways. The owner may be entitled to the difference
between the actual cost and the estimate, less cost increases attributable to
any owner changes, and a reasonable margin for error (up to 20 percent is
commonly allowed). If the project involves a commercial property, the owner
may win the difference between the cost and the fair market value of the
completed building.

If the owner seeks lump sum bids from contractors for the project and
the bids exceed the budget under which you were supposed to design the
building, the owner may not have to pay you for your work. The courts, however, usually limit the damages to a reasonable margin of error unless you
guaranteed the budgeted cost.

An owner may also seek to hold you liable for overruns resulting from
your erroneously approving defective work; or approving payment based on
an overestimate of the state of completion; or failing to verify that subcontractors got paid out of previously requisitioned funds; or erroneously authorizing
the premature release of funds due to the contractor for work performed during the course of the project but withheld from each application for payment
(known as "retainage"). Damages are then based on the additional cost of
making the situation right.

Cost overrun damages may also result from delays that create increased
expense for project supervision and field and home office overhead. Delays
may also lead to changes in the sequence of work or other disruptions to the
schedule, resulting in alleged loss of efficiency and productivity, with consequent increase in unit costs over those the contractor relied on in calculating
the bid. Other damages from delays may include overtime premiums and
other expense due to acceleration of work to make up for prior delays, and
extra financing costs. Owners may also claim extra financing expense from
the inability to use the completed project (with consequent loss of profits)

during the period of delayed completion. The usual measure of the owner's damages for this kind of claim is the rental value of the property.

A contractor may also claim that faulty plans or an erroneous report on a key test or survey led to the project's being underbid. Or the contractor may claim that you erroneously rejected shop drawings or submittals, which required him to provide work or components that were more expensive than the owner budgeted for. Or the contractor may claim that you negligently inspected and erroneously rejected completed, conforming work, forcing expensive and unnecessary changes to be made.

The contractor may blame you for the extra costs arising from delays, extended project duration, and schedule disruption in a number of ways. You may be accused of directly causing delay by taking too long to perform various construction administration phase tasks such as shop drawing and submittal review, responding to Requests for Information (RFI), or approving payment. An architect has even been held liable for procrastinating in adjudicating an owner/contractor dispute—an exception to the usual rule that shields architects from liability for their decisions in such matters.

You may also be accused of indirectly causing delay, for example, by inadequate coordination of drawings causing a later need to make costly changes to completed work to accommodate later-installed work, or by other errors requiring subsequent revisions to the plans (a particular danger in fast-track projects).

There is a small industry devoted to preparing claims of cost overruns due to "impacts and inefficiencies" from alleged scheduling delays and disruptions, often creatively argued and presented with tendentious charts, graphs, and statistics. Contractors planning to assert such claims may bombard you with RFIs asking obvious questions and then use the sheer number of RFIs as a supposed measure of the number of errors and omissions in the plans. They also may try to use statistics concerning your turnaround time for the RFIs and other submittals (the numbers or percentages that took given amounts of time for you to respond to) as a supposed measure of your nonresponsiveness.

Such presentations can often be refuted but that usually depends on your having diligent documentation of the progress of the project. As we stated in earlier chapters, diligent record keeping is critical to the defense or prosecution of all manner of construction-related claims, because of the complexity of construction projects and of the things that can go wrong in them; the fallibility of memory; the potential future unavailability of witnesses; the unpredictability of claims; and the need to reconstruct events to determine

the causes of what went wrong. Careful record keeping is particularly important in avoiding and responding to "impacts and inefficiencies" claims. Attorneys defending such cases rely on progress photographs, meeting minutes,
payment requisitions, daily reports, payroll records, time sheets, extra work
orders, bills of lading, e-mails, transmittals, and logs of every description to
reconstruct the history of a project, like historians or archeologists, to show
that the contractor's tale of woe is a tissue of chronological impossibilities,
logical fallacies, and arithmetical smoke and mirrors.

Direct Damages versus Consequential Damages

Claims for economic loss may be categorized as seeking "direct damages,"
such as repair costs, or "consequential damages," such as additional financing
costs resulting from delay. Courts differ in where they draw the line between
direct damages and consequential damages. For example, alleged lost profits
on other projects that the contractor could not pursue because of delays on
the project at issue would be considered consequential damages, whereas a
claim for lost profits on the project itself presents more of a borderline case.

Contract clauses waiving "consequential damages" offer some protection
against claims based on alleged delays, but differences in the interpretation
of this phrase make it important to spell out in such a clause what kinds of
damages the parties consider "consequential." Some owner/contractor agreements also contain clauses that purport to provide that a contractor is not
entitled to any damages for delay. Such clauses only provide partial protection against delay claims, as the courts interpret them strictly and sometimes
refuse to apply them when they consider the delays too expensive.

WHO CAN SUE ME FOR ECONOMIC LOSSES?

Obviously, an owner who has a contract with you has a straightforward basis
for seeking economic loss damages if you breach that contract. But courts in
different states differ on the issue of whether and under what circumstances
a party with whom you did not have any contractual relationship (that is,
with whom you were not "in privity of contract" as it is often phrased by the
courts) can sue you for economic losses.

The issue usually arises in one of two contexts. On the one hand, a contractor or subcontractor may sue you (or assert a cross claim or third-party

claim in a lawsuit brought by someone else), claiming to have suffered cost overruns because of your errors or omissions. On the other hand, someone who purchases a building from the original owner (your client), or some other subsequent purchaser or "remote owner," may sue you for alleged defects in the property. Claims of this nature by buyers of condominium apartment units, or their boards or associations, are especially common. Absent a direct contractual relationship (privity of contract) between the plaintiff and architect, the plaintiff cannot sue for breach of contract. Therefore, the only claim available is a tort claim such as negligence. Tort claims against an architect who is not in privity of contract with the claimant raise special issues with respect to availability of economic damages. The rules on this differ from state to state, as shown below.

Parties Foreseeably Harmed Versus Contract Parties Only

At one end of the spectrum, courts in some states consider foreseeability of harm to others to be the main focus. These courts readily hold parties liable for economic losses suffered by others if the losses were a "foreseeable consequence" of performing contractual duties negligently, regardless of whether the injured party was a party to the contract.

As the South Dakota Supreme Court reasoned in permitting a subcontractor to sue an engineering firm, the engineering firm owed a duty to the subcontractor to reasonably draft and interpret the project's specifications because it was foreseeable that failure to do so could harm the subcontractor who was following these specifications. The court wrote: "We instruct trial courts to use the legal concept of foreseeability to determine whether a duty exists."[42]

In another case influential in such jurisdictions, an architect who misinterpreted certain concrete test reports erroneously authorized the contractor to install preformed concrete structures. When the error came to light, the contractor suffered damages based on the cost to compensate for the defective structures and the resulting delay. The federal district court wrote: "Altogether too much control over the contractor necessarily rests in the hands of the supervising architect for him not to be placed under a duty imposed by law to perform without negligence his functions as they affect the contractor. The power of the architect to stop the work alone is tantamount to a power of economic life or death over the contractor. It is only just that such authority, exercised in such a relationship, carry commensurate legal responsibility."[43] And as the West Virginia Supreme Court reasoned in another construction case, "this resolution properly places the duty of care on the party who is in the best position to guard against the type of negligence herein asserted."[44]

At the other end of the spectrum, courts in some states take the view that the law of negligence provides redress only for the violation of duties involving the safety of persons or property that the courts impose to protect the broad interests of society. Leaving aside fraud (an intentional tort), they refuse to impose any tort duty to prevent even foreseeable economic losses to others in the absence of a contract.

Courts have usually based this refusal to award damages for economic loss in the absence of a contract (the so-called economic loss rule) on the concern that economic repercussions can ripple out far more widely and open-endedly than physical effects. Under this view, imposing a tort duty of care to prevent such harm would subject professionals to the risk of limitless liability to an infinite number of people in indeterminate amounts, and thereby deter much legitimate economic activity, defeat bargained-for expectations and predictability in allocating risks (especially in the construction context), overburden the court system, and cause contract law to "drown in a sea of tort."[45] As the California Supreme Court wrote, foreseeability "like light, travels indefinitely in a vacuum." It "proves too much. . . . Although it may set tolerable limits for most types of physical harm, it provides virtually no limit on liability for non-physical harm."[46]

Based on this kind of reasoning, New York's highest court wrote that "foreseeability of harm does not define duty," and even refused to permit claims for economic losses by owners of businesses in the vicinities of a 48-story construction elevator that collapsed in Times Square and a 39-story building whose façade partially collapsed onto Madison Avenue.[47]

As the Washington State Supreme Court influentially wrote, if tort and contract were allowed to overlap, "the construction industry in particular would suffer, for it is in this industry that we see most clearly the importance of the precise allocation of risk as secured by contract. The fees charged by architects, engineers, contractors, developers, vendors, and so on are founded on their expected liability exposure as bargained and provided for in the contract."[48] In the same spirit, the Nevada Supreme Court wrote, "This legal line between contract and tort liability promotes useful commercial economic activity."[49]

As a practical matter, this narrower economic loss rule recognized in some states does not completely shield the design professional from claims by contractors or subcontractors, because these parties can sue the owner for their losses, and the owner can then turn around and sue the architect for indemnification based on the owner/architect contract. Thus, the claim simply travels along the chain of contracts, where it is, however, subject to whatever limitations and protections the parties have negotiated for themselves.

Negligent Misrepresentations

Other states take an intermediate position and enforce a narrow economic loss rule subject to exceptions. The most commonly recognized exception is for negligent misrepresentation. This exception, as usually phrased, imposes liability on someone who, in the course of business or in any transaction in which he or she has a pecuniary interest, supplies information intending to influence the conduct of others in their business transactions without exercising reasonable care and competence in obtaining and communicating the information, where the information turns out to be false and causes a loss to another person who relies on it.

The exception is often held to apply only where the defendant is in the business of providing information, and provision of the information is the "end and aim" of the transaction, not merely ancillary to the sale of a service or product. A few states (for example, Oregon, California, New York, and Maryland) define this exception even more narrowly and require a "special relationship" (variously defined—under New York's and Maryland's formulation, the "functional equivalent of privity") between the supplier and recipient of the information.

The exception could clearly apply to something like a geotechnical report issued, for example, to describe subsurface soil conditions as a matter of objective fact for the guidance of parties bidding on a contract for foundation work. But courts differ as to whether it applies to errors in plans and specifications. According to one point of view, as stated by the Illinois Supreme Court, "although an architect supplies information, that information is incidental to a tangible product, i.e., a structure, and is usually transformed into the structure itself."[50] Under this view, a contractor cannot sue an architect for negligent misrepresentation on the theory that the plans misled the contractor to believe that he could build the project for a certain cost.

Unreasonably Dangerous Conditions

Certain states also observe an exception to the narrow economic loss rule for situations that, while not involving actual personal injury, are so dangerous that they warrant parties who repair building defects to recover the cost from those responsible for the defects regardless of the lack of any contract. As the Indiana Supreme Court wrote: "If there is a defect in a stairway and the purchaser repairs the defect and suffers an economic loss, should he fail to recover because he did not wait until he or some member of his family fell down the stairs and broke his neck?"[51] The issue posed by this question is moot in cases involving dwellings, since nearly all states have since adopted in one form or another implied warranties that run to subsequent purchasers of dwellings. These warranties permit a homeowner to sue responsible parties for the cost of repairing dangerous defects even though the homeowner never had a contract with those parties.

FOR HOW LONG AFTER A PROJECT CAN I BE SUED?

All states have statutes that impose time limits for bringing lawsuits against architects. Such statutes vary greatly from state to state, not only as to the lengths of time they allow for bringing suit, but also as to such things as the types of claims and parties to which they apply, the exceptions they permit, and the type of event that starts the clock running.

The most common starting date is the date of "substantial completion" of the project—a phrase itself subject to varying interpretations. A statute that imposes an absolute time limit beginning from substantial completion, or from some other date that approximately corresponds to the completion of the architect's services, is known as a statute of repose. Under a statute of limitations, in contrast, the clock may not even begin to run until the occurrence of some other event such as a personal injury, property damage, or the discovery of a defect, which may not happen until long after the project has reached completion.

In some states, the same time limits that apply to direct claims for damages also apply to claims for contribution or indemnification. In other states, the clock does not start running on such indirect claims until the direct claim is paid. Practically speaking, the clock in those states does not really run out for any party on a project until it runs out for everyone who could assert a claim for contribution or indemnification against that party.

Not only do the statutes vary widely, but so do the different courts' interpretations of similar statutory terms and provisions (the meaning of "substantial completion" is only one example). Courts in many states have even held statutes of repose unconstitutional to the extent that they cut off the right to sue for an injury before it has even occurred. Courts in other states have disagreed with this view and have upheld such statutes.

* * *

If nothing else, you should take away the following lessons from the foregoing discussion. First, the law as it relates to claims for civil damages is far from an exact science. It is in many instances a matter of opinion—namely, the judge's or arbitrator's opinion as to the meaning and relevance to your case of various statutes, contract provisions, and higher court opinions; and the opinion of your fellow architects who may testify as expert witnesses in your case regarding what an architect of normal care, diligence, competence, and judgment would have done in your situation. The outcome of your case may also turn on the opinions of witnesses and jurors as to what really happened on the project.

Second, you can reduce—or, for that matter, increase—the likelihood of a bad outcome through certain kinds of contract provisions. You should bargain (or better still, hire an attorney to bargain) for provisions that, at a minimum, limit your exposure to certain kinds or amounts of damages that are outside your control (especially specific kinds of consequential damages, and damages in excess of your insurance coverage or fee); provisions that disclaim responsibility for activities that are outside your control (for example, site safety precautions); and provisions that shift responsibility to others who are in control (for example, the actual employers of workers on the site).

You never know at the outset of a project that it is going to go wrong. Well-drafted contracts incorporate the distilled experience of generations of lawyers as to the kinds of issues that tend to lead to disputes and the kinds of opinions that judges and arbitrators in your state tend to apply to such issues when they wind up in court or arbitration.

Third, you should be absolutely punctilious about all insurance-related obligations and documentation.

Finally, be diligent and systematic about project documentation. Your defense of your conduct on a particular project may someday hinge on your ability to prove that you sent a certain document to a certain party on a certain date; or that someone made a certain statement at a certain project meeting; or that a certain type of work had or had not progressed to a certain stage on a certain floor of the building as of a certain date as shown by a payment requisition you signed or a progress photo you took.

You may have no way of knowing the importance of any of this at the time of the transmittal, meeting, or site visit. The only way to ensure that you have what you need when you need it is to stick to a rigorous routine. Write the transmittal slip, check the meeting minutes, take the photo, note the presence of any buried electrical lines on the drawings, and respond in writing to any complaints. Keep it all well organized so you can turn it all over to your attorneys in good order in case anything ever goes wrong. You just never know.

NINE

HOW DO I BECOME QUALIFIED TO PRACTICE ARCHITECTURE?

You probably already know that you can't simply wake up one morning and decide you want to "practice architecture." You must leap over a number of hurdles before you can call yourself an architect—the largest of which is the need to meet the necessary requirements to get (and keep) a license to practice architecture.

WHAT KIND OF ACTIVITIES REQUIRE A LICENSE?

While you do not have to be a licensed architect to render every type of design service, each state has its own definition of the practice of architecture (meaning the services that you need to be licensed to provide) and you need to be aware of what your state's requirements are. For example, New York defines the practice of architecture as "rendering or offering to render services which require the application of the art, science, and aesthetics of design and construction of buildings, groups of buildings, including their components and appurtenances and the spaces around them wherein the safeguarding of life, health, property, and public welfare is concerned. Such services include, but are not limited to consultation, evaluation, planning, the provision of preliminary studies, designs, construction documents, construction management, and the administration of construction contracts."[52] Simply put, this means that if you want to provide any of the listed services in the State of New York, you need to be licensed by that state.

California defines the practice of architecture as "offering or performing, or being in responsible control of, professional services which require the skills of an architect in the planning of sites, and the design, in whole or in part, of buildings, or groups of buildings and structures" and goes on to say that an architect's " professional services may include any or all of the following: (1) Investigation, evaluation, consultation, and advice. (2) Planning, schematic and preliminary studies, designs, working drawings, and specifications. (3) Coordination of the work of technical and special consultants. (4) Compliance with generally applicable codes and regulations, and assistance in the governmental review process. (5) Technical assistance in the preparation of bid documents and agreements between clients and contractors. (6) Contract administration. (7) Construction observation."[53]

According to Florida, "'Architecture' means the rendering or offering to render services in connection with the design and construction of a structure or group of structures which have as their principal purpose human habitation or use, and the utilization of space within and surrounding such structures. These services include planning, providing preliminary study designs, drawings and specifications, job-site inspection, and administration of construction contracts."[54]

Like New York, California, and Florida, many states provide that simply offering to render architectural services constitutes the "practice of architecture." If you submit a service proposal for a project in a state where you are not licensed (and where the project in question isn't otherwise exempt from licensing requirements, as discussed below), you could be "offering to render architectural services" and practicing architecture in that state. As explained further below, this could subject you to severe penalties. In addition, if you are unlicensed in certain states (such as Florida or Texas), your contracts for architectural services may be found to be invalid as a matter of law.

Many states exempt some activities that are architectural in nature from the definition of the "practice of architecture." For example, in New York you do not have to be a licensed architect to prepare shop drawings or to supervise construction. Nor do you need to be licensed to work as the employee of a licensed architect, as long as any work you do is under the supervision of the licensed architect. In New York, an out-of-state architect may solicit business in New York, as long as the architect is properly licensed in his or her home state or country and doesn't actually represent him or herself to the potential client as being licensed in, or actually perform architectural services in, New York. In Florida, you don't need to be licensed to design a one-family or two-family residence, costing less than $25,000—as long as it is for your own personal use or occupancy, and you do not offer it for sale within one year of completion of construction. In California, you do not need a license to prepare plans or drawings for single-family dwellings of wood frame construction that are not more than a basement and two stories in height.

WHY ARE ARCHITECTS REQUIRED TO BE LICENSED?

Architects must be licensed for various reasons, not for any single overriding rationale. In general, states impose licensing requirements to

- *protect the public.* Obviously the single most important feature of a building is that it be safe for people to use. One way to make sure that buildings are built safely is to require the people who are allowed to design them to be competent professionals who have gone through the necessary training process, and whom the state (or other relevant authority) determines to be qualified. In addition, since who is licensed to practice architecture is a matter of public record, members of the public can verify whether an architect who claims to be licensed actually is licensed. The licensing process thereby protects the public from hiring people who fraudulently claim to be licensed.
- *ensure accountability.* Through the licensing process, the licensing authority not only determines who can be a licensed architect, but it also keeps track of such architects. A licensing authority is in the best position to keep an up-to-date record of each architect and his or her whereabouts, so that if a design is faulty, the architect can be found and held accountable.
- *protect local professionals.* Architects cannot obtain a national license; like lawyers, architects are licensed on a state-by-state basis. Each state has different zoning and building regulations, and it makes sense for an architect who practices in a particular state to be familiar with the codes and procedures of that state. In addition, each state responds to parochial pressures to protect its local professionals against competition. By having— and imposing—its own licensing requirements, a state can keep outsiders from providing architectural services that could have been provided by local architects.

- *generate revenue.* Even though it may be the least important reason for a licensing requirement, it is a simple fact that state governments charge fees for the licensing process. Most licensing authorities administer exams as part of the licensing process, and aspiring architects must pay a fee to take these exams. Authorities also impose fees for filing applications and license renewals. These fees help to maintain the licensing authority and may raise revenue for the state's government.

WHO DECIDES WHO GETS LICENSED?

The licensing authority in each state is usually under the control of a state agency. Often referred to as the "Board of Architecture" of a particular state, different state boards use slightly different names, such as the California Architects Board, the Georgia Professional Licensing Board, the Idaho Bureau of Occupational License, and Louisiana Board of Technical Professions. Some states, such as Florida and Virginia, have combined boards that regulate architects along with other professions (such as landscape architects, engineers, and/or interior designers). In Florida, the board is called the Board of Architecture and Interior Design; in Virginia, the board is called the Virginia Board for Architects, Professional Engineers, Land Surveyors, Certified Interior Designers, and Landscape Architects.

How a board of architecture is formed and run is a matter of state law. Each state also determines who can serve on these boards, and the membership of the boards can differ greatly from state to state, although many states consistently require that a certain number of licensed architects serve on the board.

The state boards are pretty consistent when it comes to the tasks they perform: they all administer licensing exams, review applications and renewals, maintain a public record of licensed professionals, receive complaints from the public, and discipline architects where necessary. The boards are responsible for preparing the necessary examinations, administering them, determining what constitutes a "passing grade," and assisting the relevant state agency in licensing matters such as applications and license renewals. Some states, however, simply adopt the Architect Registration Examination (ARE), originally developed by the National Council of Architecture Boards (NCARB). Some states use both the ARE and their own tests. Another important function of the state board is to receive complaints from consumers, investigate the complaints, and, where the complaints are valid, conduct disciplinary proceedings. If the state requires architectural firms to register (which is discussed in Chapter 5), the board is in charge of reviewing and issuing registration for firms and other architectural entities. Of course, the board is responsible for administration of those firms' license renewals as well.

WHAT ARE THE REQUIREMENTS TO BECOME LICENSED?

Before granting you a license, most states require you to (1) achieve a certain level of education and obtain a certain level of experience, (2) pass certain written examinations, and (3) submit a written application with the requisite fee. The educational requirements, like everything else, may differ from state to state. Some states, such as Florida, do not accept a four-year bachelor's of science in architecture as sufficient, and require instead an advanced degree or a five-year bachelor's of architecture degree. In any event, the school from which you obtain your degree usually must be accredited by the National Architecture Accreditation Board (NAAB). Some state boards (such as those of Florida, Michigan, and New Jersey) may approve a school even if it is not accredited by the NAAB. Others (such as Maine, Maryland, New Hampshire, and New York) do not require a degree from an NAAB-accredited school.

After obtaining the required degree, the usual next step is to complete an architectural internship to satisfy the experience requirements necessary to become a registered architect. The length of the internship depends on your architectural degree; the more advanced the degree, the shorter the internship required. For example, in Florida, the usual internship requirement is for a period of three years if the applicant has a bachelor's of architecture; this is reduced to two years if the applicant has a master's of architecture degree.

To get licensed as an architect in New York, you must be at least twenty-one years old, be of "good moral character," comply with New York's education and experience requirements, and pass the licensing examination. In California, you have the specific requirement of not having committed certain crimes or acts that are substantially related to the qualifications, functions, or duties of an architect; this includes those crimes that if committed by an architect would constitute grounds for suspension or revocation of his or her license (including "any act involving dishonesty, fraud or deceit with the intent to substantially benefit himself or herself or another, or substantially injure another").[55]

Once you meet all the licensing requirements, you can submit your application to the state board with the required application fee. After the state board processes your application and verifies that you meet the requirements, you are issued a license to practice architecture in that state.

DO I HAVE TO BE LICENSED IN EVERY STATE WHERE I PROVIDE ARCHITECTURAL SERVICES?

While each state has its own licensing requirements, registered architects enjoy some level of reciprocity. This means that an architect who is registered in one jurisdiction can apply for a license in another by submitting documentation that he or she meets the second jurisdiction's registration requirements. Reciprocity is facilitated by NCARB, a nonprofit corporation consisting of the architectural registration boards of the 50 states plus the District of Columbia, Guam, Puerto Rico, and the U.S. Virgin Islands. NCARB facilitates the process by issuing a certificate to support an architect's application for registration in other states or Canada. To obtain an NCARB certificate, you must meet the following standard requirements:

1. Earn a professional degree from a program accredited by NAAB or the Canadian Architectural Certification Board (CACB). If you are a U.S. licensed architect who does not have such a degree, you may be able to meet this requirement through another method: NCARB's Broadly Experienced Architect Program (BEA). This offers architects the opportunity to show that they have gained the requisite knowledge through their work experience. To be eligible for the BEA program, an architect must have a current registration from an NCARB member board and must have between six and ten years' experience as a registered architect (depending on educational background). To obtain an NCARB certificate through the BEA program, an architect must (a) have established an NCARB record (by setting up an account on NCARB's website and supplying NCARB with the necessary documents), (b) have

his or her education evaluated through the Education Evaluation Services for Architects (EESA), (c) prepare and submit an education file that demonstrates that he or she has sufficient experience to make up for any education deficiencies, and (d) complete an interview with the NCARB's Broadly Experienced Architect Committee. If you were educated in a foreign country, you must have your foreign education evaluated by NAAB through its EESA.

2. Complete the Intern Development Program (IDP). In addition to certifying architects, NCARB also provides an internship program, the IDP, that enables applicants to meet the experience requirement that most state boards have in place. The IDP is a comprehensive training program created to ensure that interns in the architecture profession gain the knowledge and skills required for the independent practice of architecture. Completion of the IDP is accepted by all U.S. jurisdictions in satisfaction of their experience requirements.

3. Pass all divisions of the Architect Registration Examination (which is administered by NCARB's test consultant Prometric).

4. Have a valid license to practice from one of the NCARB member registration boards. If you are a foreign architect who does not have such a license, you may be able to satisfy this requirement through NCARB's Broadly Experienced Foreign Architect Program (BEFA). To be eligible for the BEFA program, the foreign architect must (a) have graduated with a professional degree from an accredited/validated/officially recognized architecture program, (b) be credentialed in a foreign country, and (c) have completed at least seven years of comprehensive practice as an architect exercising responsible control in his or her country. To earn an NCARB certificate through the BEFA program, an architect must have an NCARB record and submit a BEFA verification form to the NCARB Record Directorate, prepare an experience dossier that demonstrates the architect's ability to practice independently (to replace the examination requirement), and complete an interview with NCARB's Broadly Experienced Architect Committee.

Although NCARB certification alone does not qualify you to practice architecture in a particular jurisdiction, it does certify that you have met the highest professional standards set by the registration boards, and should simplify the reciprocal registration process in the 54 NCARB jurisdictions. A word of warning, however: NCARB certification for foreign architects is not yet accepted by all NCARB's jurisdictions. In those jurisdictions (Florida and Washington, for example), foreign architects have to meet the requirements of the individual jurisdiction.

DOES MY FIRM NEED TO BE LICENSED?

If you wish to set up a firm or entity such as a corporation to practice architecture, you need to comply with any requirements of the state in which you wish to form the firm. In New York, for example, only certain entities may practice architecture, and such entities need to obtain a certificate of authority from the New York State Education Department. Likewise, if your firm wishes to work on a project in another state, it must comply with that state's requirements for out-of-state firms. See the discussion in Chapter 5.

WHAT DO I NEED TO DO TO KEEP MY ARCHITECTURE LICENSE?

All states require that licenses be renewed periodically. Some states require yearly renewal while others require biennial renewal. You must usually pay a fee for renewal. In addition, most states require architects to keep their knowledge level current by taking a certain number of hours of certified continuing professional education courses. Some states, such as North Dakota, Oklahoma, Arizona, Connecticut, Maine, Michigan, Montana, North Carolina, and Pennsylvania, do not have this requirement.

WHAT HAPPENS IF I AM NOT LICENSED?

Practicing architecture without being properly licensed is a violation of law *in all states*. In some states (such as Arizona, California, and Florida) doing so can even trigger criminal liability. Certain states provide that even representing to the public that you are a licensed architect if you do not have a license is a violation of law. In New York it is a felony to practice or offer to practice a profession without authorization, or to knowingly aid and abet three or more unlicensed individuals to practice a profession. In Florida, you cannot use the title "architect," "registered architect," or any words to that effect if you do not yet have a valid license; if you are found guilty of doing so, you can be fined up to $1,000. In Texas, if the architecture work requires a licensed architect's service, performing such work without a license is a misdemeanor punishable by a fine. In California, it is a misdemeanor for an unlicensed person to practice architecture, to use the term "registered building designer" or a similar term, to use the stamp of a licensed architect, or to advertise as an architect. Anyone found guilty of these acts can be punished by up to one year in jail and/or subjected to a fine between $100 and $1,000. On a more everyday financial note: If you are not licensed, you may also not be able to sue your client in court for payment of fees.

SO IF I HAVE A LICENSE AND KEEP IT, IS THAT ALL I NEED TO DO?

No. You need to comply with any ethical rules that your state has for architects. If you violate such rules, you may be sanctioned. The rules in New York State, for example, prohibit the following:

- Practicing fraudulently, with gross negligence or incompetence on one occasion, or negligently or incompetently on more than one occasion.
- Practicing while impaired by drugs or alcohol, or because of physical or mental disability.
- Being convicted of a crime under New York state or federal law, or the law of another jurisdiction.
- Being disciplined for professional misconduct by an authorized professional disciplinary agency of another state.
- Refusing to provide professional service to someone because of the person's race, creed, color, or national origin.
- Practicing with a suspended license or failing to notify the department of changes of name or mailing address or, if a professional service corporation, violating applicable provisions of the Business Corporation Law.
- Permitting, aiding, or abetting an unlicensed individual to perform activities that require a license.

In New York, the Education Department conducts a preliminary investigation of ethics violations. If you're found to have committed an ethical violation, you are reported to the attorney general with a request for criminal prosecution.[56] Other states (Florida, for example) may likewise subject you to criminal or financial penalties, as well as revoke your license if you are found guilty of violating their ethical guidelines.

The American Institute of Architects has its own Code of Ethics and Professional Conduct for members; however, you need not be a member to file a complaint. This code is essentially divided into three types of statements: (1) canons, which describe basic principles of conduct; (2) ethical standards, which attempt to set specific goals of performance and behavior that AIA members are encouraged to attain; and (3) mandatory rules of conduct.

Some examples of ethical standards are as follows:

- Members should uphold human rights in all their professional endeavors.[57]
- Members should render public-interest professional services, including pro bono services, and encourage their employees to render such services. Pro bono services are those rendered without expecting compensation, including those rendered for indigent persons, after disasters, or in other emergencies.[58]
- Members should use sustainable practices within their firms and professional organizations, and they should encourage their clients to do the same.[59]

The mandatory rules of conduct include, but are not limited to, the following requirements:

- Members shall not discriminate in their professional activities on the basis of race, religion, gender, national origin, age, disability, or sexual orientation.[60]
- Members shall recognize and respect the professional contributions of their employees, employers, professional colleagues, and business associates.[61]
- Members leaving a firm shall not, without the permission of their employer or partner, take designs, drawings, data, reports, notes, or other materials relating to the firm's work, whether or not performed by the Member.[62]

- A member shall not unreasonably withhold permission from a departing employee or partner to take copies of designs, drawings, data, reports, notes, or other materials relating to work performed by the employee or partner that are not confidential.[63]

The AIA's National Ethics Council (NEC) enforces the Code of Ethics, and requires parties to avoid public disclosure and discussion of the complaint, the parties involved, and the issues under consideration.[64] If the party filing the complaint fails to comply with this confidentiality requirement, the NEC may choose to dismiss the complaint as a penalty; if the architect against whom the complaint is made doesn't comply, the NEC may subject him or her to discipline.

The NEC may impose one of four penalties for code violation: (1) admonition, when the NEC issues a determination that the code has been violated, but only the parties involved are aware of this decision; (2) censure, when the NEC publicizes the violation (such decisions may be published on the AIA website); (3) suspension of membership for a specific period of time; and (4) termination of membership.

If you are a member of the AIA, obtain and review the Code of Ethics and Professional Conduct to make sure that you are complying with these ethical obligations.

* * *

The most important reason for requiring that architects be licensed is to make sure, in the interest of public safety, that only competent, qualified professionals are permitted to design buildings. Architect's licenses are issued and regulated by the states' licensing authorities, which administer licensing exams, review applications and renewals, maintain a public record of licensed professionals, receive complaints and discipline architects. You must be licensed in order to "practice architecture" in any state where you wish to design buildings unless you are employed and supervised by a licensed architect. In order to obtain an architect's license, you must achieve a certain level of education, obtain a certain level of experience and pass the state licensing exam. If you are not properly licensed, you can be fined or subject to criminal liability. If you are licensed in one state and want to practice architecture in another, you must get licensed in that state as well. NCARB can facilitate this process by issuing a certificate, accepted by most states, after you have met its requirements. Once you're licensed, you must maintain your license in good standing by observing the rules and regulations in each state where you are licensed. Failure to comply can lead to your license being revoked and your being subject to criminal or financial penalties.

Some design professionals who are qualified to practice as architects regard the licensing process as a bore and a formality that they're too busy to be bothered with. Don't be one of them.

TEN

HOW DO I CHOOSE AN ATTORNEY TO HELP ME?

Representing design professionals is a highly specialized area of the law. The number of attorneys concentrating in this area is relatively small, so you need to be careful when looking for legal help. Corporate attorneys who advise businesses day in and day out may not have a clue about what the AIA contracts say or even what the AIA is. They may have no knowledge of the special requirements various states have for ownership of an architecture firm. Attorneys who are commercial litigators are likely to have little understanding about how to read drawings or specifications or about the legal nuances of a construction dispute.

The first step in locating a competent attorney is finding the pool of lawyers who claim to be qualified. Since the pool is limited, it is always a good idea to ask your professional colleagues for a reference when you need an attorney. Local AIA chapters may also be a resource. Bar associations (American, state, or city) can be resources as well. Your professional liability insurance broker should also know of firms in the field and make suggestions. Be sure to speak to the attorney yourself, ask any pertinent questions, and get references if you feel you need them.

When engaging an attorney, you should start by focusing on what you want him or her to do. If you are in need of help with an agreement, you want an attorney well versed not only in the AIA agreements, but also with the issues that owners and architects frequently argue about. Keep in mind that an attorney who is very familiar with construction could also be one who primarily represents owners or contractors. Finding an attorney who has represented both sides in a negotiation of a construction agreement may prove beneficial since that attorney brings a useful and important perspective to any negotiation.

When engaging an attorney specifically for dispute resolution, verify that she has demonstrable experience with construction issues. Although expert consultants are often brought into a complex construction dispute, having an attorney who can read plans, understand at least some aspects of the building code, and knows what a door jamb is (without looking it up in a construction dictionary) will serve you well. Construction disputes often do not involve a lot of issues requiring lawyers to research case law to support their positions. Rather, much of what happens in a construction dispute involves poring over meeting minutes, e-mails, letters, and plans to reconstruct what happened on a project site perhaps years ago. Having an attorney who is familiar with the paperwork that construction projects generate is a big plus. You need someone who knows enough to ask you the right questions so you can provide the information needed for your defense or prosecution of a claim. Here are some questions you should ask a potential attorney:

- Tell me about your experience representing architects, both as plaintiffs and defendants.
- Have you ever seen a contract of the kind involved here? If so, when and in what kind of matter?
- Have you worked with insurance companies that provide professional liability insurance? (If your carrier is going to provide you a defense).
- Are you able to read and understand architects' plans and specifications?
- What are some of the special issues you have experience with that are unique to the representation of architects?

An attorney who is used to being in the courtroom and cross-examining witnesses in an adversarial environment may not be the best person to represent you in a mediation, where there is no cross-examination and where an aggressive courtroom style definitely is not going to help you. Here are some questions to ask potential counsel who would handle a mediation:

- Have you represented architects in mediation before?
- Describe the mediation process and how it might work in our case.

If you are engaging an attorney to advise you on issues of employment law and to help you draft an employment handbook for your office, the best attorney for the job may well be the same attorney who can negotiate an AIA agreement, but maybe not. You just need to ask the right questions to see if the lawyer you are working with can help you in this area as well. Here are some questions to ask an attorney who would help you on employment matters:

- Have you advised architects on employment matters and, if so, in what areas?
- Have you ever handled discrimination claims for or against an architecture firm?
- What government agencies have you dealt with/appeared before on employment matters?

* * *

What it all comes down to at the end is finding an attorney who is best suited for the assignment at hand. The same attorney who set you up in business may not be the best person to represent you in a negotiation of an agreement with an owner for the design of a new house. The attorney who helps you negotiate the agreement for the new house may not be the best person to advise you when you are in a dispute with the owner over delays on the project.

Having professional liability insurance helps you sleep well at night knowing there is coverage if you make a mistake. Having an attorney or attorneys you can consult on a regular basis with questions about your practice gives you even more peace of mind.

NOTES

1. www.whitehouse.gov/omb/intellectualproperty/ipec, "About the Office of the U.S. Intellectual Property Enforcement Coordinator (IPEC)."
2. U.S. Const., art. I, § 8.
3. 17 U.S.C. § 101.
4. *Id.*
5. Paul Goldstein, Copyright, § 2.15.1, at 2:183 (1999).
6. 2010 WL 5175171 (W.D. La. Dec. 7, 2010).
7. *Id.* at *4.
8. 17 U.S.C. § 101.
9. 17 U. S. C. § 120 (a).
10. 17 U. S. C. § 120 (b).
11. 201 F.3d 50 (2d Cir. 1999).
12. *Id.* at 54.
13. *Id.* at 55.
14. *Id.* at 56 (emphasis added).
15. *Id.*
16. 303 F.3d 460 (2d Cir. 2002).
17. 303 F.3d at 468-469.
18. 382 F. Supp. 2d 602 (S.D.N.Y. 2005).
19. *Id.* at 611.
20. *Id.* at 612.
21. *Id.* at 614.
22. *Id.* at 615.
23. *Kootenia Homes, Inc. v. Reliable Homes, Inc.*, 69 U.S.P.Q.2d 1675, 1680 (D.Minn. 2002).
24. *Arthur Rutenberg Corp. v. Parrino*, 664 F. Supp. 479, 481 (M.D. Fl. 1987).
25. *Nelson-Salabas, Inc. v. Morningside Holdings*, 2001 SL 419002 (D. Md. 2001).
26. *Kootenia Homes Inc. v. Reliable Homes, Inc.*, 69 U.S.P.Q.2d 1675, 1680 (D. Minn. 2002). The court went on to state that "Any overall general similarities between the Hoeffel Home and the Purtell Home extend only to unprotectable concepts or ideas." *Id.*
27. *Oravec v. Sunny Isles Luxury Ventures, L.C.*, 527 F.3d 1218, 1226-27 (11th Cir. 2008).
28. *Kootenia Homes, Inc. v. Reliable Homes, Inc.*, supra, 69 U.S.P.Q.2d at 1680.
29. *John Alden Homes, Inc. v. Kangas*, 142 F. Supp. 2d 1338, 1345 (M.D. Fl. 2001).
30. *LaJoie v. Pavcon, Inc.*, 146 F. Supp. 2d 1240, 1248 (M.D. Fla. 2000).
31. *Attia v. Society of New York Hosp.*, 47 U.S.P.Q.2d 1154, 1156 (S.D.N.Y. 1998), *aff'd*, 201 F.3d 50 (2d Cir. 1999), *cert. denied*, 531 U.S. 843 (2000).
32. *Sturdza v. United Arab Emirates*, 281 F.3d 1287, 1298 (D.C. Cir. 2002).
33. 848 F. Supp. 682, 686 (E.D. La. 1994).

34. 17 U.S.C. 504(c)(1).

35. 858 F.2d 247 (6th Cir. 1988).

36. "The Contractors' Guide to BIM," edition 1, p. 3.

37. www.gsa.gov/portal/content/105075.

38. 35 U.S.C. § 284.

39. This text is based upon wording in an XL Specialty Insurance Company policy and is similar to text found in other professional liability policies.

40. *City of Mounds View v. Walijarvi*, 263 N.W.2d 420, 424 (Minn. 1978).

41. *Mallow v. Tucker, Sadler & Bennett, Architects & Engineers, Inc.*, 245 Cal. App. 2d 700, 703, 54 Cal. Rptr. 174, 176 (Cal. App. 4th Dist. 1966).

42. *Mid-Western Electric, Inc. v. DeWild Grant Reckert & Associates Co.*, 500 N.W.2d 250, 254 (S. Dak. 1993).

43. *U.S. ex rel. Los Angeles Testing Laboratory v. Rogers & Rogers*, 161 F. Supp. 132, 136 (S.D. Cal. 1958).

44. *Eastern Steel Constructors, Inc. v. City of Salem*, 209 W. Va. 392, 401, 549 S.E.2d 266, 275 (W. Va. 2001).

45. *East River S.S. Corp. v. Transamerica Delaval, Inc.*, 476 U.S. 858, 866, 106 S. Ct. 2295, 2299, 90 L. Ed. 2d 865 (1986).

46. *Bily v. Arthur Young & Co.*, 3 Cal. 4th 370, 398, 11 Cal. Rptr. 2d 51, 68, 834 P.2d 745, 762 (1992).

47. *532 Madison Ave. Gourmet Foods, Inc. v. Finlandia Center, Inc.*, 96 N.Y.2d 280, 289, 727 N.Y.S.2d 49, 53, 750 N.E.2d 1097, 1101 (2001).

48. *Berschauer/Phillips Constr. Co. v. Seattle Sch. Dist. No. 1*, 124 Wash. 2d 816, 826–827, 881 P.2d 986, 992 (1994).

49. *Terracon Consultants Western, Inc. v. Mandalay Resort Group*, 206 P.3d 81, 89 (Nev. 2009).

50. *Fireman's Fund Ins. Co. v. SEC Donohue, Inc.*, 176 Ill. 2d 160, 168, 233 Ill. Dec. 424, 428, 679 N.E.2d 1197, 1201 (1997).

51. *Barnes v. Mac Brown and Company*, 264 Ind. 227, 230, 342 N.E.2d 619 (1976).

52. N.Y. Educ. Law § 7301.

53. California Business and Professions Code § 5500.1.

54. Florida Statutes § 481.203.

55. California Business and Professional Code § 480(a).

56. N.Y. Educ. Law § 6514(1).

57. AIA 2007 Code of Ethics & Professional Conduct, E.S. 1.4

58. *Id.*, E.S. 2.2

59. *Id.*, E.S. 6.3

60. *Id.*, Rule. 1.401.

61. *Id.*, Rule 5.301.

62. *Id.*, Rule 5.302.

63. *Id.*, Rule 5.303.

64. AIA National Ethics Council, *Rules of Procedure* (rev. January 2011) §§ 3.5 and 4.5.

INDEX

Page numbers in italic refer to illustrations.

additional services, 21–23, 35

administrative remedies, 165–66

alternative dispute resolution, 166. *see also* arbitration; mediation

American Arbitration Association, 162, 167

American Institute of Architects code of ethics, 208–9

American Institute of Architects forms of agreement
  advantages of, 15
  client perceptions of, 15
  on digital data licensing, 74, 75
  review and modification of, 15–16
  trends, 13
  see also Standard Form of Agreement Between Owner and Architect

Americans with Disabilities Act, 39

arbitration, 40, 158, 166–70

Architect Registration Examination, 202

Architectural Works Copyright Protection Act, 57–58

asset purchase agreement, 124–25

Associated General Contractors of America, 76

Attia, Eli. *see Eli Attia v. Society of New York Hospital*

attorney, selecting, 211–13

automobile, business use of, 92

B101 Agreement. *see* Standard Form of Agreement Between Owner and Architect

basic services, 16, 18–21

Berne Convention for the Protection of Literary and Artistic Works, 57, 73

board of directors, 106, 107–8

boards of architecture, state, 122–23

Brunelleschi, Filippo, *80,* 81

Building Information Modeling software, 76–77

business structure
  advantages, 105, 125
  corporation, 106–9

firms offering multiple design services, 120
  forms of, 90
  insurance coverage, 90
  legal liability and, 105, 106–7
  licensing requirements, 206
  limited liability company, 109–10
  officers and directors, 106, 107–8
  partnerships, 110–11
  permission to work in other states based on, 121–22
  sole proprietorship, 105–6
  see also owners' agreement

capital account valuation, 115–16

C106 Digital Data Licensing Agreement, 74, 75

Certificate for Payment, 33–35

change orders, 22

Chartered Institute of Arbitrators, 162

Childs, David. *see Shine v. Childs*

Civil Rights Act, 129

client
  agreement with contractor, 51–53
  confidentiality issues, 72–73
  identifying decision making authority, 23
  indemnification, 37–38
  ownership and use of design, 25–26
  see also copyright
  responsibilities, 23
  termination rights, 44–45

codes and ordinances, 22

common law, 180, 188

computer professionals, 139

condominium work, 91, 193

confidentiality
  mediation proceedings, 163
  owners' agreement provisions, 118–19
  promotional use of client's or architect's name, 72, 73

ConsensusDOCS, 15

consequential damages, 40–41, 192

Consolidated Omnibus Budget Reconciliation Act, 148–49

construction administration

contractor payment, 33–35
contract provisions, 28–29
determination of substantial
    completion, 35
owner–contractor agreement, 51–53
punch list documentation, 35–37
rejecting or stopping work, 30–31
see also construction disputes;
    contractors; cost of work
construction disputes
    attorney selection, 211–12
    documentation of claims, 155–57,
        197–98
    indications for legal counsel, 154–55
    response to claims, 156
    risk of, 151–53, 177–78, 179, 197
    shifting of liability in, 187
    statute of limitations, 157
    see also dispute resolution;
        malpractice suits
construction worker injury, 185–86
consultants
    contractual agreement on use of,
        45–46
    coordination of services, 46
    insurance issues, 46, 94
    written agreements with, 45–46
contractors
    addressing faulty work, 30–31
    contractual obligations for payment
        to, 33–35
    insurance coverage, 93–94
    owners agreement with, 51–53
    punch list completion, 35–37
    scope of architect's services, 15–16, 22
contracts
    arbitration clause, 167
    building information modeling
        issues, 76–77
    client indemnification in, 37–38
    for design architects, 50
    documentation provisions, 43–44
    economic loss claims in absence of,
        192–93, 194–95
    guarantee of work product
        provisions, 38–39
    indemnification provisions, 187–89
    individual differences in, 53–54
    insurance requirements, 43, 95

legal protections of, 197
limitations on damages, 40–41
malpractice claims based on violation
    of, 180–81, 183, 184
owner–contractor, 51–53
payment terms, 97, 98–99, 100, 104
trends, 13
on use of clients or architects names,
    72, 73
on use of images of building, 71–73
for work in foreign countries, 47–49
see also Standard Form of Agreement
    Between Owner and Architect;
    written agreements
copyright
    alterations to built works and, 59
    definition, 56
    duration, 63
    evaluation of infringement claims,
        63–70
    notice requirements, 63
    ownership, 59–62
    protection for derivative works,
        58–59
    protection for works of architects,
        56–58
    registration, 62
    remedies for infringement, 70–71
    software, 75–76
    use of images of building, 71–73
corporation, 106–9
cost of work
    basic contract provisions, 23–24
    estimates, 26–27
    overruns, 24, 190–92
    payment as percentage of, 98–99
    redesign to meet budget, 27
cost-plus agreements, 33
defaults, 42
delays
    compensation for, 22–23
    contract provisions, 22–23, 27–28
    economic loss claims arising from,
        190–91
    not caused by architect, 28
    work stoppage based on faulty work,
        30–31
depositions, 169–70
design architect, contracts for, 50

design patent, 80–81
design professional service corporation,
    106
discrimination in workplace
    complaint investigation, 137
    Equal Pay Act, 140
    hiring process protections, 129–31
    prevention, 136–37
dispute resolution
    administrative remedies, 165–66
    arbitration, 40, 158, 166–70
    contractual provisions, 40
    documentation, 161
    employment agreement, 134
    in foreign countries, 48
    informal negotiations, 158–61
    mechanisms of resolution, 157–58,
      161–62
    by mediation, 40, 158, 162–66
    monetary negotiations, 159
    nonmonetary claims, 159–61
    owners' agreement on, 120
    see also litigation
documentation
    concerns of design architects, 50
    of construction dispute claims, 155–
      57, 161
    contractual provisions, 43–44
    electronic transfer, 43–44, 73–76
    employee performance evaluations,
      136, 143, 144–45
    good practice, 157
    insurance policy, 88
    for litigation, 173–74, 191–92, 197–98
    new employee paperwork, 135
    for patent protection, 81
    site visit minutes, 29–30
due process, 171
duty of care, 181–83, 193–94
economic loss
    in absence of contract, 192–93,
      194–95
    categories of, 189
    consequential damages, 192
    cost to correct or repair, 189–90
    direct damages, 192
    due to cost overruns, 190–92
    foreseeability of harm in liability for,
      193–94

    from negligent misrepresentations, 195
    in repair of dangerous conditions,
      195–96
    source of claims for, 192–93
E201 Digital Data Protocol Exhibit, 75
electronic document transfer, 43–44,
    73–76
Eli Attia v. Society of New York Hospital,
    64–66, 71
e-mail claims, 155
Employee Retirement Income Security
    Act, 133
employees
    advantages of employment contract,
      131–34
    at-will employment, 131
    benefits, 133
    compensation arrangements, 132–33
    discrimination laws, 129–31
    dispute resolution, 134
    employment practices insurance, 93
    handbooks, 131, 146
    independent contractors versus,
      127–29
    leaves of absence, 140–42
    noncompete and nonsolicitation
      provisions, 119, 133–34
    ownership of work created by, 134
    performance evaluations, 136, 142–
      43, 144–45
    required paperwork, 135
    restrictive covenants, 133–34
    stated duration of employment,
      131–32
    termination procedures and
      restrictions, 132, 146–50
    wage and hour regulations, 138–40
    whistleblower protection, 137–38
    workplace injuries, 140
engineering services, 15, 18–19
environmentally responsible design,
    20–21
Equal Employment Opportunity
    Commission, 147
Equal Pay act, 140
errors and omissions coverage, 16, 88
Espinel, Victoria, 55
E202 Standard Agreement for
    Integrated Projects, 77

ethical practice, 207–9
Fair Labor Standards Act, 138–39
Family and Medical Leave Act, 140–41
fixed fee payment, 98
force majeure, 28
foreign jurisdictions, work in, 47–49
    insurance issues, 49, 89–90
    intellectual property rights, 73
foreseeability of harm, 193–94
fraud, 184
general business corporation, 106, 107
General Conditions of the Contract for
        Construction, 52
Goldstein, Paul, 58
guarantees of work, 38–39
*Guillot-Vogt Associates, Inc. v. Holly &
    Smith,* 70
Hartford Civic Center, *181*
Hellmuth Obata & Kassabaum, 64
indemnification, 37–38, 125, 187–89
initial decision maker, 52
insurance
    additional insured status, 93–94
    after termination of employment,
        148–49
    binder, 86
    broker's role in, 85–86, 96
    business office coverage, 92–93
    business use of automobile, 92
    certificate, 86–88, 94
    claims-made policies, 84
    client indemnification, 37–38
    commercial general liability, 91
    conceptual basis, 84
    considerations in firm mergers and
        acquisitions, 124
    for consultants, 46, 94
    contractor's, 93–94
    contractual requirements, 43
    coverage for firm, 90
    declarations, 84
    deductible, 85, 90
    disability, 135
    document review, 88
    employment practices liability, 93
    endorsements, 85
    fidelity bond coverage, 93
    geographic coverage area, 89–90
    liability coverage, 88–91

liability for failure to acquire, 186–87
life insurance for partners, 117
maintenance of coverage, 88, 89, 96
notice requirements, 85, 90–91
occurrences policies, 84–85
premium calculation, 95–96
project, 95
rationale, 83
scope of coverage for architects, 83,
    84
substantial completion of project
    and, 35
tail coverage, 89
time period of coverage, 89
use of consultants and, 46
waiver of subrogation, 95
workers' compensation, 92, 135, 140,
    187–88
for work in foreign countries, 49,
    89–90
intellectual property rights
    conceptual basis, 55–56
    electronic transfer of documentation
        and, 73–76
    in foreign countries, 73
    limits of protections, 81–82
    ownership and use of design, 25–26
    ownership of employee work, 134
    provisions in proposal letter, 14
    see also copyright; patents;
        trademarks
International Chamber of Commerce,
    162
internships, 203
jury duty leave, 142
Lanham Act, 64
layoffs, 149–50
Leadership in Energy and
        Environmental Design (LEED)
        certification, 20–21, 39
LEED. *See* Leadership in Energy and
        Environmental Design (LEED)
        certification
legal fees
    insurance coverage for, 85, 90, 93–94
    recovery of, 71
lenders
    obligations for borrower's debt, 42–43
    right to legal action, 42

Libeskind, Daniel, 66–67
licensing, state
  authority for, 202–3, 209
  differences between states, 120–21
  for firms, 206
  penalties for practice without, 206–7
  professional activities requiring,
    199–201
  rationale, 201–2, 209
  reciprocity among states, 204–6,
    209
  registration with boards of
    architecture, 122–23
  registration with secretary of state,
    121–22
  renewal, 206
  requirements, 122, 203–4
liens, 101, *102–3*
limited liability company, 109–10, 113,
  115
limited liability partnerships, 110–11
litigation
  appeals process, 176–77
  causes of, 171–72, 179
  civil liability for violation of statute,
    183–84
  contractual protections, 197
  discovery process, 173–75
  dispositive motions, 175
  essential elements, 171
  judgments, 176
  legal basis for, 172
  legal fees, 71, 85, 90, 93–94
  parties to, 172–73
  pleadings, 172
  pretrial proceedings, 173
  representation, 172
  structure of U.S. court system, 171
  trial procedure, 175–76
  see also malpractice suits
Looney Ricks Kiss Architects, Inc. v.
  Bryan, 58
malpractice suits
  common law basis for, 180
  contractual protections, 197
  contribution to damages, 188
  damages, 179
  indemnification rights, 188
  legal basis for, 180–83

liability for breaches of duty by
  others, 186–87
personal injury claims, 184–86
spreading of liability, 187
statute of limitations, 185, 196–97
see also economic loss; insurance,
  liability coverage; litigation
maternity leave, 142
mediation, 40, 158, 162–66, 212
mergers and acquisitions, 123–25
minimum wage laws, 138–40
National Architecture Accreditation
  Board, 203
National Council of Architecture
  Boards, 202, 204–6
negligent misrepresentations, 195
noncompete and nonsolicitation
  provisions, 119, 133–34
office management
  complaint investigations, 137
  insurance coverage for, 92–93
  legal advice for, 212–13
  preventing discrimination and
    harassment, 136–37
  resources, 150
  see also employees
oral agreements, 13
overtime pay, 138
owners' agreement
  buy and sell arrangements, 113–17
  confidentiality provisions, 118–19
  dispute resolution provisions, 120
  life insurance policies, 117
  on management structure and
    function, 118
  noncompete and nonsolicitation
    provisions, 119
  on profit and loss allocations, 112–13
  rationale, 111–12, 125
  statement of capital contributions,
    112
ownership and use of design, 25–26. *see
  also* copyright
partnerships, 110–11, 115
patents
  definition, 56, 80
  documentation for, 81
  duration, 80
  first, *80,* 81

penalties for infringement of, 81
registration, 80
types of, 80–81
payment terms
for additional services, 22
claims for payment, 155
client's failure to comply, 100, 101, 104
for consultants, 46
contractor terms, 33–35
contract provisions, 14
cost of work calculations, 23–24
design changes, 24
duration of project and, 22–23
fixed fee payment, 98
guaranteed maximum price, 52
hourly basis, 99
owner's agreement with contractor, 52
percentage of construction cost, 98–99
provisions in proposal letter, 14
retainer deposit, 99
substantial completion of project and, 35
termination of services, 44
timeliness, 100
types of arrangements, 97
for work in foreign countries, 48–49
phases of project design and construction, 19
payment schedule, 98
plant patent, 80–81
professional service corporation, 106
professional service limited liability company, 109–10
property insurance, 92–93
proposal letter, 14
public hearings, 22
punch lists, 35–37
regulations, civil liability for violation of, 183–84
remedies
arbitration awards, 170
client's failure to pay, 100, 101, 104
judgment after litigation, 176
malpractice damages, 179
penalties for patent infringement, 81
penalties for trademark infringement, 79

recovery of attorney's fees, 71
remedies for copyright infringement, 70–71
retainer deposit, 99
revisions of design
additional services required by, 21–22
alterations to built works, copyright law and, 59
for budget reasons, 27
contract coverage, 20, 24
limitations on, 20
ownership and use of original design, 25–26
Robert R. Jones Architects, Inc., 71
schedule of services, 27–28
scope of work, 14, 19–20
secretary of state, 121–22
service mark, 77–78
Shine, Thomas. *see Shine v. Childs*
Shine v. Childs, 66–67
shop drawings, 31–32, 50
sick leave, 142
site plan, 19–20
site visits, 29–30
Small Business Administration, 135
software
building information modeling, 76–77
copyright, 75–76
sole proprietorship, 105–6
Sparaco v. Lawler, Matusky, Skelly Engineers LLP, 65
Standard Form of Agreement Between Owner and Architect
additional services provisions, 21–23
basic services provisions, 18–21
construction administration provisions, 28–29
contractor payment provisions, 33–35
cost of work provisions, 23–24, 26–27
dispute resolution provisions, 40, 162, 166, 168
on identification of stages of project completion, 35–37
initial information, 16
limitations on damages, 40–41
limitations on third-party liability, 42–43

on ownership and use of instruments
of service, 25–26, 60–62
owner's responsibilities under, 23
on rejecting or stopping work, 30–31
on responsibility for shop drawings
and submittal reviews, 31–32
schedule for services provisions,
27–28
site visit provisions, 29
standard of care provisions, 16–18
supplemental agreements, 21
termination provisions, 44–45
on use of images of building, 72
see also contracts
standard of care
contract provisions, 16–18
litigation based on violation of, 182–
83
state laws
on employee termination, 147
new employee information, 135
see also licensing, state
statute of limitations, 157, 185, 196–97
Subchapter S corporations, 108, 109–
10, 112–13
submittal reviews, 31–32
substantial completion of project, 35
supplemental agreements, 21
taxes
for corporations, 108–9
employee versus independent
contractor, 127–29
new employee paperwork, 135
retention of records, 157
for sole proprietorships, 106
Taylor Clark Associates, 64
temporary restraining order, 171
termination
contractual provisions, 44–45

licensing arrangements after, 62
ownership and use of design after,
25–26, 61–62
provisions in proposal letter, 14
time is of the essence, 27–28
tort law, 180–82, 183, 193, 194
trademarks, 56
definition, 77–78
duration, 79
eligibility for, 78–79
penalties for infringement, 79
registration, 78, 79
Uniformed Services Employment and
Reemployment Rights Act, 141
United States Department of Labor,
138
United States Patent & Trademark
Office, 78
Universal Copyright Convention, 73
unjust enrichment, 181
U.S. Green Building Council, 20–21
utility patent, 80–81
waiver of lien, 101, 103
waiver of subrogation, 95
whistleblower protection, 137–38
workers' compensation, 92, 135, 140,
187–88
work made for hire, 25
written agreements
arbitration clause, 167
basic provisions, 14
with consultants, 45–46
employment contract, 131–34
importance of, 13–14
mergers and acquisitions, 123–25
trends, 13
see also American Institute of
Architects forms of agreement;
contracts; owners' agreement

ABOUT THE AUTHORS

Robert F. Herrmann

Robert F. Herrmann, a lifelong New Yorker, is a partner in the New York City law firm of Menaker & Herrmann LLP. He is a graduate of Yale College and Columbia University School of Law. For nearly thirty years Bob has advised architects, engineers, interior designers, owners and contractors. He is a professional affiliate of the New York Chapter of the American Institute of Architects, where he has organized and participated as a panel member in many seminars for design professionals. Bob serves as a mediator of construction claims for the American Arbitration Association and the Commercial Division of the New York State Supreme Court. He is also a member of the Board of Directors of the Sir John Soane's Museum Foundation and the Broadway Mall Association.

Yao Fu Bailey

Yao Fu Bailey was born and raised in China. She is a partner of Menaker & Herrmann LLP. Yao's law practice focuses on real estate transactions and on advising design professionals. She received a bachelor of laws degree from Peking University and a master of laws degree from the University of Washington School of Law. Yao practiced law in Beijing before moving to the U.S. in 1997; she joined the firm in 1999. Yao has assisted American architects negotiating professional service agreements with developers in China, and has co-presented contract programs to design professionals. Mandarin is Yao's native language.

Michiel A. Bloemsma

Michiel A. Bloemsma is a partner of Menaker & Herrmann LLP and represents privately held companies and professional service entities, including architecture firms, with respect to general corporate and commercial law matters. Michiel's practice includes the structuring of business and professional service entities, and drafting and negotiating agreements between the owners of corporations, LLCs and partnerships. Michiel received law degrees from Leyden University School of Law in the Netherlands, Columbia Law School, and Cardozo Law School. He is fluent in Dutch.

Cheryl L. Davis

Cheryl L. Davis is a litigator who concentrates in intellectual property matters (particularly copyright and trademark cases), employment, and real estate/construction related matters. She is a graduate of Princeton (A.B. 1983) and Columbia (M.S.J. 1986 and J.D. 1987) Universities, and is an active member of the New York City Bar Association, where she has served on the Committees on Copyright and Literary Property and on Communications and Media Law, the American Bar Association, where she is the Vice Chair of the Arts and Museums Committee and Diversity Liaison of the ABA Forum on the Entertainment and Sports Industries, as well as the co-Chair of the Diversity Committee for the Entertainment, Arts and Sports Law Section for the New York State Bar Association. She is also Vice President of Communications for the League of Professional Theatre Women.

Paul M. Hellegers

Paul M. Hellegers is a partner of Menaker & Herrmann LLP and a commercial litigator with experience in domestic and international business disputes in the state and federal courts, including complex cases involving construction, accounting, and finance issues. Paul received his B.A. and M.A. degrees from Oxford University, where he earned a "double first" in classical history, literature and philosophy, and his J.D. from Georgetown University in 1984, following which he clerked for Judge Christine Nettesheim of the United States Claims Court in Washington. Paul has been Chair of the Civil Court Committee of the New York City Bar.

Richard G. Menaker

Richard G. Menaker, a founding partner of Menaker & Herrmann LLP, has practiced as a trial and appellate lawyer in business and construction cases since 1975. His main areas of concentration have included partnership and corporate governance disputes, antitrust, employment and severance issues, and financial and accounting matters. Dick has been an arbitrator for the American Arbitration Association and has had cases in the United States Supreme Court and several of the federal Courts of Appeals. He is a graduate of Columbia College and the University of Virginia School of Law. He also holds a D. Phil. in English legal history from the University of Oxford, where he was a Rhodes Scholar, and is a member of the Executive Committee of Legal Services of the Hudson Valley, which serves indigent clients in the seven counties north of New York City.

Rebecca Northey

Rebecca Northey has been practicing employment law in New York City for more than 30 years, representing businesses, municipalities and individuals. She is an honors graduate of Vassar College and Boston University School of Law and a partner at Menaker & Herrmann LLP.